VIEWPOINT

STUDENT'S BOOK

MICHAEL MCCARTHY
JEANNE MCCARTEN
HELEN SANDIFORD

CAMBRIDGE
UNIVERSITY PRESS

CAMBRIDGE
UNIVERSITY PRESS

University Printing House, Cambridge CB2 8BS, United Kingdom

One Liberty Plaza, 20th Floor, New York, NY 10006, USA

477 Williamstown Road, Port Melbourne, VIC 3207, Australia

4843/24, 2nd Floor, Ansari Road, Daryaganj, Delhi – 110002, India

79 Anson Road, #06–04/06, Singapore 079906

Cambridge University Press is part of the University of Cambridge.

It furthers the University's mission by disseminating knowledge in the pursuit of education, learning and research at the highest international levels of excellence.

www.cambridge.org
Information on this title: www.cambridge.org/9780521131865

© Cambridge University Press 2012

This publication is in copyright. Subject to statutory exception and to the provisions of relevant collective licensing agreements, no reproduction of any part may take place without the written permission of Cambridge University Press.

First published 2012
40 39 38 37 36 35 34 33 32 31 30 29 28 27 26 25 24 23

Printed in the United Kingdom by Latimer Trend

A catalog record for this publication is available from the British Library.

ISBN 978-0-521-13186-5 Student's Book 1
ISBN 978-1-107-60151-2 Student's Book 1A
ISBN 978-1-107-60152-9 Student's Book 1B
ISBN 978-1-107-60277-9 Workbook 1
ISBN 978-1-107-60278-6 Workbook 1A
ISBN 978-1-107-60279-3 Workbook 1B
ISBN 978-1-107-60153-6 Teacher's Edition 1
ISBN 978-1-107-63988-1 Classroom Audio 1
ISBN 978-1-107-62978-3 Classware 1

Cambridge University Press has no responsibility for the persistence or accuracy of URLs for external or third-party Internet Web sites referred to in this publication and does not guarantee that any content on such websites is, or will remain, accurate or appropriate. Information regarding prices, travel timetables and other factual information given in this work is correct at the time of first printing but Cambridge University Press does not guarantee the accuracy of such information thereafter.

Cover and interior design: Page 2, LLC
Layout/design services and photo research: Cenveo Publisher Services/Nesbitt Graphics, Inc.
Audio production: New York Audio Productions

Authors' acknowledgements

The authors would like to thank the entire team of professionals who have contributed their expertise to creating *Viewpoint 1*. We appreciate you all, including those we have not met. Here we would like to thank the people with whom we have had the most personal, day-to-day contact through the project. In particular, Bryan Fletcher for his incredible vision, publishing ability, and drive – we deeply appreciate his confidence in us and our work; Sarah Cole, for her extraordinary editorial flair, market knowledge, technical skills, and superb direction of the project; Mary Vaughn for her usual outstandingly perceptive comments on our drafts and her excellent contributions to the material; Desmond O'Sullivan for his skills in managing the project successfully with unfailing good humor; Karen Davy for her tireless attention to detail; Catherine Black for her invaluable and timely help in the proofing stages; Graham Skerritt and Sabina Sahni for their detailed editorial comments; Dawn Elwell for her flawless design and production skills and especially her never-ending patience; Ellen Shaw for sharing her expertise so generously and for her continued support, which we value; Lorraine Poulter for her assiduous and supportive role in the creation of the Workbook; Sue Aldcorn for her work on creating the Teacher's Edition; Peter Satchell for his careful editorial support; Lisa Hutchins for making the audio program happen; Rachel Sinden for her role in setting up the online component. Carol-June Cassidy for her meticulous work with the wordlists; Tyler Heacock and Kathleen Corley, and their friends and family for the recordings they made, which fed into the materials; Ann Fiddes and Claire Dembry for their corpus support; Andrew Caines for corpus research support; Mike Boyle for contributing the articles in Units 4 and 7; Melissa Good for arranging access to the English Profile wordlists; Jenna Leonard, Sarah Quayle, and Helen Morris for making all kinds of things happen; Dr. Leo Cheng and Mercy Ships for the interview and photographs in Unit 5; Chris Waddell for the interview and photographs in Unit 12.

We would also like to express our appreciation to Hanri Pieterse and Janet Aitchison for their continued support.

Finally, we would like to thank each other for getting through another project together! In addition, Helen Sandiford would like to thank her husband, Bryan, and her daughters, Teia and Eryn, for their unwavering support.

In addition, a great number of people contributed to the research and development of *Viewpoint*. The authors and publishers would like to extend their particular thanks to the following for their valuable insights and suggestions.

Reviewers and consultants:
Elisa Borges and Samara Camilo Tomé Costa from **Instituto Brasil-Estados Unidos**, Rio de Janeiro, Brazil; Deborah Iddon from **Harmon Hall** Cuajimalpa, México; and Chris Sol Cruz from **Suncross Media LLC**. Special thanks to Sedat Cilingir, Didem Mutçalıoğlu, and Burcu Tezvan from **İstanbul Bilgi Üniversitesi**, İstanbul, Turkey for their invaluable input in reviewing both the Student's Book and Workbook.

The authors and publishers would also like to thank additional members of the editorial team: John Hicks, Lori Solbakken, and our **design** and **production** teams at Nesbitt Graphics, Inc., Page 2, LLC and New York Audio Productions.

Thank you to the models as well as all those who allowed us to use their homes and businesses for our Lesson C photographs, especially Nina Hefez; Tokyo Eat, the restaurant at the Palais de Tokyo, Paris, France; Panam Café, Paris, France; Thanksgiving grocery store, Paris, France; and Majestic Bastille Cinéma, Paris, France. Special thanks to the photographer, Fabrice Malzieu, for his skill, direction and good humor.

*And these Cambridge University Press **staff** and **advisors**:*
Mary Lousie Baez, Jeff Chen, Seil Choi, Vincent Di Blasi, Julian Eynon, Maiza Fatureto, Keiko Hirano, Chris Hughes, Peter Holly, Tomomi Katsuki, Jeff Krum, Christine Lee, John Letcher, Vicky Lin, Hugo Loyola, Joao Madureira, Alejandro Martinez, Mary McKeon, Daniela A. Meyer, Devrim Ozdemir, Jinhee Park, Gabriela Perez, Panthipa Rojanasuworapong, Luiz Rose, Howard Siegelman, Satoko Shimoyama, Ian Sutherland, Alicione Soares Tavares, Frank Vargas, Julie Watson, Irene Yang, Jess Zhou, Frank Zhu.

Viewpoint Level 1 *Scope and sequence*

	Functions / Topics	Grammar	Vocabulary	Conversation strategies	Speaking naturally
Unit 1 **Social networks** pages 10–19	• Ask questions to get to know someone • Talk about friends and social networking habits	• Use the present tense, *tend*, and *will* to talk about habits	• Personality traits (e.g. *open-minded, pushy, talkative*) • Formal verbs (*obtain, withhold, accuse*)	• Ask questions to find out or check information • Use *And*, *But*, and *So* to start questions which link back to what the previous speaker said	• Questions with answers *page 138*
Unit 2 **The media** pages 20–29	• Talk about the influence of the media and celebrities • Share views on the impact of TV, online videos, and video games	• Use defining and non-defining relative clauses to give and add information • Use *that* clauses to link ideas	• Nouns and prepositions (*increase in, impact on*) • Formal expressions (*complex issue*)	• Use *which* clauses to comment on your own and others' statements • Use *You know what . . . ?* to introduce a comment on what you're going to say	• *which* clauses *page 138*
Unit 3 **Stories** pages 30–39	• Talk about life lessons and experiences • Tell stories about your childhood	• Use the past tense and present perfect forms • Use the simple past, past perfect, and past perfect continuous	• Expressions for school-related experiences (*count toward a grade*) • Verbs (*slip, tug, etc.*)	• Interrupt a story you are telling to make a comment and then come back to it • Use *(It's) no wonder* to say something is not surprising	• Auxiliary verbs *page 139*
Checkpoint 1 Units 1–3 pages 40–41					
Unit 4 **Working lives** pages 42–51	• Discuss and give advice on finding and changing jobs • Share opinions about perks and benefits offered by employers • Discuss and prepare to answer interview questions	• Use countable and uncountable nouns • Generalize and specify using definite and indefinite articles	• Verb + noun collocations on the topic of finding a job (*achieve a goal*) • Word families (*solve – solution*)	• Show your attitude toward what you say with *-ly* adverbs • Use *As a matter of fact* or *In fact* to give new information that you want to emphasize, or to correct what someone assumes or expects	• Word stress *page 139*

Listening	Reading	Writing	Vocabulary notebook	Grammar extra
Reasons for ending friendships • Four people talk about solutions to relationship problems *But is it fair?* • Two students debate whether it is fair for employers to check out job applicants online	*Future college students and employees, beware!* • An article about the importance of posting only appropriate content online	• Write a script for a debate over whether or not employers should judge applicants by their online profile • Plan an argument • Contrast ideas and arguments • Avoid errors with *whereas*	*The right choice!* • Identify new vocabulary as formal or informal	• Questions • Frequency expressions • State verbs *pages 144–145*
It's really interesting that . . . • Five people discuss the effects of TV on young people *They're just games* • A professor delivers a lecture on violence and the media	*Not just a game* • An article about the impact of violent video games on young people	• Write a paragraph in an essay about whether songs with violent lyrics should be banned • Use topic sentences • List ideas • Avoid errors with listing expressions	*What an effect!* • When you learn a new noun, find out what prepositions are used with it	• Verbs in subject and object relative clauses • Using *that* clauses • *what* clauses *pages 146–147*
It just goes to show . . . • Three conversations about life lessons *How friendly are people?* • Three students describe the people in their cities	*Saturday* • A short story about a woman who suddenly feels invisible	• Write a narrative article about a positive or negative experience with people • Brainstorm and plan • Use verbs to structure an article • Avoid errors with the past perfect	*Catch up!* • Write a definition to help you remember a new expression	• Time expressions with the simple past and present perfect • Time expressions with the past perfect *pages 148–149*
Checkpoint 1 Units 1–3 pages 40–41				
The best perks • Five people discuss and give examples of perks and benefits offered to employees *Interview rules* • Five applicants are interviewed for a job	*Career help: What questions should I ask at a job interview?* • An article outlining questions a job applicant should and shouldn't ask during an interview	• Write a personal statement for an application form • Use nouns in formal writing • Avoid errors with uncountable nouns	*Meet that deadline!* • When you learn a new word, write down its collocations	• Making uncountable nouns countable • More about uncountable nouns • More about the definite article *pages 150–151*

	Functions / Topics	Grammar	Vocabulary	Conversation strategies	Speaking naturally
Unit 5 **Challenges** pages 52–61	• Talk about world issues and ways to help • Share wishes, hopes, and regrets about the world • Hypothesize on making the world a better place	• Use conditional sentences to talk about hypothetical events in the present or past • Use *wish* and *hope* to talk about wishes, hopes, and regrets	• World problems and solutions (*eradicate poverty*) • Word building (*devastate, devastation, devastated*)	• Suggest possible scenarios or ideas with *What if . . . ?, suppose,* and *imagine* • Use *I suppose* to show that you're not 100 percent sure	• Shifting word stress *page 140*
Unit 6 **Into the future** pages 62–71	• Talk about the future of money, technology, clothing, travel, entertainment, and everyday life • Give a presentation	• Describe future events with *be going to, will, may, might,* and the present • Use modal verbs for expectations, guesses, offers, necessity, requests, etc.	• Expressions used in giving presentations (*As you'll see on the slide.*) • Nouns for people (*climatologists*)	• Use *would* or *'d* to soften your opinions • Respond with expressions such as *I think so, I don't think so,* and *I guess not*	• Silent consonants *page 140*

Checkpoint 2 Units 4–6   pages 72–73

	Functions / Topics	Grammar	Vocabulary	Conversation strategies	Speaking naturally
Unit 7 **Getting along** pages 74–83	• Talk about getting along with friends and family • Compare experiences of growing up in different types of families • Share views on dealing with difficult friends	• Use phrasal verbs • Use infinitives and *-ing* forms after adjectives, nouns, and pronouns	• Phrasal verbs on the topic of house rules (*have friends over*) • Idiomatic expressions (*drive your friends away, tag along with someone*)	• Make your meaning clear with expressions like *What I'm saying is* and *I mean* • Use expressions such as *I have to say* to show that you want to make a strong point	• Conversational expressions *page 141*
Unit 8 **Food science** pages 84–93	• Talk about farming, food, and nutrition • Share ideas for eating a healthy diet • React to statistics	• Use the passive to focus on information when talking about the past, present, and future • Use complements of verbs that describe causes and effects	• Human body parts and processes (*heart, metabolism*) • Noun and verb forms of the same root (*discovery, discover*)	• Use rhetorical questions to make a point • Give examples with expressions such as *such as, like, take,* and *for instance*	• Strong and weak forms of prepositions *page 141*

Listening	Reading	Writing	Vocabulary notebook	Grammar extra
What would you give away? • Three people talk about ways to help others *Inspiring people* • An interview with a doctor about his work with the charitable organization Mercy Ships	*On the Mercy Ships* • An interview with Dr. Leo Cheng, whose volunteer work with Mercy Ships changes lives in developing countries	• Write an email inquiry about volunteering • Use *it* as subject and object • Avoid errors with verb forms	*Wealthy = rich* • When you learn a new word, write down its synonyms or a paraphrase of it	• Continuous forms for conditions • *even if* and *unless* to talk about conditions • Use of *wish* with *would* • Strong wishes with *If only* *pages 152–153*
Going cashless – the pros and cons! • Two friends discuss the advantages and disadvantages of a cashless society *Future entertainment* • Four conversations about entertainment in the future	*What does the future look like?* • Four short news articles about developments and changes that could occur in the future	• Write a one-paragraph article about how our everyday life will be different in the future • Use modal verbs with adverbs • Structure a paragraph with topic, supporting, and concluding sentences • Avoid errors with adverbs	*Present yourself!* • Create an "idea string" for a new expression by thinking of different ways you can use it	• Plans and intentions with *be going to* and *will* • Present forms in clauses that refer to the future • More on necessity modals • Possibility modals in the affirmative and negative *pages 154–155*

Checkpoint 2 Units 4–6   pages 72–73

My worst roommate • Four people talk about their negative experiences with roommates *"Boomerang" kids* • Two parents talk about their "boomerang" children – grown children who move back home	*Now That I've Driven All My Friends Away, I Finally Have Time For Me!* • A satirical article with suggestions for ways to get rid of friends and make time for yourself	• Write an introduction to an essay about whether family relationships are more important than friendships • Use a thesis statement • Use *what* clauses to give the most important information • Avoid errors with subjects	*Look forward to it!* • When you learn a new expression, use it in a true sentence about someone you know	• Objects with separable phrasal verbs • Phrasal verbs followed by the *-ing* form of the verb • More patterns with infinitives and *it* clauses *pages 156–157*
A food revolution! • Two radio show hosts and five listeners talk about the British chef Jamie Oliver *Backyard beekeeping* • A man talks to an interviewer about his unusual hobby – beekeeping	*Where did all the bees go?* • An article about "colony-collapse disorder" and why the disappearance of bees is a serious threat to the world's food supply	• Write a report about trends, using information in graphs and charts • Use prepositions after verbs and nouns • Use expressions for approximate numbers • Avoid errors with *fall, rise* and *grow*	*Picture this!* • Create a picture dictionary on your computer	• Question forms in the passive • Verb + object + infinitive • More verb patterns *pages 158–159*

	Functions / Topics	Grammar	Vocabulary	Conversation strategies	Speaking naturally
Unit 9 **Success and happiness** pages 94–103	• Define and discuss success and happiness • Share stories about happy moments and times when things went wrong	• Use the determiners *all, both, each, every, neither, none of, no* • Use *-ing* forms as reduced relative clauses, to describe simultaneous events, and as subjects and objects	• Expressions with *get* (*get off the ground, get under way, get off to a good start*) • Synonyms (*study = analyze*)	• Use expressions like *As far as (success) is concerned* to focus in on a topic • Use expressions like *As far as I'm concerned / can tell* to give and soften opinions	• Stress in expressions *page 142*
Checkpoint 3 Units 7–9 pages 104–105					
Unit 10 **Going places** pages 106–115	• Describe travel and vacation experiences • Report conversations • Share views on what to take on trips • Discuss the effects of tourism	• Use reported speech to report statements • Use reported speech to report questions and instructions	• Adjectives ending *-ed* and *-ing* (*amazed, amazing*) • Synonyms (*industries, businesses*)	• Use expressions such as *you mean, so what you're saying is*, and *so I guess* when drawing conclusions • Ask for more details about someone's ideas or opinions, using *In what way?*	• Silent vowels *page 142*
Unit 11 **Culture** pages 116–125	• Talk about weddings, gifts, and other traditions • Discuss the positive and negative aspects of globalization	• Use relative clauses with *when, where,* and *whose* • Use verbs with direct and indirect objects	• Expressions to describe wedding customs (*bride, walk down the aisle*) • Opposites (*loss ≠ preservation*)	• Soften your comments with expressions like *kind of, a little,* and *not really* • Use *Yeah, no* to agree with someone and then make a comment of your own	• Consonant groups *page 143*
Unit 12 **Ability** pages 126–135	• Talk about intelligence, skills, and abilities • Discuss views on parents' and teachers' roles in developing children's talents	• Use adverbs before adjectives and adverbs • Use *as . . . as* and comparative and superlative adjectives and adverbs	• Expressions to describe types of intelligence and abilities (*linguistic, articulate*) • Collocations (*raise awareness*)	• Use vague expressions like *and that kind of thing* when you don't need to be precise • Show that you strongly agree with someone, using *No doubt*	• Stress and intonation *page 143*
Checkpoint 4 Units 10–12 pages 136–137					

Listening	Reading	Writing	Vocabulary notebook	Grammar extra
Happy moments gone wrong! • Three people talk about happy occasions and the things that went wrong *Happiness and the community* • A sociology professor lectures on policies that can make communities happier	*Unhappy? Maybe you're not in the right country!* • An article describing ways that governments can take responsibility for their citizens' happiness	• Write a paragraph for an essay about whether governments are responsible for citizens' happiness • Use expressions to add ideas • Avoid errors with *in addition to*, etc.	*Get started!* • When you learn a new expression, imagine using it in an everyday situation. Write the situation and what you would say	• Singular or plural verbs with determiners • Determiners with and without *of* • Verbs followed by an *-ing* form or an infinitive • Verbs of perception + object + base form or *-ing* form *pages 160–161*

Checkpoint 3 Units 7–9   pages 104–105

Listening	Reading	Writing	Vocabulary notebook	Grammar extra
More adventures in Bolivia • A woman tells a friend about her plans for a trip to Bolivia *Responsible tourism* • An eco-tour guide discusses things people can do to be responsible tourists	*The tourist threat* • An article about the benefits and dangers of the tourist industry	• Write a survey article for a student magazine • Contrast ideas • Avoid errors with *although*	*So amazing!* • When you learn a new word, make word forks with other words in the same family	• Reported speech: verbs and pronouns • Reported speech: time and place expressions • Other reporting verbs • Reporting verb forms *pages 162–163*
Gift giving around the world • An interview about certain gifts in different cultures *Reviving a dying language* • Students and their professor discuss ideas for saving endangered languages	*Are we losing our culture?* • An article discussing the different aspects of culture and things that can threaten it	• Write a concluding paragraph in an essay about the effects of globalization on culture • Explain cause and effect • Avoid errors with *due to*	*Wedding bells!* • Write new vocabulary on word webs	• More on relative clauses • Prepositions in relative clauses • More on verb + direct object + prepositional phrase • Passive sentences *pages 164–165*
Minds for the future • Two friends discuss an article about the five minds that Howard Gardner identified *The genius in all of us* • Two radio show hosts talk about natural talent and giftedness	*Seeing things in a completely different way . . .* • An interview with Chris Waddell, whose disability didn't stop him from becoming a world champion skier	• Write an essay about someone you admire • Brainstorm, then plan an essay • Explain purpose and intention • Avoid errors with *so that*	*It's just the opposite!* • When you learn a new adjective or descriptive expression, find out how to express the opposite meaning	• *well* + adjective • Adverb and adjective collocations • Patterns with comparatives *pages 166–167*

Checkpoint 4 Units 10–12   pages 136–137

Social networks

What RU doing?

In Unit 1, you . . .

- talk about friends and social networking.
- use the present tense, *tend*, and *will* to talk about habits.
- ask questions to find out or check information.
- use *And, But,* and *So* in follow-up questions.

Lesson A *Speed-friending*

1 Getting to know each other

A ◀))) CD 1.02 **Read the article. Why do people go to speed-friending events? What happens at this kind of event?**

Make New Friends and Network Fast!

These days we live life in the fast lane. We insist on fast food, quick service, high-speed downloads, instant messaging, and immediate responses. So why should we spend time making new friends? At a speed-friending event, you have just a few minutes to ask and answer questions before moving on to the next person. If you find people you'd like to get to know better, you can contact them after the event. Here are the kinds of questions that people ask.

1. How do you like to spend your free time?
2. What music are you listening to these days?
3. What was your most valuable possession as a child? And now?
4. Can you say no to chocolate?
5. When did you last stay out after midnight? Where were you?
6. Who's your favorite celebrity?
7. Have you ever won a prize or a contest?
8. What word describes you best?

About you

B Pair work **Take turns asking and answering the questions in the article.**

C **Write six interesting questions you'd like to ask at a speed-friending event. (For help with questions, see page 144.)**

How often do you go out with your friends?

D Class activity **Hold a speed-friending event in class. You have two minutes to ask each person your questions.**

2 Vocabulary in context

A ◀))) CD 1.03 **Listen. Tanya is describing people she met at a speed-friending event. Who do you think she will get in touch with again? Who won't she contact? Say why.**

What can I say? Greg wasn't very **talkative**, and when he did talk, he seemed kind of **narrow-minded**.

Lauren was very **intelligent**, but she seemed kind of **eccentric** – you know, a little **weird**, but fun.

I thought Kayla was kind of **aggressive** – you know, a little too **pushy** for me. I bet she can be **a pain** at times.

Rickie seemed really **sweet** and **thoughtful** – but a little too **sensitive**, maybe? He got a little **touchy** about some of the questions.

Victor sounded really, you know, **self-confident** but in a nice way – not at all **arrogant**. And he was interested in my answers.

Emma was very **open-minded** and **relaxed** about things – pretty **laid-back**. And she had a good sense of humor. We laughed a lot.

Word sort

B **Complete the chart with personality traits from Tanya's descriptions. Add more ideas.**

I like people who are . . .	I don't like people who are . . .	I don't mind people who are . . .
open-minded		

Vocabulary notebook

See page 19.

About you

C **Pair work** **Do you know anyone with the personality traits in your chart? Take turns asking and answering questions.**

A *Do you know anyone who is open-minded?*

B *Actually, my sister is very open-minded. She always listens to new ideas.*

3 Viewpoint What makes a good friend?

Group work **Discuss the questions. Do you share the same views on friendship?**

- Think of three good friends. How would you describe them?
- Are there things about your friends or people you know that you don't like?
- How do friendships differ? Is it possible to be equally close to everyone?
- Would all your friends get along if they met one another?
- What do you think about speed-friending as a way to make new friends?

"Well, . . . my friend Martha is really sweet. She . . . "

Why don't my friends talk to ME?

DONNELLY

In conversation . . .

You can use *Well, . . .* to take time to think.

Lesson B *Networking*

1 Grammar in context

A Class survey Read the information. What percentage of your class uses these methods of communication every day? Vote on the methods you use, and complete the chart.

How do you keep in touch?

Most people use several different ways to keep in touch. Here are the percentages of young people who use these methods of communication every day.

The percentage of young people who . . .		Your class
talk on a cell phone	70%	
send text messages	60%	
use instant messaging	54%	
use social networks	47%	
talk on a landline	46%	
send email	22%	

B ◀)) CD 1.04 Listen. Four people talk about how they communicate. What methods of communication do they use?

We asked four people how they like to communicate. Here's what they said.

Jeff Gordon, 25

"I go on my social networking site five or six times a day. I'll log in when I'm taking a break. I like to check out my friends' pages and see what they're up to."

Victoria Garza, 40

"Personally I use email, but my kids are constantly texting. Occasionally my son will email someone like my sister, but with friends he tends to text."

David Smith, 31

"At work I'm on the phone all the time, but when I'm traveling, I normally use my laptop to make calls over the Internet. It doesn't cost anything, so . . ."

Sarah Wang, 19

"Every once in a while, I'll instant message with a friend. Some of my friends don't use IM, so mostly I just call on my cell to catch up with them."

About you

C Pair work Find things in the interviews that you do and don't do. Tell a partner.

"I go on my social networking site a lot, like Jeff. And I . . ."

② Grammar Talking about habits

Figure it out

A Find sentences in the interviews with a similar meaning to the ones below. Rewrite the sentences, changing the words in bold. Then read the grammar chart.

1. With friends he **usually texts**.
2. Every once in a while, I **instant message**.
3. My kids **text all the time**.
4. When I **travel**, I normally use my laptop.

The present tense, *tend*, and *will* ⬇

Grammar extra
See page 145.

To talk about habits, you can use the simple present, the verb *tend*, or the modal verb *will*. Here, *will* does not have future meaning.
*Mostly I **call** on my cell. I'**m** on the phone all the time. My friends **don't use** IM.*
*My son **tends to** text. He **doesn't use** IM. Occasionally he'**ll email** someone.*

You can use the present continuous for a "longer" activity that happens at the same time as another habit.
*When I'**m traveling**, I normally use my laptop to make calls.*

You can use *always* and *constantly* with the present continuous for a habit that is noticeable or more frequent than is usual.
*My kids **are constantly texting**.*

> **In conversation . . .**
>
> People often use *will / 'll* in statements to talk about their habits. Questions and the negative forms *will not / won't* are rarely used in this meaning.

B Complete the conversations with a correct form of the verbs given. Then practice.

1. *A* How do you normally catch up with your friends? By phone?
   B Yeah. I _____ (tend / call) them when I'm taking my lunch break.
   A Yeah? I _____ (not call) my friends much. We _____ always _____ (email) each other, so . . .

2. *A* How much time do you spend on your social networking site?
   B I _____ probably _____ (will / spend) a few hours a day on it. I _____ (tend / use) it to make plans with friends. Mostly I _____ (check out) my friends' photos and stuff.
   A Yeah? I'm not on one. But occasionally I _____ (will / get) invites from people. But I _____ (not reply) to them.

3. *A* What do you mostly use your cell phone for? Texting?
   B Yeah. I _____ constantly _____ (text) my kids to find out where they are.
   A That's funny. In my family, we _____ (not text) a lot. We _____ (tend / talk). Like, my sister regularly _____ (call) me after dinner when she _____ (watch) TV.

About you

C Pair work Write your own answers to the questions in Exercise B. Then take turns asking the questions and giving your own answers.

D Group work Prepare a short presentation about your family's communication habits to give to your group. Listen to your classmates' presentations, and ask questions.

"Mostly I text my friends and family. My dad'll text me when he's working, and . . ."

③ Speaking naturally Questions with answers *See page 138.*

Lesson C *And why's that?*

1 **Conversation strategy** Finding out or checking information

A How would you feel if someone "unfriended" you (removed you from their list of friends on a social networking site)? Would you take it personally and be offended?

B ◀))CD 1.07 Listen. What does Stan think about "unfriending" someone? How do you think Alexa feels about it?

Stan I ran into Tammy today. She's really upset.

Alexa Oh, yeah? And why's that?

Stan Because I "unfriended" her.

Alexa Oh, that's awkward. How did she find out?

Stan I'm not sure, actually.

Alexa Huh. So why did you "unfriend" her?

Stan Well, it was nothing personal. It's just that every once in a while, you know, when I'm updating my profile, I'll remove people – if we haven't been in touch for some time.

Alexa But you emailed her, right? I mean, you let her know?

Stan No. I didn't think she'd be offended.

Alexa So you just delete people that you're not in touch with?

Stan Yeah. It's no big deal.

C **Notice** how Alexa asks some questions to find out new information.

She asks other questions in the form of statements to check information or her understanding of what was said or done. Find examples of both types of questions in the conversation.

> *"And why's that?"*
>
> *"But you emailed her, right?"*

D ◀))CD 1.08 **Complete the rest of Stan and Alexa's conversation with the questions in the box. Then listen and check. Practice with a partner.**

Alexa So has anyone ever "unfriended" you?

Stan You mean, taken me off their friends list? I don't think so.

Alexa _____ It wouldn't bother you?

Stan No. I wouldn't mind at all. _____

Alexa It's not *bad*. It's just Tammy didn't do anything wrong.

Stan _____

Alexa Well, if they post obnoxious comments, for example.

Stan Hmm. _____

Alexa Well, yeah. That's probably a good reason, too.

Stan Right. _____

Alexa I don't know. Just make sure you never "unfriend" me! OK?

a. So you think it's bad, then?

b. And it's OK when you stop dating?

✓ c. So has anyone ever "unfriended" you?

d. But you'd be fine with it if they did?

e. So when *is* it OK, do you think?

f. But what should I do about Tammy?

2 Strategy plus Linking with *And*, *But*, and *So*

🔊 CD 1.09 You can start questions with **And,** **But,** or **So** to link back to things the previous speaker said. It makes the conversation "flow."

She's really upset.

And why's that?

A 🔊 CD 1.10 **Underline the best question to continue each conversation. Then listen and check your answers. Practice with a partner.**

1. *A* Have you ever removed someone from your list of friends online?
   B Actually, I don't have one. I'm not on a social networking site.
   A **And you just tend to add people? / So how do you keep in touch with people?**

2. *A* Do you think it's OK to "unfriend" people?
   B Oh, yeah. People do it all the time, I'm sure.
   A **Yeah. But why do they do it? / So they never remove anyone?**

3. *A* What would you do if someone deleted you from their friends list?
   B It depends. I probably wouldn't say anything.
   A **But you'd say something if it was a good friend? / And you'd call them, right?**

About you | **B** **Pair work** **Ask and answer the questions. Can you continue each conversation?**

3 Listening and strategies Reasons for ending friendships

A 🔊 CD 1.11 **Listen to the first part of four conversations. What would each person say the problem is with his or her friendship? Number the issues 1–4. There are two extras.**

_____ We've lost touch.   _____ My friend is two-faced.
_____ My friend is too serious.   _____ We can't agree on things.
_____ My friend posts annoying stuff on my wall.   _____ We don't like each other's friends.

B 🔊 CD 1.12 **Listen again. Circle the best question to continue each conversation.**

1. a. So you don't agree on *anything*?
   b. But do you agree on politics?

2. a. But she never posts photos, right?
   b. And does she post obnoxious comments, too?

3. a. But why does she do that?
   b. So does she talk about you behind your back?

4. a. So you mostly call each other?
   b. So she just dropped you?

C 🔊 CD 1.13 **Listen to the complete conversations. Check your answers. What solutions do the speakers have for their friendship problems?**

About you | **D** **Pair work** **Agree on six good reasons for ending a friendship and the best ways to do it.**

A Well, if you don't agree on anything, it's probably a good reason to end a friendship.
B But do you only want friends who agree with you on everything?

Good reasons to end friendships
1. You don't agree on important issues.
The best ways to do it . . .

Lesson D *Online footprints*

① Reading

A Prepare Guess the meanings of *online footprint* and *digital dirt*. Then scan the article and find the explanations.

B ⬇ **Read for main ideas** Read the article. What examples of digital dirt can you find?

Future college students and employees, beware!
Clean up that digital dirt – now!

When student-teacher Ms. S. posted a photo from a party on the wall of her social networking site, she had no idea of the consequences. Just weeks away from obtaining a teaching degree, Ms. S.'s diploma was withheld after school administrators viewed the photo and accused her of promoting underage drinking – a charge that she denied. Her case is not an isolated one. Increasingly, employees are being fired from their jobs and students are having their college applications rejected because of "digital dirt," or inappropriate online content.

These cases highlight the need to be careful about the type of content you post online. Each time you post a photo or comment, or write a profile online, you create an image, or "online footprint," of yourself that is difficult to erase. If you think your friends are the only ones checking your profile, think again. It's increasingly common for colleges and employers to look closely at the online pictures and profiles of actual and prospective students and employees. A survey conducted by ExecuNet reported that 83 percent of job recruiters regularly use Internet searches to find out more about candidates. Nearly half said they will reject candidates based on the "digital dirt" they find.

How can you still have fun online without making a bad impression on future college admissions officers and employers? Here are five basic steps you can follow.

1. **Check what's online already.** Type your name into several search engines to see your digital footprint. Then check all of your privacy settings, and remove anything you don't want others to see. If you have "friends" who are always posting off-color jokes or rude comments about you on your wall, then block their comments.

2. **Avoid writing anything you might regret later.** Don't badmouth a current or previous employer online. The same applies to teachers, professors, classmates, or co-workers.

3. **Create a positive online image.** The Internet is the perfect place to showcase your talents and skills. Use a blog or website to promote your work, research, and interests.

4. **Use a professional email address.** An employer or a college admissions officer is more likely to contact annsmith@cup.com than smoothiefan@cup.com.

5. **Join online groups selectively.** Instead of joining groups and campaigns with names like "Sleeping in class," connect to a professional organization. When it comes time to apply for a job or place in college, you'll be glad you did.

Reading tip

Writers often begin an article with an example to illustrate their argument.

C Check your understanding Are the sentences true (T) or false (F)? Write T or F. Correct the false sentences.

1. Ms. S. was unable to graduate from college. _____
2. Her school said she was encouraging young people to drink. _____
3. It's becoming more common for employers to check people out online. _____
4. Eighty-three percent of job recruiters reject candidates with "digital dirt." _____
5. The article recommends "unfriending" people who post rude comments. _____
6. The article suggests that you shouldn't join social network campaigns. _____

About you

D React **Pair work** What do you think of Ms. S.'s story? Have you heard of similar cases? Which advice in the article do you intend to follow?

② Focus on vocabulary Formal verbs

A Find the verbs in bold below in the article. Match the two parts of the sentences to find the meanings. Write the letters a–g.

1. If you **obtain** something, you _____
2. If you **withhold** something (**from** someone), you _____
3. If people **accuse** you **of** (doing) something, they _____
4. If you **promote** something, you _____
5. If you **deny** (doing) something, you _____
6. If employers **reject** a job applicant, they _____
7. If you **regret** (doing) something, you _____

a. say it is a good thing.
b. say you didn't do it.
c. don't want that person.
d. are sorry that you did it.
e. keep it and don't give it to that person.
f. say you did something bad or wrong.
g. get or achieve it.

B Pair work Take turns using the verbs above to ask questions about Ms. S.'s story.

"What happened before Ms. S. obtained her teaching degree?"

③ Listening and speaking But is it fair?

A Pair work Read the question below. How many reasons can you think of to support a "yes" and a "no" answer? Make two lists.

> **Today's online debate:** Is it fair for employers to check out job applicants online?

B ◀)) CD 1.14 Listen to two people debate the question above. Who answers, "Yes, it's fair" and "No, it's not fair" to the question? Which of the reasons in your lists did they use?

Rosa says _____

Daniel says _____

C ◀)) CD 1.15 Listen again and write the two missing words in each sentence.

1. a. On the one hand, Rosa believes that what you do online shows your _____ .
   b. On the other hand, Daniel argues that your online profile is _____ .
2. a. Rosa says online profiles tell you what you won't see in _____ .
   b. Daniel thinks social networking sites don't tell you what a person is like _____ .
3. a. Rosa argues that it's _____ to recruit and train new staff.
   b. Daniel believes that everyone has a right to _____ in his or her free time.
4. a. Rosa says companies want people who will fit in and _____ with other people.
   b. Daniel argues that people behave in a different way _____ .

About you **D** Class debate Prepare a response to the debate question with a partner, and then present your arguments to the class. How many people answer "yes"? How many answer "no"?

Writing *Making judgments*

In this lesson, you . . .
- plan an argument.
- contrast ideas.
- avoid errors with *whereas*.

Task Write a script for an online debate.
Should employers judge applicants by their online profiles?

A **Brainstorm** Read the question above. Write three reasons to answer "yes" and three reasons to answer "no."

B **Look at a model** Read the debate script. Circle three more expressions that contrast ideas.

> Many employers check the Internet for information about job applicants. However, this is not a fair way to judge a person. On the one hand, employers need people who will fit into the company. An online profile gives information that employers will not see on a résumé – for example, if the person is aggressive or has extreme views. On the other hand, an online profile is for friends, whereas a résumé is for employers. A résumé provides the most relevant details about qualifications and work experience. An online profile may contain information that employers should not use to judge an applicant, such as age or religion. In conclusion, while there are good reasons to check an applicant's online profile, it is not a professional document. For this reason, it is not fair, in my opinion, to judge candidates by their personal online profiles.

C **Focus on language** Read the grammar chart. Then use your ideas from Exercise A to complete the sentences below.

Contrast ideas in writing ⬇

On the one hand, employers need workers who will fit into the company.
On the other hand, an online profile is for friends.

A résumé is for employers. *However,* an online profile is for friends.
A résumé is for employers, *while/whereas/but* an online profile is for friends.
While there are reasons to check an online profile, it is not fair to do this.

Writing vs. Conversation

whereas ▮ ▮ ■ Conversation ▮ Writing

however ▮▮▮▮▮▮▮▮▮▮▮▮▮▮▮

1. Introduction: *Many employers _____ . Some people think _____ . However, _____ .*
2. Say why it is fair: *On the one hand, an online profile _____ , whereas a résumé _____ .*
3. Say why it is not fair: *On the other hand, an online profile _____ .*
4. Conclusion: *In conclusion, while _____ . In my opinion, _____ .*

D **Write and check** Now write your own script for the debate. Then check for errors.

Common errors

Do not start a sentence with *Whereas* to contrast ideas with a previous sentence.
*An online profile is for friends. **However,** a résumé is for employers.* (NOT ~~Whereas~~ . . .)

Vocabulary notebook *The right choice!*

Learning tip Formal or informal?

When you learn informal vocabulary, write down a more formal equivalent. Don't use informal words in formal writing.

weird (informal) = odd, strange, or eccentric
touchy (informal) = sensitive, easily upset

Dictionary tip

Dictionaries often label extremely informal words as *inf(ormal)*, *slang*, *colloqu(ial)*, *rude*, or *taboo*.

A Match the spoken sentences on the left with the more formal written sentences on the right.

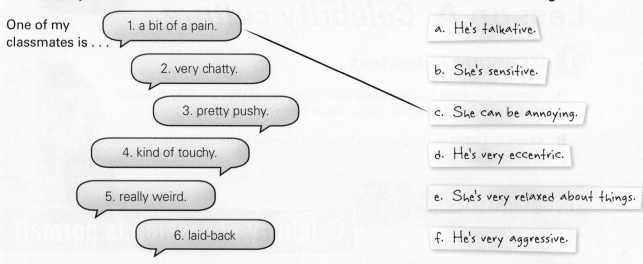

One of my classmates is . . .

1. a bit of a pain.
2. very chatty.
3. pretty pushy.
4. kind of touchy.
5. really weird.
6. laid-back

a. He's talkative.
b. She's sensitive.
c. She can be annoying.
d. He's very eccentric.
e. She's very relaxed about things.
f. He's very aggressive.

B Think of three people you know. Describe each person informally and more formally.

Person	Informal	More formal
1. _____	" _____ "	_____
2. _____	" _____ "	_____
3. _____	" _____ "	_____

C Word builder Find the meanings of the verbs below. Match the informal and more formal verbs. Then use each verb to say and write something true about people you know.

Informal

badmouth	bug	chill out (with)
get a kick out of (doing)		hang out (with)

More formal

annoy	criticize	enjoy (doing)
relax (with)		socialize (with)

One guy in my class is always <u>badmouthing</u> other people.

One of my classmates is always <u>criticizing</u> other people.

brainy = intelligent

On your own

Make a dictionary of informal expressions. Write down an informal word or expression and a more formal synonym that you can use in writing or formal speech.

The media

In Unit 2, you . . .

- talk about the influence of the media and celebrities.
- add information with relative clauses.
- link ideas with *that* clauses.
- make comments with *which* clauses.
- use *You know what . . . ?* to introduce what you say.

Lesson A *Celebrity culture*

1 Grammar in context

A Who are the most popular celebrities in the news? Why are they famous? How do people follow the news about them?

B 🔊 CD 1.16 Listen to the podcast. Why is it normal to be interested in celebrities?

ONE-MINUTE PODCASTS

Celebrity obsession is normal!

Everywhere we look these days, we see images of celebrities. Celebrity magazines, which outnumber news magazines, are on every newsstand. We love to read about the people that celebrities date, the clothes they wear, and especially their problems, which the media will often invent. Then there's reality TV. Millions of viewers avidly follow reality and talent shows, which make ordinary people into instant celebrities. There are even shows that pay for plastic surgery, so people can look like their favorite celebrity. So, why *are* we so obsessed?

Well, there's a simple scientific reason for it, which might make you feel better about your own interest in celebrity gossip. Psychologists say it's natural for us to talk about or imitate the people who are the most successful in our society. In ancient times, people gossiped about kings and leaders, who were the celebrities of their day. Nowadays, it's actors, musicians, or athletes. And with TV and the Internet, they come right into our homes, which almost makes them part of the family.

So our obsession with celebrity is perfectly normal, which is reassuring – don't you think?

About you

C Pair work Answer the questions about the podcast. Then give your own view and add more information on each answer.

1. Which are more popular – celebrity magazines or news magazines?
2. Why can't we always believe celebrity gossip?
3. What do some people do to look like their favorite celebrities?
4. Why are celebrities so familiar to us?

❷ Grammar Adding information

Figure it out

A Check (✔) the sentence that has a complete meaning if you remove the words in bold. Then read the grammar chart.

1. We love to read about celebrities' problems, **which the media will often invent.** ☐
2. There are even shows **that pay for plastic surgery.** ☐

Defining and non-defining relative clauses ⬇

Grammar extra
See page 146.

Defining relative clauses define, identify, or give essential information about a noun.
*There are shows **that/which pay for plastic surgery**.*
*We love to read about the people **(who/that) celebrities date** and the clothes **(that) they wear**.*

Non-defining relative clauses give extra information about a noun.
They do not begin with *that*. Notice the use of commas.
*Celebrity magazines, **which outnumber news magazines**, are everywhere.*
*It's natural to talk about celebrities, **who we see as successful people**.*

A *which* clause can add information or a comment to the clause before it.
*This obsession is normal, **which is reassuring**.*
*Celebrities come into our homes, **which almost makes them family**.*

In conversation . . .

That is more common than *which* in defining relative clauses.

Non-defining and *which* clauses often give opinions as well as information.

Common errors

Do not use *which* for people, or *what* in relative clauses.

B Complete the interview extracts with *who, that,* or *which*. If you can leave them out, write parentheses ( ) around them. Sometimes there is more than one correct answer.

1. *Miki*   I like to read about the problems (*that*) celebrities are having, _____ makes me feel better about *my* problems. I don't want to know all the details of their marriages, _____ should be private, but . . . just a few things.

2. *Tariq*   I'm interested in celebrities _____ can do other things. For example, there's Natalie Portman, _____'s a scientist. She's published in journals, _____ is interesting.

3. *Miguel*   Well, I'll occasionally read the gossip in magazines, _____ is probably all untrue anyway. It's a distraction from work, _____ I think we all need. And it gives me something to talk about with my co-worker Jo, _____'s really into celebrity gossip and stuff.

4. *Salwa*   Actually, I'm not interested in celebrities, _____ I feel set a bad example. You know, they often think they can do anything just because they're famous, _____ is ridiculous, really.

❸ Viewpoint Who's into celebrity gossip?

Class activity Ask your classmates the questions. Are you a celebrity-obsessed class?

• Are you interested in celebrities? If so, what interests you about them?
• How closely do you follow celebrity gossip? Which celebrities are in the news at the moment?
• What other celebrity gossip have you heard about in the last year?

"I'm interested in the clothes that celebrities wear. I mean, they wear some weird things, which is always fun."

In conversation . . .

Use *I mean, . . .* to repeat your ideas or say more.

❹ Speaking naturally *which* clauses See page 138.

Lesson B *The impact of TV*

1 Vocabulary in context

A 🔊 CD 1.19 **Read the article. Which research did you already know?**

The problem with TV

Young people tune into TV for over four and a half hours every single day. That's an **increase in** TV viewing **of** 40 minutes a day compared to a few years ago. But it's not surprising that we're watching more TV. With all the latest technology, TV is now viewed online, on mobile devices such as phones and tablets, or on digital video recorders (DVRs). What's clear is that TV is central to our lives. But what kind of **impact** does it have **on** us?

1 Language development There is a lot of **research on** TV and its effects on children. What is most disturbing is that TV may have a negative **effect on** children's language development. While the results of studies vary, the opinion of most experts is that children under two should not watch TV.

2 Obesity An average teenager sees 6,000 food commercials a year, and most are **advertisements for** fast foods, candy, and sugary cereals. It is also likely that increased TV-viewing time contributes to inactivity. Experts claim that these are two of the main **reasons for** the **rise in** obesity among young people.

3 Literacy One **problem with** TV is that it reduces the time that students spend reading. Research shows that there is a direct **link between** reading and good test scores, and it's possible that TV viewing is one **cause of** poor test results.

4 Social skills There is also some **concern about** TV and its **influence on** behavior. In one survey, teachers complained that some shows encourage their students to behave badly. Other reports suggest that there is a **relationship between** watching too much TV and bullying.

B Complete the questions with prepositions. Use the article to help you. Then ask and answer the questions with a partner.

1. What's one reason _____ the increase _____ TV viewing over the last few years?
2. What does the article say about the effects of TV _____ children under two?
3. What foods are most food advertisements _____ ? Is there a problem _____ this?
4. What's another cause _____ the rise _____ obesity levels among young people?
5. What's the link _____ watching TV and reading? Why is there concern _____ this?
6. What impact does TV have _____ students' behavior?

Word sort

C Which nouns in the article are followed by these prepositions? Write them in the chart. Some nouns take more than one preposition.

_____ about	_____ between	_____ for	_increase_ in
_____	_____	_____	_____
_____ of	_____ on	_____ with	
_____	_____	_____	
	_____		

Vocabulary notebook
See page 29.

2 Grammar Linking ideas

Figure
it out

A Rewrite each pair of sentences as one sentence. Use the article on page 22 to help you.
Then read the grammar chart.

1. Children under two should not watch TV. This is the opinion of most experts.
2. We're watching more TV. It's not surprising.
3. TV is central to our lives. It's clear.
4. There is a direct link between reading and good test scores. Research shows this link.

---

that clauses ⬇

Grammar extra
See page 147.

You can use a *that* clause after these structures. In conversation people often leave out the word *that*.

noun + *be*	*One problem with TV is (that) it reduces students' reading time.*
be + adjective	*It's clear (that) TV viewing contributes to inactivity.*
What's + adjective + *be*	*What's disturbing is (that) TV may have an effect on language development.*
verbs, e.g., *know, think, say, show*	*Experts claim (that) watching TV is one cause of obesity.*

In conversation . . .

Common expressions with *that* clauses:
The thing / problem / point is that . . .
What I'm saying is that . . .
My feeling / opinion is that . . .

B Rewrite the sentences using a *that* clause. Start with the
words given, and add a verb when necessary.

1. People who watch TV spend more on consumer goods. *Experts . . .*
2. The majority of families have TV on during mealtimes. *It's disturbing . . .*
3. Most people multitask and do other things while watching TV. *What's interesting . . .*
4. Young people who watch a lot of TV are not very happy with their lives. *One recent study . . .*
5. It's not good for anyone to have a TV in the bedroom. *My feeling . . .*
6. TV is a good thing because there are lots of good educational programs. *My opinion . . .*
7. There are too many commercials and not enough good shows. *The problem with TV . . .*
8. Children are watching so much TV these days. *Teachers are concerned . . .*

About
you

C **Pair work** Discuss your reactions to the sentences in Exercise B.

"I'm not surprised that there's a link between spending and watching TV. What I'm saying is that . . ."

3 Listening and speaking It's really interesting that . . .

A 🔊 CD 1.20 Listen. Five people are reacting to information from the article on page 22.
Which topic does each person talk about? Write the letters a, b, c, or d.

1. Maggie _____
2. Howard _____
3. Daniela _____
4. Isabel _____
5. Tony _____

a. Language development
b. Obesity
c. Literacy
d. Social skills

B 🔊 CD 1.21 Listen again. Write the alternative opinion each person gives.

1. Maggie says one good thing about TV is that . . .

About
you

C **Pair work** Discuss your sentences in Exercise B. Do you agree with the points each person makes?

"I think Maggie is right. What's interesting is that people never talk about how good TV can be."

Lesson C *You know what gets me?*

① Conversation strategy Adding comments

A How often do you watch online video clips? What different kinds of clips are there? Do you watch movies online, too?

B ◀)) CD 1.22 Listen. What does Anna think about video clips? How about Pedro?

Anna Did you see that video clip I emailed you?

Pedro Um, no. I don't generally tend to watch them, which is unusual, I guess. What was it?

Anna Oh, it's a couple of talking cats. It's hilarious.

Pedro Yeah? I don't mind the funny ones. You know what I don't like? People do really dangerous things and video it – like riding bikes off walls.

Anna Which is stupid, I know.

Pedro You know what gets me, too? Some of the home videos people post. They're so boring.

Anna That's true. But you know what's amazing? The number of hits they can get. I mean, they get millions.

Pedro Which is incredible. I just don't get it.

C **Notice** how Anna and Pedro use relative clauses with *which* to comment on their own and each other's statements. Find more examples in the conversation.

> *"People do really dangerous things and video it . . ."*
>
> *"Which is stupid, I know."*

D ◀)) CD 1.23 **Complete the conversations with the comments in the box. Then listen and check. Practice with a partner.**

1. *A* What kinds of video clips do you tend to watch?
   B Mostly music. I subscribe to a few websites, _____ .

2. *A* Do you ever watch those video debates on news sites?
   B Yeah, they're good. People have very different views on things.
   A _____ . I like to hear different opinions – it makes you think.

3. *A* Do you ever upload your own videos online?
   B My brother does. He'll video anything – even the wall – _____ .

4. *A* Do you email video clips to your friends all the time?
   B No. It's a pain. I have a friend who's *always* sending clips, _____ . I'll only send one if it's really interesting or funny.
   A _____ .

a. which is kind of weird

b. which is a great way to find new bands

c. Which is interesting

d. Which is fine

e. which is really annoying

About you

E **Pair work** Ask the questions in Exercise D, and give your own answers. Add comments with *which* . . . where possible.

2 Strategy plus *You know what . . . ?*

CD 1.24 You can use **You know what . . . ?** to introduce a comment on what you are going to say.

You know what's *amazing?*
You know what *gets me?*
You know what *I don't like?*

But you know what's amazing? The number of hits they can get.

A Circle the best option to complete the *You know what . . . ?* expression. Compare with a partner.

1. You know what **interests me / I hate**? We like to watch people's home videos – why is that?
2. You know what's **amazing / so nice**? People waste so much time watching this stuff.
3. You know what**'s bad / I like**? Anyone can be creative and make a video to upload.
4. You know what**'s great / gets me**? People upload videos of their friends without permission.
5. You know what **scares me / I love**? I might be on an embarrassing video and not know.
6. You know what's **fun / annoying**? Some of the ads. They can be hilarious.

About you

B Pair work Start conversations with six of the *You know what . . . ?* expressions in Exercise A. Do you agree with each other's views?

A You know what I hate? All those advertisements that come on before the videos.
B I know. They can be annoying. But they're not before every video.

3 Strategies Watching movies

A Complete the *You know what . . . ?* expressions with your own ideas, and circle the best *which . . .* comments. Then practice the conversations with a partner.

1. *A* It's good that you can watch movie trailers online before you see a movie.
   B But you know what _____ ? The trailers always look exciting. But then, when you see the movie, it's often not that good, which is **fun / a pain**.

2. *A* We usually watch movies on DVD. But you know what _____ ?
      They often get stuck – like right at the best part . . .
   B Which is really **annoying / nice**. The problem is they get scratched.

3. *A* You know what _____ ? Even though you can watch movies online and everything, the research shows that people still like to go to movie theaters.
   B Which **is terrible / isn't surprising**, really. It's more fun to watch on a big screen.

4. *A* I hate it when people tell you how a movie ends before you watch it.
   B Yeah. But you know what _____ ? When people tell you every detail about a movie they've just seen, which is just so **exciting / boring**.

About you

B Class activity Prepare answers to the questions. Give reasons. Then survey the class. What is the consensus?

- What do you think about online movies and videos?
- Do you have any concerns about their content?
- What are the good things about them? What are the problems?

A Well, one problem with some of the music videos is that they can be offensive.
B I agree. You know what gets me? All that bad language, which is just awful.

Lesson D *A bad influence?*

① Reading

A **Prepare** **Which of these statements about violence in the media do you agree with?**

1. It can make people aggressive.
2. It's just harmless entertainment.
3. It's harmful to children.
4. It should be banned.

B ⬇ **Understanding viewpoints** **Read the article. Which of the statements in Exercise A would the writer agree with? Find reasons for your answers in the article.**

NOT JUST A GAME

1 Whether we like it or not, violence is part of all mass media. It's on TV and the Internet, in movies, music, and the video games people play. What is most disturbing perhaps is that it's not just in adult entertainment. On a typical Saturday morning, children's television shows up to 25 acts of violence per hour, which means that by the age of 18, the average person has witnessed around 200,000 violent acts. [1 __d__]

2 What kind of impact does this have on young people? Over 25 years ago, psychologists found that elementary-school children who watched many hours of violence on television had more aggressive behavior as teenagers. In recent years, however, researchers have turned their attention to the problem of violence in video games, which are now a more popular form of entertainment than movies.

3 One disturbing trend in video-game design is the number of games that include extreme violence and killing. Critics of video games are concerned about the impact that these types of video games can have, especially on young people. Violent games are often blamed for aggressive behavior on school playgrounds and, in extreme cases, for the rise in school shootings.

4 However, are violent video games the cause of violent behavior? [2 __e__]

5 Psychologists claim that there *is* evidence to suggest that playing violent video games really does make people feel, think, and behave more aggressively.

[3 __a__] The research also suggests that video games have a greater influence than television because they are interactive and players identify with and take on the role of the killers in the games.

6 There *are* games that reward players for positive, pro-social behaviors such as cooperating or sharing. However, children tend to prefer games that require them to be aggressive, violent, or competitive in order to win. One point that critics of violent video games make is that these games are regularly used as part of military training, where the aim is to desensitize the players to killing. The same seems to be happening to young people, they say.

7 [4 __b__] In one study, 80 percent of junior high school students said they were familiar with a particular violent computer game, but fewer than 5 percent of parents had even heard of it, which proves how little parents are engaging with this complex issue.

8 Isn't it time for us all to take more interest in the effect that media violence has on us, and do something about it?

Reading tip

Writers often ask a question and then answer it to build their argument. (See paragraphs 2 and 4.)

C **Read for detail** **Where do these sentences fit in the article? Write the correct letters in the spaces. There is one extra sentence.**

a. Furthermore, children who enjoy aggressive video and computer games show less pro-social behavior, such as helping people.
b. Parents need to be more aware of the violent games that their children are playing.
c. Parents of teenagers are also concerned about violent music lyrics.
d. By the age of 11, a U.S. child will typically have seen 8,000 murders on TV.
e. The short answer seems to be "yes."

② Focus on vocabulary Formal expressions

A **Find more formal ways in the article of expressing the underlined ideas. Write the number of words indicated.**

turned their attention to

1. Researchers have <u>started looking at</u> video games. (4 words: para. 2)

2. Some games have <u>really bad</u> violence and killing. (1 word: para. 3)

3. <u>People who don't like</u> video games say they are harmful. (2 words: para. 3)

4. Players <u>think they are like</u> the characters in the games. (2 words: para. 5)

5. Children <u>knew about</u> games that their parents hadn't heard of. (3 words: para. 7)

6. Violence in video games is a very <u>difficult subject</u>. (2 words: para. 7)

About you

B **Pair work** **What new facts did you learn from the article? How did the information affect your views on violence in the media? Discuss with a partner.**

"I think it's interesting that the average person sees 200,000 violent acts by the age of 18. That has to have an effect on you . . ."

③ Listening and speaking They're just games!

A ◀)) CD 1.25 **Listen to part of a lecture about violence and the media. Choose the best phrase to complete the summary of the speaker's argument.**

There _____ between violence in the media and crime.

a. is a clear link   b. is no proof of a link   c. are a number of links

B ◀)) CD 1.26 **Listen again. Circle the correct option to complete the information about the lecture.**

1. The speaker **agrees / does not agree** that violent entertainment makes people aggressive.
2. Over the last 25 years, there has been a **rise / drop** in violent youth crime.
3. Around 90 percent of boys and **14 / 40** percent of girls play video games.
4. He says that people **can / can't** tell the difference between fact and fiction.
5. He claims that there is **some / no** evidence that games turn people into killers.

About you

C **Group work** **Discuss the questions. Give reasons for your answers.**

1. Were you surprised by anything the speaker said? What did you find most interesting?
2. Do you think there is too much violence in the media?
3. Do you know people who enjoy violent entertainment? Do they tend to be more aggressive?
4. Should we have the right to choose what we watch and play?
5. Is it possible to stop children from seeing extreme violence? If so, how?

DONNELLY

Writing *Should it be banned?*

In this lesson, you . . .
- use topic sentences.
- list ideas.
- avoid errors with listing expressions.

Task | **Write a paragraph.**

Songs with violent lyrics make people more violent and should be banned. Do you agree or disagree?

A **Look at a model** Read the paragraph from an essay. Check (✔) the two good topic sentences below, and choose one to write in the space.

> While many people feel that music with violent lyrics should be banned, we need to look closely at this argument. _____ First, the main problem with banning this music is that it becomes more attractive, especially to young people. People who did not listen to it before might become interested in it, which may make it even more popular. Second, there is no proof that this music makes people violent. A lot of people enjoy it, which does not mean that they are violent people. Finally, people can find all kinds of music on the Internet, which means that a ban will not work.

☐ a. Music is something that everyone loves.
☐ b. I like this type of music.
☐ c. It is unlikely that a ban will work for several reasons.
☐ d. This music does not make people more violent.
☐ e. There are at least three problems with banning this type of music.

Topic sentences

A topic sentence gives the main idea or topic of a paragraph. The other sentences should support the main idea.

B **Focus on language** Circle two more expressions in the paragraph in Exercise A that organize the ideas. Then read the grammar chart.

Listing ideas in writing ⬇

There are at least three problems with banning this music. **First,** *it may become more attractive to young people.* **Second, . . . Third, . . . Finally, / Lastly,** *people can find all kinds of music on the Internet.*

Writing vs. Conversation

- *First, Second, Finally,* and *Lastly* are much more common in writing.
- *First of all* is more common in conversation.

C **Brainstorm** What's your answer to the essay question? Think of three reasons to support your answer. Complete the sentences with your ideas. Then compare with a partner.

1. Say if you agree or disagree: *I agree/disagree with the statement that* _____
2. Give reason 1: *First,* _____
3. Give reason 2: *Second,* _____
4. Give reason 3: *Finally,* _____

D **Write and check** Now write a paragraph that gives your answer to the essay question and the reasons for it. Include a clear topic sentence. Then check for errors.

Common errors

Use *First* and *Lastly* when you list ideas.
There are two reasons for this.
First, *this music is . . .* (NOT ~~At first, . . .~~)
Lastly, *the Internet has . . .* (NOT ~~At last, . . .~~)

Vocabulary notebook *What an effect!*

Learning tip Nouns and prepositions

When you write down a new noun, find out what prepositions (if any) are used with it. Write a short sentence and complete it with two or more ideas.

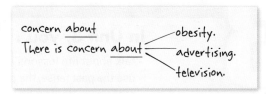

concern <u>about</u>
There is concern <u>about</u> — obesity.
— advertising.
— television.

A **Complete the notes and sentences with prepositions. Then add another idea that could replace the bold words in each sentence.**

children's toys

1. advertisement <u>for</u>   There are a lot of advertisements <u>for</u> **fast food** on television.

2. cause _____   One cause _____ low test scores may be **TV viewing**.

3. concern _____   There is a lot of concern _____ **childhood obesity**.

4. effect _____   Advertising may have an effect _____ **children's diets**.

5. influence _____   TV has a big influence _____ **children's behavior**.

6. impact _____   Television has an impact _____ **young children**.

7. link _____   There is a link _____ TV viewing and **language development**.

8. problem _____   One problem _____ television is **the number of commercials**.

9. relationship _____   There's a relationship _____ reading and **test scores**.

10. reason _____   What are the reasons _____ **obesity**?

11. research _____   The research _____ **TV viewing** is very clear.

12. rise _____   There has been a rise _____ **bullying in schools**.

B **Word builder Find out which prepositions you can use with these nouns, and complete the sentences. Then use your own ideas to write one more sentence for each noun + preposition.**

1. attitude _____   We should change our attitude _____ television and what it can offer.

2. connection _____   There seems to be a connection _____ the amount of television kids watch and their ability to pay attention.

3. information _____   We need more information _____ the effects of bullying.

4. need _____   There's a need _____ better programming on TV.

link between . . .

There's a link between advertising and diet.

On your own

Make a flip pad of nouns and prepositions. Write a different noun on every page.

Stories

In Unit 3, you . . .

- talk about life lessons and experiences.
- use the past tense, the present perfect, and the past perfect.
- make comments when telling a story.
- use (It's) no wonder . . . to say something is not surprising.

Lesson A *Highlights*

1 Grammar in context

A What are some typical highlights in people's lives? Make a list.

"Well, getting into college seems to be a real highlight for a lot of people."

B ◀))) CD 1.27 Listen to the interviews. What special things has each person done?

We interviewed people and asked,
"What are some of the highlights of your life so far?"

JANIE, 35
Vancouver, Canada:
high school teacher

"Oh, I've been pretty lucky up until now. For one thing, I've traveled a lot. I lived in Italy a couple of years ago. That was amazing. Then after Italy, I went to Central America and worked with a team of volunteers. We were rebuilding homes after a major earthquake for two months. It was hard work but so rewarding. Life has definitely been interesting so far."

MARCOS, 25
Belo Horizonte, Brazil:
college student

"Um, I've done some interesting things in the last few years. I started a band the year before last, though it didn't last – we broke up after six months. But it was fun. And I've been coaching a local soccer team for the last two years. That's been good. We've won most of our matches. I still haven't decided what I want to do after I graduate. I haven't thought too much about it . . . yet. But that's OK!"

JING-WEI, 25 and SHENG, 27
Beijing, China: designer
and graduate student

"Well, we haven't really done anything except work over the last few years. We met when we were in college. Sheng was getting his master's, and I was studying design. Then Sheng started his PhD. Since then, he's just been concentrating on school."
"Jing-Wei got an internship at a fashion company last year. That was a big thing for her. You've been enjoying it so far, haven't you?"

About you **C** **Pair work** Discuss the questions about the people. Give your own opinions.

Who . . .

1. has the most initiative?
2. works very hard?
3. makes the most out of life?
4. is doing something you'd like to do?
5. has the most exciting life?

"I think Janie has the most initiative. It's great that she did that volunteer work and . . ."

2 Grammar Talking about the past

Figure it out

A Find the sentences below in the interviews. Do they refer to a completed past time (C) or a past time that continues up to now (N)? Write C or N. Then read the grammar chart.

1. After Italy I went to Central America. _____
2. Life has definitely been interesting so far. _____
3. I started a band the year before last. _____
4. Since then, he's been concentrating on school. _____

The past tense vs. the present perfect ⬇

Grammar extra
See page 148.

Use the past tense for situations and events that are part of a completed past time, not connected to now.

| past time | now |

I **lived** in Italy a few years ago. (I'm not there now.)
The band **didn't last**. We **broke up** after six months.

Use the present perfect for situations and events that are part of a past time that continues up to now.

| past time → now |

Life **has been** interesting so far. (It still is.)
Marcos **hasn't decided** what he wants to do yet.

Use simple verbs for completed events or permanent situations.
Marcos's band **broke up**.   I**'ve been** pretty lucky.

Use continuous verbs for background, ongoing, or temporary events or situations.
We **were rebuilding** homes.   He**'s been coaching** a soccer team.

B Complete the conversations with an appropriate form of the verbs given. Sometimes more than one option may be possible. Then practice with a partner.

1. **A** Have you had any interesting opportunities in the last couple of years?
   B Um, last year I _____ (join) a gymnastics team. Since then, we _____ (compete) at several events, but so far we _____ (not win) anything.

2. **A** Have you traveled much over the last few years?
   B Well, I _____ (not go) away last year, but the year before, when I _____ (study) geography in college, we _____ (take) a trip to Alaska. That _____ (be) fun. I _____ (not travel) much since then.

3. **A** What's been the highlight of your year so far?
   B Actually, up until now, I _____ (not do) anything special because I _____ (be) so busy with school. I _____ (work) on my thesis all year, so I _____ (not have) much time for anything else. I _____ (take) a short break last weekend, though, and I _____ (go) hiking, but that's all.

About you

C Pair work Take turns asking and answering the questions in Exercise B. Give your own answers.

3 Viewpoint So far . . .

Group work Tell your group about three highlights in your life so far. Ask your classmates questions to find out more information.

A *One highlight for me is that I met my favorite baseball player. He was giving out baseball jerseys at a game.*
B *That's so cool. Did he sign them?*

In conversation . . .

Use expressions like these to react to people's stories.
That's so great/amazing/ cool/interesting.

Lesson B *Life lessons*

① Vocabulary in context

A Read the blog. What is the story about? Can you guess what the professor said?

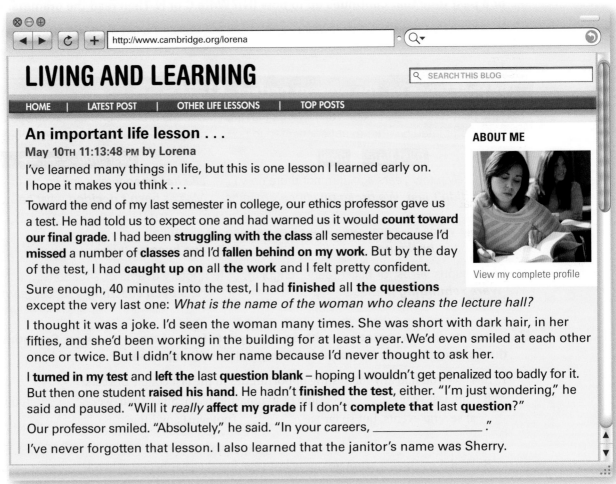

http://www.cambridge.org/lorena

LIVING AND LEARNING

SEARCH THIS BLOG

HOME | LATEST POST | OTHER LIFE LESSONS | TOP POSTS

An important life lesson . . .
May 10TH 11:13:48 PM by Lorena

I've learned many things in life, but this is one lesson I learned early on.
I hope it makes you think . . .

Toward the end of my last semester in college, our ethics professor gave us
a test. He had told us to expect one and had warned us it would **count toward
our final grade**. I had been **struggling with the class** all semester because I'd
missed a number of **classes** and I'd **fallen behind on my work**. But by the day
of the test, I had **caught up on** all **the work** and I felt pretty confident.

Sure enough, 40 minutes into the test, I had **finished** all **the questions**
except the very last one: *What is the name of the woman who cleans the lecture hall?*

I thought it was a joke. I'd seen the woman many times. She was short with dark hair, in her
fifties, and she'd been working in the building for at least a year. We'd even smiled at each other
once or twice. But I didn't know her name because I'd never thought to ask her.

I **turned in my test** and **left the** last **question blank** – hoping I wouldn't get penalized too badly for it.
But then one student **raised his hand**. He hadn't **finished the test**, either. "I'm just wondering," he
said and paused. "Will it *really* **affect my grade** if I don't **complete that** last **question**?"

Our professor smiled. "Absolutely," he said. "In your careers, _____."

I've never forgotten that lesson. I also learned that the janitor's name was Sherry.

ABOUT ME

View my complete profile

About you

B 🔊 CD 1.28 Listen to the story. Did you have a similar ending? What do you think of the
professor's response?

C Pair work Prepare answers to the questions. Give reasons using expressions from the
story. Then compare with a partner.

1. Why was the ethics test an important one?
2. What was Lorena's experience with her ethics class?
3. What problem did she have with the test?
4. Why was she concerned that she would get penalized?
5. How did the professor answer the student who raised his hand?

Word sort

D How many expressions from the blog can you find that include these words? Add other
ideas. Then take turns using each expression to ask your partner a question.

___miss___ a class	_____ a grade	_____ a test
_____ your work	_____ your hand	_____ a question (_____)

Vocabulary notebook

See page 39.

"Have you ever missed a class?"

2 Grammar Sequencing events

Figure it out

A When did each event below happen: on the day of the test (D) or before the day of the test (B)? Write D or B. What do you notice about the verb forms? Then read the grammar chart.

1. The professor gave us a test. _____
2. He had told us to expect it. _____
3. I'd been struggling with the class. _____
4. I felt pretty confident. _____

The simple past, past perfect, and past perfect continuous ⬇

Grammar extra
See page 149.

Use the simple past for two or more events that are part of the same past time period.

past event + past event	now

past event 1   past event 2
He **raised** his hand and **asked** a question.

Use the past perfect for an event that is part of a time period before another event in the past.

earlier past event	past event	now

earlier past event   past event
He **had told** us to expect a test. We **took** it last week.

Use the past perfect continuous for background, ongoing, or temporary events or situations.

ongoing earlier past event	past event	now

ongoing earlier past event   past event
I**'d been struggling** . . ., but I **felt** confident on the day.

In conversation . . .

People often use the past perfect to give reasons or explanations.
I didn't know her name **because I'd never thought to ask her.**

B Complete the anecdote with the verbs given. Use one simple past and one past perfect verb in each sentence.

"Right before I _____ (move) here, I _____ (lose) my job. I _____ (not have) an interview for weeks, and I _____ (be) concerned, you know. And I _____ (think) about going back to school, but actually, I _____ (not want) to. And then out of the blue, I _____ (get) an email from an old friend that I _____ (not contact) in ages."

C Complete the rest of the anecdote with the past perfect or past perfect continuous form of the verbs given. Sometimes both are possible. Then take turns retelling the story to a partner.

"And it turned out that he _____ (start up) his own company. But he _____ (struggle) to find someone to work for him for some time, and he _____ (not found) anyone suitable. Well, actually, he _____ (hire) one woman, but she _____ (quit) after the first month because she _____ (not be able) to travel so much. Anyway, I _____ (look) for a job in sales, and he offered me the job. So, yeah, I learned it's good to keep in touch with people!"

3 Listening and speaking It just goes to show . . .

A What do these sayings mean? Check (✔) the ones you agree with.

☐ a. You can't judge a book by its cover.
☐ b. You've got to stop and smell the roses.
☐ c. Truth is stranger than fiction.
☐ d. Life's too short.

B ◀)) CD 1.29 Listen to three stories. How will each story end? Number the sayings above 1–3.

C ◀)) CD 1.30 Listen and check your answers.

About you

D Group work Take turns telling about an important life lesson you've learned.

"I've learned to think positively. In high school, I'd been applying to lots of different colleges, but . . ."

4 Speaking naturally Auxiliary verbs *See page 139.*

Lesson C *Anyway, back to my story . . .*

1 Conversation strategy Telling stories

A Look at these expressions from a conversation. What do they mean? Can you guess what the conversation is about?

picture day at school	it was a big deal	scruffy-looking	my hair was sticking up

B ◀))) CD 1.33 Listen. Why was picture day a big deal for Brad's family?

Arnold Look at this old class photo. I mean, look at our hair!

Brad I know. You should see one of my school photos. We'd forgotten it was picture day, and looking back, picture day was a big deal in our house. My mom showed the photos to everybody and sent them out to my aunts. I hated it.

Arnold No wonder.

Brad Yeah. And she made me wear a shirt and tie. It's no wonder I hated it. But anyway, back to my story . . . so this one day I went to school as usual, which means I hadn't combed my hair and I was wearing an old T-shirt. I mean, when I think about it, I was always really scruffy-looking.

Arnold Yeah, me too. I didn't care how I looked back then.

Brad No, me neither. So anyway, where was I?

Arnold You went to school on picture day all scruffy . . .

C **Notice** how Brad interrupts his story to make a comment and comes back to it with expressions like these. Find examples in the conversation.

Interrupting a story:	Coming back to the story:
Looking back, . . .	*(But/So) anyway, . . .*
When I look back, . . .	*Anyway, (getting) back to*
When I think about it, . . .	*my story, . . .*

D ◀))) CD 1.34 Listen to more of their conversation and write the missing expressions. Then practice the conversation with a partner. Practice again, using different expressions.

Brad . . . Oh, yeah. So there I was in the front row – with my hair sticking up and a hole in my shirt. Right next to our teacher, Mr. Gray.

Arnold Yeah? That's funny.

Brad Yeah. _____ *(interrupt)*, he was a funny guy – nice but eccentric. He wore a bow tie and these little glasses, which he was always losing. _____ *(back to the story)*, when we got the photos the following week, my mom took one look at them and cried.

Arnold She did? She actually cried?

Brad Oh, yeah. I mean, _____ *(interrupt)*, picture day was the one day a year I looked good. It was a special day to her! _____ *(back to the story)*, she took me to a photographer and had my picture taken there.

2 Strategy plus *No wonder.*

> I hated it.
>
> No wonder.

CD 1.35 You can use *No wonder* as a response to a comment on an experience that is not surprising.

You can also use (*It's*) *no wonder* (*that*) to introduce a comment.

It's no wonder I hated it.

In conversation . . .

People mostly say *No wonder* . . .

No wonder . . . . . ■■■■■
It's no wonder . . . ■

A Match the sentences and the responses. Write the letters a–e. Then practice with a partner.

1. French classes were my favorite. _____
2. I walked two miles to school every day. _____
3. Lunch was always hot dogs and fries. _____
4. I couldn't wait for the summer. _____
5. I always fell behind in math. I hated it! _____

a. It's no wonder that kids are overweight.
b. No wonder. It's the best time of year.
c. Me too. It's no wonder we were fit.
d. No wonder. It's no fun if you're struggling.
e. It's no wonder you're so fluent.

About you

B Pair work Make the sentences true for you, and add a comment with (*It's*) *no wonder* . . .

"French was my least favorite class. It's no wonder I can't speak a word of it."

3 Strategies Childhood stories

A Complete each anecdote with the expressions in the box. Then take turns telling the stories. Listen to your partner and make comments.

anyway	But anyway	It's no wonder	when I look back

1. "One day my teacher asked me for help. We'd been painting pictures of flowers. We painted a lot in that class. So _____ , I picked up this cup and said, 'I can put it away.' You know, _____ , I was always trying to help the teacher. I was a good kid. _____ , I had this cup, which was full of dirty paint water, and I spilled it all over her skirt. _____ she never asked for my help again!"

But anyway, back to my story	looking back	No wonder	When I think about it

2. *A* I won first prize one time in a bicycle-safety contest. And _____ , it was really special because I'd never come first in anything. I wrote this slogan: *A five-minute check might save your neck.* _____ , I loved playing with words, even then. _____ . I was so excited – I thought the prize was a bike. But I just got a pen. I was so disappointed.

   B _____ .

About you

B Group work Use a chart like this one to prepare a story about your childhood (e.g., a fun or scary time, or a time you got into trouble). Then take turns telling your stories.

The story	Comments
1. I heard some noises in the yard one night.	I was a nervous kid – always scared at night.

Lesson D *Good fiction*

1 Reading

A **Prepare** What good fiction have you read recently? Who are your favorite authors?

B ⬇ **Read for main ideas** Read the winning entry in a short-story contest. What is Janet's problem?

Saturday
By Susan Ingram

¹ Janet couldn't remember when she'd first realized she was invisible. She supposed it had started, well, maybe it had started before, but she first noticed it when she would look into someone's eyes, say a passerby on the street, or even someone in the hallway at work when she was pushing the mail cart from office to office.

² She had always thought it was only human. What you did as a part of a community, a part of society. When someone passes by, you look them in the eyes, smile and say hi, or hello, or how's it going?

³ Janet always did. To everyone. Of course, not everyone responded. Some people looked away. Some acted like they didn't see her, or didn't hear her. She always felt sorry for people like that. What was it like not to be able to smile and say hi? She couldn't imagine.

⁴ But lately, she had noticed that not only was no one saying hi back, no one was even acknowledging her. As if she weren't even there. Just as if they couldn't see her at all.

⁵ Then stranger things happened. One day, when she was in line at her local donut shop, the woman behind the counter waited on the guy in front of her, then looked through her and asked the girls behind her, "May I help you?"

⁶ She began ordering from the drive-through window. They could hear her voice, apparently, through the cheap speakers. Could see at least her truck when she pulled up to the window. They would slip her the medium half-decaf with vanilla cream and take her bills and give her change. All without making eye contact.

⁷ She would drive away, smiling, eyes wide, and shake her head and sip her coffee and wonder what was happening in the world.

⁸ This morning, a clear, hard winter morning, a Saturday, Janet pulled out of the drive-through, doubled back into the parking lot still piled high with mountains of snow, and parked. She'd been stuck in the house for three days, the office closed, her neighborhood like something from another planet.

⁹ She grabbed the newspaper from the seat next to her. It was the first paper she'd gotten since the day before the storm. She found it sitting in the sun on top of a six-foot mound of snow at the end of her driveway like a yellow-plastic-bagged Valentine's Day gift.

DONNELLY

¹⁰ With her coffee and bag in one hand and the newspaper tucked under her arm, she pushed through the door of the donut shop, where she hadn't ventured in months, and made her way to a small table by the window. There were a few people at a high-top at the opposite window. A couple of workers in headsets and caps moved behind the counter. No one looked up as she crossed to her table and sat down.

¹¹ Janet sipped at the coffee. It was hot and almost burned her tongue. She slipped the newspaper out of the plastic sleeve and spread it out on the table. A small, wrinkled man was making his way toward her, sliding a large rag mop across the already clean floor. Janet lifted her feet as he mopped under her table. He put the mop in the bucket and reached over for her newspaper, sliding it halfway off the table before Janet slapped her hand down, stopping it. The man looked puzzled and tugged again.

¹² "Hello," Janet said and smiled. The man looked up into her eyes.

¹³ "Oh, hello," he said, smiling back. "I didn't see you."

¹⁴ "Now you do," she said. "Now you do."

Reading tip
Fiction writers often break up sentences into small parts to create interest and drama.

To everyone. All without making eye contact.

These sentences can be ungrammatical, so don't use them in your writing for school.

C **Pair work** **Understand and react** **Discuss the questions.**

- What kind of woman do you think Janet is?
- Why did Janet feel invisible?
- How do you think Janet felt on the Saturday morning after the storm?
- What do you think the restaurant worker was thinking about while he was cleaning?
- Was he rude to Janet, do you think? Do you think Janet was rude to him?

2 Focus on vocabulary Verbs

A **Find the verbs in the story. Match them with their meanings. Write the letters a–h.**

1. say (para. 1) _____
2. acknowledge (para. 4) _____
3. slip (para. 6) _____
4. make eye contact (para. 6) _____
5. venture (para. 10) _____
6. make (your) way (para. 11) _____
7. slap down (para. 11) _____
8. tug (para. 11) _____

a. nod or smile to show you see someone
b. move something quickly so people don't notice
c. hit with a flat hand
d. walk toward
e. for example, like
f. go somewhere risky or unpleasant
g. look at someone directly in the eye
h. pull hard

B **Pair work** **What can you remember about the story? Take turns retelling the story in your own words. Try to include as many details as you can.**

"It's about a woman who noticed people had been ignoring her. They didn't . . ."

3 Listening and speaking How friendly are people?

A **Which statement below best describes people in your town or city? Give examples.**

☐ a. People are extremely friendly.
☐ b. People are friendly if you're friendly to them.
☐ c. People are very unfriendly.
☐ d. People are polite but not that friendly.

B ◀))CD 1.36 **Listen to three students describe the people in their cities. Which statement in Exercise A summarizes what they say? Number the statements 1–3. There is one extra statement.**

C ◀))CD 1.37 **Listen again. Each person tells an anecdote to illustrate a point. Where were the people and what happened? Make notes and compare with a partner.**

About you

D **Group work** **Create a list of rules that would make your city a friendlier place to live.**

"Well, I think people should acknowledge other people when they come into contact with them. Like, if you get into an elevator with someone, you should at least smile."

In conversation . . .

You can use *like* to give examples.

Writing *What do you expect?*

In this lesson, you . . .
- brainstorm and then plan an article.
- use verbs to structure an article.
- avoid errors with the past perfect.

Task | **Write a narrative article.**

Write an article for a college magazine about a time you experienced good or bad behavior.

A **Look at a model** Number the paragraphs in the correct order. Find an introduction (1), background events (2), main events (3, 4), and a conclusion (5). Which verb forms are used in each part?

_____ Since then, I've often thought about that day. I know if I ever find someone's bag, I'll do the right thing.

_____ I ran across the platform, but the doors of the train started to close, and in a last effort to get on the train, I threw my bag onto it. The doors slammed shut, and I stood on the platform as the train pulled slowly away. I felt so stupid. I'd just thrown my bag with my computer and wallet onto a train!

_____ I remember one day, I was running to catch the subway to go to an interview. I was feeling stressed because I was late and I'd been running around all morning.

_____ I looked around for help, but of course, everyone ignored me. The next day, I called the lost and found department to ask if they had my bag. They didn't. Someone had taken it.

__1__ I like to think, generally, that people are honest and that they will always do the right thing. Unfortunately, this is not always the case.

B **Focus on language** Read the chart. Then complete the article below with appropriate forms of the verbs given. Sometimes more than one option may be possible.

> ### Verbs in narrative writing
>
> You can use:
> - the present tense to introduce your article: I **like** to think that people **are** honest.
> - continuous forms for background events: I **was feeling** stressed. I**'d been running** around.
> - simple past forms for main events: I **threw** my bag onto it. The doors **slammed** shut.
> - the present perfect to link events to now: I**'ve** often **thought** about that day.

It _____ (be) simply good manners to hold doors open for people, but not everyone _____ (be) so considerate. One day I _____ (go) into an office building. I _____ (carry) a big box of paper, which I _____ (deliver) to a business. Suddenly, a woman who _____ (walk) behind me _____ (push) right in front of me. She _____ (open) the heavy glass door and _____ (not hold) it for me. The door _____ (slam) in my face, and I _____ (fall) backwards on the sidewalk. Since then, I _____ always _____ (make) sure that I hold doors open for people.

C **Brainstorm and plan** Think of ideas for your article. Then use the headings to help you plan it.

1. Introduction: _____
2. Background events: _____
3. Main events: _____
4. Conclusion / link to now: _____

> **Common errors**
>
> The past perfect is *had* + a past participle. Do not use *had* + a simple past form of the verb.
>
> I'd just **thrown** my bag onto a train. (NOT I'd just ~~threw~~ . . .)

D **Write and check** Write your article. Then check for errors.

Vocabulary notebook *Catch up!*

Learning tip   Writing definitions

When you learn a new expression, write a definition to help you remember it.

> If you struggle with a class, you have a difficult time with it (for example, because the work is hard or there's too much to do).

A   **Complete the definitions with a correct form of the expressions in the box.**

affect your grade	count toward your final grade	leave a question blank
catch up on your work	fall behind on your work	✓ raise your hand

1. If you _____ raise your hand _____ , you put it in the air to get someone's attention – for example, when you want to ask a question in class.
2. If you _____ , you can't do all the things you are supposed to do on time.
3. If you _____ , you don't write an answer to it.
4. If tests or assignments _____ , they are part of your final score.
5. If assignments _____ , they can make a difference to your grade.
6. If you _____ , you do all the work on your desk that you had to do or that is late.

B   **Now write definitions for these expressions.**

1. miss a class _____
2. complete a question _____
3. turn in a test _____
4. finish a test _____

C   **Word builder**   **Find the meanings of the expressions in the box, and write definitions for them.**

attend a class	drop a class	fail a class	hand in an assignment	repeat a class/grade

1. _____
2. _____
3. _____
4. _____
5. _____

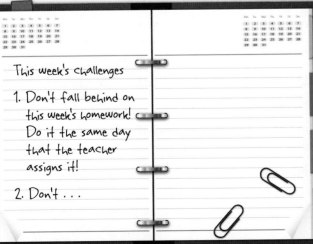

This week's challenges

1. Don't fall behind on this week's homework! Do it the same day that the teacher assigns it!

2. Don't . . .

> **We *catch up* on . . .**
>
> The things people talk about *catching up on* most are: *sleep, reading, correspondence, paperwork.*

> **On your own**
>
> What can you do to improve your work for your classes? Make a list in English in the front of your notebook. Review the list in a week. Are you sticking to the challenges?

Checkpoint 1 *Units 1–3*

1 TV time

A Complete the conversations with a correct form of the verbs given. Then practice in pairs.

1. **Kamal** Do you ever eat dinner in front of the TV?

   Lynn Not really. Though on Friday nights, we _tend to watch_ (tend / watch)
   a movie and often we _____ (will / order) a pizza or something.
   But we _____ (tend / sit) at the table. And when we _____ (have) dinner,
   you know, we _____ (talk) about our day and things.

   Kamal Which _____ (be) nice. My son _____ always _____ (text) – even
   at the table! He _____ (play) around with his phone all through dinner, so I
   guess we _____ (not talk) much as a family.

2. **Diego** What do you think about all the TV commercials for fast-food places?

   Nagwa Well, there are way too many. But you know what _____ (get) me?
   The fast-food places _____ always _____ (advertise) toys, too,
   which _____ (be) annoying because the kids want to eat there then.

   Diego I know. My kids _____ constantly _____ (complain) because I
   _____ (not take) them to fast-food places. But my wife _____ (not want)
   them to eat fast food, so . . .

3. **Colin** Do you watch a lot of TV?

   Minh Um, not really. But my brother _____ (live) in front of the TV. He even
   _____ (do) his homework when he _____ (watch) TV, which I'm sure
   _____ (have) an effect on his grades.

About you

B Pair work Discuss the questions in Exercise A. Comment on your partner's answers using *which* clauses.

A We never have the TV on during dinner. We tend to listen to music.
B Which is always nice. We listen to the radio when we're having dinner.

2 What are they like?

A Complete the sentences with *who*, *that*, or *which*. If you can leave them out, write parentheses ( ) around them. Sometimes there is more than one correct answer.

1. My best friend has a great sense of humor, _which_ is something I like a lot.
2. My sister, _____ is really talkative, is very open-minded.
3. I like people _____ are relaxed, but my boss, _____ is very sweet, is just too laid-back.
4. The most interesting person _____ I know is my Uncle Rick, _____ is a bit eccentric.
5. My dad's a sensitive guy, _____ makes him a little touchy – especially with people _____ are pushy.

About you

B Pair work Take turns describing people you know. Ask your partner checking or information questions with *So*, *And*, or *But*.

A My sister's a really thoughtful person. She always remembers everyone's birthday.
B So she sends a lot of cards? OR But how does she remember?

3 It has an influence on you

Pair work Write a preposition for each noun. Then use each phrase in a sentence.

1. advertisement _for_   3. effect _____   5. increase / rise _____   7. problem _____   9. relationship _____
2. cause _____   4. impact _____   6. link _____   8. reason _____   10. research _____

"I saw an advertisement today for those new smart phones."

4 At school

About you

Complete the sentences with the expressions in the box. Use the correct form of the verbs. Then use each expression in a true sentence.

affect my grades	count toward	leave a lot of questions blank	not raise my hand	turn in my test paper
catch up on	fall behind on	✓ miss a class		struggle with

1. I _missed a class_ last week, which is too bad. The teacher reviewed stuff for the final exam.
2. I'm not doing very well in school. I've been _____ my classes. Two assignments that _____ my final grade are late. I really need to _____ my work.
3. I hate asking questions in class. I mean, I _____ once this semester!
4. I haven't been studying enough recently, and I know it's been _____ .
5. Math was really hard for me last semester. I'd been _____ the class all year, actually. But on the final exam, I _____ . I couldn't do them. So I just _____ and left.

Actually, I've been going to all my classes this semester. I haven't missed one class.

5 Problem solved!

A Complete the story with the verbs given. Use the simple past, past perfect, or past perfect continuous. Sometimes more than one form may be possible.

"When I was 17, I _wanted_ (want) to go to college, but I _____ (not finish) high school. I _____ (need) one more credit, so I _____ (decide) to take art history at night school. It was great. ☐ I _____ always _____ (like) art – even before I took that course. ☐ the teacher_____ (be) pretty cool. She _____ (play) classical music in class. ☐ I guess that's when I _____ (learn) to love Mozart. ☐ she _____ (ask) us to write an essay on a famous artist, so I _____ (choose) Vincent van Gogh. I _____ (not start) my essay until the night before it was due because I _____ (work) at my uncle's store all semester. I sat down to write, but I _____ (leave) all my art books at work. I only _____ (have) a book of van Gogh's letters to his brother, Theo. Also, I _____ (forgot) to buy paper. So for my essay, I _____ (write) letters from Theo to Vincent on my mother's fancy writing paper! My teacher _____ (love) it. ☐ I leave things till the last minute. It often works out!"

B Add these expressions to the story. Write the numbers 1–5 in the boxes. There may be more than one correct answer. Then take turns telling the story with a partner.

1. When I think about it,   3. Looking back,   5. So anyway,
2. It's no wonder that   4. Anyway, getting back to my story,

About you

C **Pair work** Was it fair that the writer got a good grade? Is it OK to leave things to the last minute? Is it good to work *and* study? Discuss your answers using the expressions below.

My feeling is that . . .	What's interesting is that . . .	I think that . . .
It's possible that . . .	What I'm saying is that . . .	You know what I think?

4

Working lives

In Unit 4, you . . .

- talk about work and finding a job.
- use countable and uncountable nouns.
- generalize and specify with articles.
- use *-ly* adverbs to express your attitude.
- use *As a matter of fact* and *In fact* to give or correct information.

Lesson A *Stand out from the crowd!*

① Vocabulary in context

A ◀))CD 2.02 **What do you think employers look for in job applicants? Make a list. Then read the article. Which of your ideas are mentioned?**

WHAT EMPLOYERS WANT ...

AND OUR ADVICE!

In today's job market, candidates **face** stiff **competition**. The evidence suggests that applicants who do their homework on an employer before they **submit an application** stand out from the crowd. Recent research shows what employers look for in new hires. Information like this is often the key to landing your dream job.

EMPLOYERS OFTEN LOOK FOR ...

1. PEOPLE WHO HAVE LONG-TERM POTENTIAL In interviews, **show interest** in moving ahead in your career. Ask about the career paths of other employees and possible promotions.

2. EVIDENCE YOU CAN WORK WELL WITH OTHERS Give an example of how you collaborated with others on a project to **make progress, meet deadlines,** or **achieve** a **goal.**

3. AN ABILITY TO MAKE MONEY FOR THE COMPANY Explain how your work can **make** or **save money** for the company.

4. AN IMPRESSIVE RÉSUMÉ Highlight the experience and skills that are relevant for each employer, as well as details of your education. Show your résumé to a career counselor or someone with experience in management, and **follow** their **advice.** Their feedback is invaluable.

5. RELEVANT WORK EXPERIENCE Emphasize the **skills** and **knowledge** you **have acquired** in other jobs, and include any relevant **training** you **have had**.

Word sort

B **Which nouns in the article go with the words below? Write them in the chart. Then ask a partner which things he or she has done in the last 12 months.**

achieve a ___goal___	make _____ with a project
acquire _____ or _____	meet a _____
face _____ in school or at work	save or make _____
follow someone's _____	show _____ in a job
have some (job) _____	submit a job _____

Vocabulary notebook

See page 51.

About you

A *Have you achieved any goals in the last 12 months?*
B *Well, one thing I did was pass an accounting exam.*

2 Grammar Types of nouns

Figure it out

A Find these three nouns in the article: *candidate, application, research.* Answer the questions below for each noun. Then read the grammar chart.

| Is it used with *a/an*? | Is it singular? | Is it plural? |

Countable and uncountable nouns ⬇

Grammar extra See page 150.

Countable nouns can be singular. You can use them with *a/an*.
*Give **an example** of how you achieved **a goal**.*

Uncountable nouns are only singular. Do not use them with *a/an* or add *-s*.
*Explain how your **work** can save **money**.*

Singular countable nouns take a singular verb. Plural countable nouns take a plural verb.
***An impressive résumé is** important.*
***Candidates face** stiff competition.*

Uncountable nouns take a singular verb.
***Feedback** from a counselor **is** invaluable.*
***Research shows** what employers look for.*

Common errors

Don't make these uncountable nouns plural or use them with *a/an* or with plural verbs: *information, equipment, advice, research, knowledge, software, work, homework, training, help, evidence, permission.*

About you

B Complete the questions with a correct form of the nouns given. Sometimes there is more than one answer. Then ask a partner the questions.

1. Do you have <u>a job</u> (job)? How hard is it to find _____ (work) that pays well?
2. Has anyone given you _____ (advice) on your résumé? Did you use the _____ (information)?
3. Do you need _____ (permission) from your school before you take _____ (job)?
4. What do you need to know about _____ (company) before you submit _____ (application)?
5. Where can _____ (graduate) go to get _____ (help) with career planning?
6. What _____ (skill) do you need to start your own business? Where can you get _____ (training)?

C Circle the correct form of the nouns, and write in the correct form of the verb *be.*

"The **information / informations** in the article _____ interesting, especially now when **work / works** _____ hard to find. Any **help / helps** you can get _____ useful. The point about getting **feedback / feedbacks** on your résumé _____ **a good advice / good advice**. My **research / researches** on employers _____ still at an early stage. I want to work in developing **software / softwares**, and I still need **a training / training**, though my **knowledge / knowledges** _____ good."

3 Viewpoint The best advice

Group work Discuss the questions. Draw up a five-point plan with the best advice for landing your dream job. Read your classmates' plans. How are they different from yours?

- Which advice in the article on page 42 is most relevant to you right now?
- What do you personally need to do to make sure you land your dream job?
- What else do candidates need to do to stand out in today's job market?

"Actually, the best advice for me was about the relevant work experience."

In conversation . . .

You can use *actually* to give new information.

4 Speaking naturally Word stress *See page 139.*

Lesson B *Perks and benefits*

1 Grammar in context

A What are some common perks and benefits that people have at work? Share ideas.

Transit Pass

B ◀)) CD 2.05 Read the survey. Which perks or benefits are common? Which had you not heard of?

In a recent poll, 65% of companies believe perks help attract employees. Here are some desirable benefits and perks that are offered by a number of major employers. How do you rate them?

RATE THE PERKS

1 = not at all desirable
5 = extremely desirable

I'd like to work for a company that . . .

	1	2	3	4	5
▶ offers free transportation to work.	○	○	○	○	○
▶ gives subsidized child care.	○	○	○	○	○
▶ has good health insurance.	○	○	○	○	○
▶ lets you make personal calls from work.	○	○	○	○	○
▶ has a quiet room for employees to take a nap after lunch.	○	○	○	○	○
▶ lets you take the kids to work if you need to.	○	○	○	○	○
▶ offers free exercise classes after work.	○	○	○	○	○
▶ provides an on-site doctor.	○	○	○	○	○
▶ has a salon that gives discounted haircuts.	○	○	○	○	○
▶ lets you listen to music while you work.	○	○	○	○	○
▶ offers regular training or reimburses tuition fees.	○	○	○	○	○
▶ lets you bring your pet to the office.	○	○	○	○	○

What other perks would you like to have?

▶ _____

▶ _____

▶ _____

About you | **C** Pair work Add three more perks or benefits that you would like to have. Then rate all the perks on a scale of 1–5.

A *I think free transportation is a great benefit. You could save a lot with that, so I gave that a 5.*
B *I agree. Monthly subway passes are so expensive. I gave it a 4.*

2 Grammar Generalizing and specifying

Figure it out

A **Which sentences below contain errors? Use the survey to help you correct them. Then read the grammar chart.**

1. Some employers offer the free exercise classes.
2. Others give you dental insurance.
3. Some let you take the kids to office.
4. Some companies have doctor.

Articles 🔽

Grammar extra
See page 151.

Generalizing

Use *a/an* with a singular countable noun to make a generalization, or when you don't mean a specific person or thing.
*I want to work for **a company** that has **a salon**.*

Do not use *the* to make generalizations with a plural countable noun or an uncountable noun.
***Classes** after work are a great idea.*
*I like to listen to **music** at work.*

Specifying

Use *the* when the idea is known to the reader or listener, or when it is clear which specific person or thing you mean.
*I'd like to take **the kids** to **the office**.*

Use *the* when you are specific about which thing you mean.
***The classes that I take** are very expensive.*
*My colleagues don't like **the music I listen to**.*

B **Circle *a/an, the,* or – (no article) in the conversations. Then practice with a partner.**

1. *A* Would you like to work for **a / the / –** company that offers **a / the / –** benefits like **a / the / –** free food?
   B Well, **a / the / –** perks are nice, but I think things like **a / the / –** paid overtime are better. Actually, **a / the / –** company that I work for has **a / the / –** good cafeteria. But I just have **a / the / –** sandwich at lunch, so free food isn't really worth much to me.
2. *A* If your company had **an / the / –** on-site gym, would you use it?
   B Maybe. But I'd prefer **a / the / –** pool. Then I could take **a / the / –** kids.
3. *A* Do you think perks like **a / the / –** free massages are worth having?
   B Oh, yeah. I'd love **a / –** job that has stuff like that. My friend's company has **an / the / –** exercise class during **a / the** lunch break every day. She loves it.

About you

C **Pair work** **Take turns asking and answering the questions above. Give your own answers.**

3 Listening and speaking The best perks

A 🔊CD 2.06 **Listen to the perks or benefits that five people discuss. Number them 1–5. Then listen again. Complete the specific examples of each perk in the chart.**

_____ paid time off	You can get paid leave to work _____ or _____ .
_____ tuition fees	You can get _____ or extra _____ .
_____ flexible work time	You can _____ early or _____ .
_____ a pleasant atmosphere	You work with _____ people and get _____ .
_____ a health club	You get free _____ , and there's _____ .

About you

B **Pair work** **Which perks are worth giving up a higher salary for? Why? Agree on the top five ideas. Then present your ideas to another pair.**

A I think free meals are worth giving up a higher salary for. Food is expensive.
B Yeah, I agree. And anyway, I hate cooking when I get home in the evening.

Lesson C *Obviously, . . .*

1 Conversation strategy Showing your attitude

A Replace the words in bold with your own ideas. How many ideas can you think of?

1. One factor to consider before taking a job is **the salary**.
2. **Being stuck in an office all day** is definitely not "me."
3. There's a shortage of **nurses**, so that would be a good choice of career.

B ◀))) CD 2.07 **Listen. What is Tori's job situation right now?**

Jake	How are the interviews going? Any luck yet?
Tori	Yeah, as a matter of fact, I just had an offer from a biotech company . . . but I'm having second thoughts about it.
Jake	And why's that?
Tori	Well, it's a fabulous opportunity with a great salary and everything, but you know, I don't know if it's really "me" – being stuck in a lab all day. I'm not sure it would be rewarding enough.
Jake	So you're not tempted by the money, then?
Tori	Not really. I mean, money *is* a factor, obviously. But seriously, it's not *that* important. As a matter of fact, I've been considering teaching. I just want to do something that involves people more. But I don't know if they need teachers, really.
Jake	Well, interestingly enough, I just read an article that said there's a real shortage of science teachers – so, in fact, teaching might be a good choice for you.

C **Notice** how Jake and Tori show their attitude toward what they say by using *-ly* adverbs like these. Find examples in the conversation.

seriously	*(un)fortunately*
obviously / clearly	*interestingly enough*
luckily	*(not) surprisingly*

In conversation . . .

Interestingly, *strangely*, and *oddly* are often used with *enough*.
Importantly is usually used in the expressions *More importantly . . .* or *Most importantly . . .*

About you

D Add *-ly* adverbs to the sentences using the ideas given. Add *enough* where appropriate. Then discuss the sentences with a partner. Which are true in your situation?

1. _____ (fortunate), I made my own career choices. My parents never forced me into a career I didn't want. _____ (lucky), I've never had second thoughts, either.
2. One of my friends is stuck in a job he really hates, _____ (unfortunate). But _____ (strange), he's not making any effort to leave.
3. _____ (odd), I've never really been tempted by money. I mean, _____ (obvious) a good salary is nice to have. But _____ (more important), you want a job that's really "you."
4. It takes years to train to be a doctor, _____ (not surprising). I mean, doctors make a lot of money, but _____ (serious), I don't want to be in school that long.
5. _____ (interesting), one of my friends has just had a job offer. _____ (unfortunate), they didn't offer him any benefits.

2 Strategy plus *As a matter of fact*

CD 2.08 You can use *As a matter of fact* or *In fact* to give new information that you want to emphasize.

As a matter of fact, I just had an offer . . .

You can also correct what someone assumes or expects.

There's a real shortage of science teachers – so ***in fact***, *teaching might be a good choice.*

A **CD 2.09** Match each question with two answers. Write the letters a–f. Then listen and check.

1. Have you decided what your next career move will be? _____ _____
2. Do you know anyone who has had second thoughts about their job or career? _____ _____
3. Do you think some people still expect to stay in the same job all their lives? _____ _____

a. I don't think so. In fact, most people's careers change and develop over time.
b. Not really. As a matter of fact, most of my friends love their work.
c. Yeah, I have, as a matter of fact. I'm planning on going into engineering.
d. No. As a matter of fact, nowadays most people are forced to change jobs every few years.
e. Actually, yeah. One of my friends hates his job. In fact, he's looking for something else, so . . .
f. No, I haven't. In fact, I probably should start thinking about that.

About you

B Pair work Discuss the questions in Exercise A. Use *In fact* and *As a matter of fact* in your answers.

3 Strategies Changing careers

A **CD 2.10** Circle the best expressions to complete the conversation. Then listen and check your answers. Practice in groups of three.

Branka I wonder why people change careers.
Josh Well, **obviously, / oddly enough,** a higher salary is one reason.
Pam Yeah. **Unfortunately, / Luckily,** I have a pretty good salary, so . . .
Josh What if your job isn't very rewarding? **In fact, / Fortunately,** that happened to a friend of mine, and he quit his job. **Fortunately, / Seriously,** it worked out for him.
Pam And **luckily, / not surprisingly,** people just get bored.
Branka That's true. **Clearly, / Amazingly,** you don't want to be stuck in a job that's not challenging.
Josh And **in fact, / oddly enough,** it's a good way to get other experience.
Pam **Interestingly enough, / Clearly,** I read an article that said there'll be no more "jobs for life."
Josh I saw that, too, **as a matter of fact / seriously.** We'll all be changing jobs and **more importantly, / strangely enough,** going back to school!

About you

B Pair work Agree on six good reasons to change careers. What are good reasons not to change careers? Make a list of your ideas.

"Well, one reason would be because you're bored with the career you have. Obviously, if your job's not rewarding enough, you'll get tired of it and . . ."

Reasons to change careers . . .
1. It's not rewarding enough . . .
Reasons not to change careers . . .

Lesson D *Ace that interview!*

1 Reading

A **Prepare** Which of these are good questions for a candidate to ask at a job interview? Which are not? Why?

a. How does the position fit into the company's structure?

b. What opportunities are there to get training?

c. What projects are you currently working on?

d. Can I work from home?

e. How is performance reviewed?

f. How much vacation will I get?

B ⬇ **Read for main ideas** Read the article. Where do the questions in Exercise A fit in the article? Write the questions.

CAREER Help

What questions should I ask at a job interview?

So when can I take my first vacation?

DONNELLY

¹ Congratulations! After submitting dozens of applications, you've finally landed an interview. You've done your research on the company, printed out extra copies of your résumé, and even rehearsed answers to questions like, "What is your greatest weakness?" But have you prepared for the most difficult interview question of all: "Do you have any questions for us?"

² "A candidate can't afford to trip up on this question," says Erica Lee, a career advisor in Los Angeles. "Employers need evidence that you're interested in the position." To avoid this fate, follow Lee's advice and impress your future boss by asking questions like these:

³ [1.] _____
"Listen carefully to the answer," advises Lee. "Then show how you can help them achieve their goals." Try to sell yourself as a solution to a manager's problems. "Managers spend most of their time worrying," says Lee. "Clearly, an employee who takes that stress away is like gold to them."

⁴ [2.] _____
Employers want people who care about the company as a whole, not just about their own paycheck. Lee says this question also helps you see if the job has long-term potential. "If they make the job sound unimportant, do you really want to be working there five years from now?"

⁵ [3.] _____
This shows your desire to acquire skills and knowledge that will benefit the company. In addition, says Lee, "it shows you're interested in working your way up the organization. You want a promotion – who doesn't? – but you are willing to work for it."

⁶ [4.] _____
This question demonstrates that you appreciate the importance of being accountable, meeting deadlines and targets. It also shows that you understand the value of constructive criticism and guidance.

⁷ Lee also warns her clients *not* to ask questions like these.

⁸ [5.] _____
If you ask this, employers will worry that you're not fully committed to the job. "Focus on getting offered the job first," says Lee. "Then you can discuss annual leave, benefits, and, of course, compensation."

⁹ [6.] _____
It's never a good idea to show an interest in this at the interview. "The managers I know all prefer staff to work in the office first to make an assessment of their work and training needs," says Lee. "Again, just try to get the job first." Similarly, avoid questions like, "Do I have to work overtime?" or "Can I listen to music at work?"

¹⁰ Remember an interview is a two-way process. You need to find out if the job is right for you, so don't be afraid to ask questions. Just make sure they're the right ones.

Reading tip

Writers use *this* (instead of *it* or *that*) when they focus on something important. (See paragraphs 5 and 8.)

C Paraphrase **Read the sentences below. Underline the sentences in the article that they paraphrase.**

1. You need to prepare not just to answer questions but to *ask* questions, too.
2. Interviewees shouldn't make a mistake when answering this question.
3. Workers who are able to deal with difficult problems are extremely valuable.
4. It demonstrates you are willing to learn new skills to make the company more successful.
5. Asking this question shows you see the benefit of getting useful feedback.
6. Make sure you don't give the impression that you won't be dedicated to your work.

About you **D** React **Which parts of the article did you find most useful? Which questions have you asked at an interview? What other questions should you ask?**

❷ Focus on vocabulary Word families

About you **Complete the sentences with the noun form of the words given. Use the article to help you. Then work with a partner. Give examples from your own experience.**

Give an example of . . .

1. how you usually find a _____ to a difficult problem. (solve)
2. the _____ of preparing for an interview. (important)
3. a skill you have that employers put a high _____ on. (value)
4. a time someone gave you constructive _____ . (criticize)
5. a time you offered someone _____ on something important. (guide)
6. a good way to make an _____ of a future employer. (assess)
7. a skill that most employers have a _____ for. (need)

"If I need to find a solution to a difficult problem, I usually think of all the possible options and . . ."

❸ Listening and speaking Interview rules . . .

A Pair work **Read the advice a–e about how to answer interview questions. Why are these good rules to follow? What other rules can you think of?**

Candidate	Advice: when you answer interview questions, . . .
1. Elizabeth	a. give actual examples of relevant experience to support your answers.
2. Marcus	b. be clear and concise, but don't just say yes or no.
3. Esma	c. never criticize a professor or previous boss.
4. Carlos	d. don't try to be funny.
5. Hugo	e. be prepared beforehand so you know what to expect.

B 🔊 CD 2.11 **Listen to extracts from five interviews. Match each person in Exercise A with the rule he or she breaks. Draw lines.**

About you **C** 🔊 CD 2.12 **Think of a job you might want to interview for. Listen to the interview questions again, and prepare your own answers. Then compare answers with a partner.**

"For question 1 I wrote, I've applied for this position as a receptionist because I'd like to work in a job that gives me opportunities to use my English."

Writing *My responsibilities included . . .*

In this lesson, you . . .
- use paragraphs for different topics.
- use nouns in formal writing.
- avoid errors with uncountable nouns.

Task **Write a personal statement.**
Give personal information in support of an application.

A **Look at a model** Read the excerpts from a personal statement on an application for a graduate program. Which topic does each paragraph address? Write the letters a–e.

a. Introduction	b. Leisure time	c. Studies	d. Summary	e. Work experience

1. ☐ My interest in business began in high school. I was team leader of the investment club. My responsibilities included organizing the meetings and writing reports. (. . .)
2. ☐ In college my major was financial management, which is critical to the success of any company. (. . .)
3. ☐ Last year I completed an internship in the management office of a hotel, which gave me some invaluable experience in meeting deadlines and achieving goals. The decision to do this internship was based on my wish to pursue a career in the hospitality industry. (. . .)
4. ☐ In my free time, I volunteer at a senior center. This experience has taught me the importance of patience and understanding. (. . .)
5. ☐ I am now ready to take on a further challenge by studying for a master's degree in business administration. (. . .)

B **Focus on language** How does the writer express the ideas below? Underline the sentences in the personal statement in Exercise A. Then read the grammar chart.

I was interested in business.   I was responsible for writing reports.   I decided to do this internship.

Using nouns in formal writing ⬇

Use nouns to make your writing more formal and varied. Don't start every sentence with *I* + verb.
I was interested in business in high school. → **My interest** in business began in high school.
I was responsible for writing reports. → **My responsibilities** included writing reports.
I decided to do this internship. → **The decision** to do this internship was based on . . .

C Rewrite the sentences, using noun forms of the words in bold.

1. I was **responsible** for advertising student events and raising money. *My responsibilities included . . .*
2. I have grown more **interested** in the media over the last three years.
3. I **worked** in a software company, and it helped me improve my time-management skills.
4. I **decided** to go into nursing because I **wish** to pursue a career in caregiving.

D **Brainstorm** Write ideas for an application to college, to graduate school, or for a job. Use the model in Exercise A to help you.

E **Write and check** Write your personal statement. Then check for errors.

Common errors

Check your use of uncountable nouns.
*This gave me **some** invaluable **experience**.*
(NOT ~~an invaluable experience~~)
*My work **experience** includes an internship at a hotel.*
(NOT ~~experiences include~~)
*I would like **a job / a position** in hotel management.*
(NOT ~~a work~~)

Vocabulary notebook *Meet that deadline!*

Learning tip   Collocations

When you learn a new word, write down its collocations –
the words that are used with it. For example, write the verbs
and adjectives that go with a noun.

have, meet, miss, set a deadline
a tight deadline

A Complete the vocabulary notes with the verbs in the box.

| achieve | acquire | ✔ face | follow | make | make | save | show | submit |

1. _face___ competition

2. _____ or _____ money

3. _____ progress

4. _____ interest

5. _____ an application

6. _____ knowledge

7. _____ a goal

8. _____ advice

B Look back at page 42. Write an adjective that can go before each noun. Can you add other adjectives?

1. _stiff___ competition

2. _____ job

3. _____ résumé

4. _____ skills

5. _____ feedback

6. _____ training

C **Word builder** Add nouns from Exercises A and B to these sets of verbs and adjectives. Sometimes there
is more than one answer.

Verbs

1. give, offer, take, ignore, seek _advice___

2. fill out, complete _____

3. set, achieve, reach _____

Adjectives

1. fierce, intense _____

2. positive, negative _____

3. formal, vocational _____

4. social, technical _____

5. good, practical, helpful _____

Dictionary tip

Dictionaries often tell you
if a noun is countable [C],
uncountable [U], or both [C/U].
Read the example sentences
to find a noun's collocations.

interest (INVOLVEMENT)
noun [C/U]

  *I lost interest halfway
  through the book.*

get some formal training

get a promotion

get some advice from colleagues

On your own

Make a poster for your own career goal. Write
a career goal in the center of the poster, and
then write all the things you have to do to
achieve it. Put the poster on your wall.

Challenges

In Unit 5, you . . .

- talk about world issues and ways to help.
- use conditional sentences to talk about wishes, hopes, and regrets.
- use *what if*, *suppose*, and *imagine* to suggest possible scenarios or ideas.
- use *I suppose* to show you're not 100 percent sure.

Lesson A *Giving away your things*

1 Grammar in context

A Are there a lot of homeless people in your area? How do people generally react toward the homeless?

B 🔊 CD 2.13 Read the article. What did Hannah Salwen's family do and why?

THE POWER OF *half*

What would you do if you saw a homeless person begging in the street? Walk on by? Give a few spare coins? Not the Salwen family . . . they gave much more than that. Read their story and ask yourself, *"What would I have done?"*

Kevin Salwen was driving his 14-year-old daughter, Hannah, back from a sleepover. Hannah had often seen homeless people begging for food at the stoplight near their home. But on this particular day, while they were waiting for the light, Hannah noticed an expensive car in front of them and a homeless man standing on the side of the road.

"If that guy didn't have such a nice car, the man over here could have a meal," Hannah said. The scene clearly made a deep impression on Hannah, and she continued to discuss it with her parents and brother for some time. She wanted her family to make a difference in the world – even if it was a small difference.

"How much are you willing to give up?" her mom asked. "This house?" Eventually, that's exactly what the family did. They sold their $2 million dream home and donated half the proceeds to the Hunger Project's work in Africa.

The Salwen family in front of the house they sold

If Hannah hadn't seen the homeless man alongside the car that day, maybe the Salwens would still be in their dream home. But would they be as happy? In their new, smaller house, they found they were spending more time together and became closer as a family. They admit they might not have become so close if they had stayed in their old home.

If you want to learn more about the Salwens' remarkable story, visit their website.

C Pair work Close your book. Then retell the story with a partner. How much detail can you remember?

2 Grammar Imagining situations

A Circle the correct verb forms to complete the sentences below. Use the article to help you. Then read the grammar chart.

1. What would you do if you **see / saw** a homeless person?
2. The family might not **have become / become** so close if they hadn't moved to a smaller house.
3. If Hannah **didn't see / hadn't seen** the man and the car, the family might still live in the big house.

Conditional statements and questions ⬇

Grammar extra
See page 152.

You can use *if* clauses to talk about hypothetical events in the present or past. Notice the commas.

| **Present** | What **would** you **do** if you **saw** a homeless person on the street? |
| *If* + past form; modal + verb | If he **looked** hungry, I**'d** probably **give** him some money. |

| **Past** | If you**'d been** in the car with Hannah, what **would** you **have done**? |
| *If* + past perfect form; modal + *have* + past participle | I **might not have thought** about it if she **hadn't mentioned** it. |

| **Mixed present and past** | If they still **lived** in their big house, **would** they **have raised** any money? Maybe. But they **might not be** so close now if they **had stayed** there. |

About you

B Complete the conversations with a correct form of the verbs given. Sometimes there is more than one correct answer. Then ask the questions and give your own answers.

1. *A* <u>Would</u> the Salwens <u>have had</u> (have) the idea to sell their home, do you think, if Hannah _____ (not see) the expensive car that day?
   B Maybe not. If the car _____ (not stop) in front of them, she _____ (might not decide) to do something. But maybe she _____ (do) something later.
2. *A* If you _____ (be) in the car with Hannah that day, how _____ you _____ (react)?
   B You mean, if I _____ (see) the homeless man, too? I _____ (not do) anything.
3. *A* If you _____ (be) Hannah, how would you have _____ (feel) when the house was sold?
   B I _____ (be) really upset if I _____ (have to) move. But I guess I _____ (agree) to it.
4. *A* What _____ you _____ (do) if someone _____ (ask) you for money on the street?
   B It depends. Maybe I'd give them a few coins – if I _____ (have) change.

3 Listening and speaking What would you give away?

A ◀))CD 2.14 Listen to three people talk about ways to help others. Number the summaries of what they say 1–3. Then listen again and complete the sentences for each person.

If I wanted to help, I'd . . .	I'd be able to do it if I . . .	I'd give to . . .
☐ use the car less.		
☐ donate my time.		
☐ watch my spending on groceries.		

About you

B Class activity Make a chart like the one above, and ask your classmates questions. Complete the chart with your classmates' ideas.

"So, what would you do if you wanted to do something for charity?"

Unit 5: Challenges **53**

Lesson B *A better future?*

① **Vocabulary in context**

A 🔊 CD 2.15 **What are some of the biggest problems that the world faces today? Make a list. Then listen to four people. Which of your ideas are mentioned?**

WE ASKED PEOPLE, **"WHAT'S THE BIGGEST CHALLENGE FACING THE WORLD TODAY?"**

Here are some of their views and hopes for the future.

Aya HIROSHIMA

"Well, I wish we could **eradicate poverty**. The gap between the rich and the poor keeps getting bigger. There's something like two billion people who live below the poverty line. I just wish we **distributed wealth** more fairly."

"I guess I'd choose **protecting** the **environment**. And **pollution** is, I think, the biggest problem. I just wish everywhere hadn't gotten so **polluted**. **Environmental protection** is critical if we're going to survive. I also wish we **invested** more in "green" projects. I hope that makes sense."

Luis SAN SALVADOR

Pin CHIANG MAI

"The biggest challenge? The **eradication** of **hunger**. I really wish someone would find a solution. You see all these **poor, starving** people – 16,000 kids die every day from **starvation**. No one should be **hungry** in this day and age. The problem is mostly one of food **distribution**. There are enough **wealthy** countries to solve it. I just wish I knew what to do about it."

"Um, there are so many **unemployed** people, especially with the economy the way it is right now. I wish the government would do something to reduce **unemployment** and **create** new jobs. I hope they put more **investment** in job **creation**."

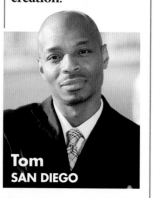
Tom SAN DIEGO

About you

B **Circle the correct form of the words to complete the sentences. Then discuss the sentences with a partner. Do any reflect your views?**

1. **Unemployed / Unemployment** is not a big problem. There's plenty of **invest / investment** in jobs.
2. There's no solution to the problem of **poor / poverty**. Its **eradicate / eradication** is impossible.
3. There's definitely a problem with the distribution of **wealth / wealthy**.
4. I know people are **starving / starvation**, but **hungry / hunger** isn't the biggest issue.
5. My priority would be environmental **protect / protection** – sorting out **polluted / pollution**.
6. There should be more job **create / creation** programs for young people.

Word sort

C **Write the words in bold in the article in a chart like this. Add any other words you know. Then, in pairs, use each noun in a sentence about world problems.**

Noun	Verb	Adjective
poverty	—	poor

Vocabulary notebook
See page 61.

54 Unit 5: Challenges

2 Grammar Talking about wishes, hopes, and regrets

Figure it out

A Are the sentences below true (T) or false (F)? Write T or F. Underline the sentences in the interviews that tell you. Then read the grammar chart.

1. Aya thinks that wealth is distributed fairly. _____
2. Luis feels bad that the world has become polluted. _____
3. Pin says someone has found a solution to hunger. _____
4. Tom wants someone to invest in new jobs. _____

Grammar extra
See page 153.

wish and hope

Use *wish* + past form to imagine a different situation in the present.	*Aya wishes we **could** eradicate poverty. She wishes the gap between rich and poor **was / were** smaller.*
Use *wish* + past perfect to imagine the past.	*Luis wishes everywhere **hadn't gotten** so polluted.*
Use *wish* + *would* + verb for things you want other people to do or for things you can't control.	*Pin wishes someone **would solve** the hunger problem. Tom wishes the government **would do** something.*
Use *hope* to talk about things that you want to be true about the future, present, or past.	*Tom hopes they **(will) create** more new jobs. I hope that **makes** sense / I **didn't say** anything silly.*

In conversation . . .

I wish I were . . . and *I wish it were . . .* are considered correct in writing. However, people often say *I wish I was . . .* and *I wish it was . . .*

About you

B Rewrite the sentences starting with the words given. Sometimes there is more than one answer. Then discuss the sentences with a partner. Do any of them represent your views?

1. Big industries shouldn't pollute the rivers. *I wish . . .*
   I wish big industries wouldn't / didn't pollute the rivers.
2. Someone needs to do something to help the homeless. *I hope . . .*
3. The government should have invested in public transportation years ago. *I wish . . .*
4. It's difficult to find a solution to problems like starvation and hunger. *I wish . . .*
5. Governments need to do more to protect wildlife, but they probably won't. *I wish . . .*
6. I don't know how to eradicate poverty in our cities. *I wish . . .*
7. We shouldn't have ignored all the environmental problems in our country. *I wish . . .*
8. I didn't want to upset you when we were discussing the distribution of wealth. *I hope . . .*

3 Viewpoint Good solutions

A **Pair work** How can we make the world a better place? Complete the sentences.

I hope our government will . . .

I wish we hadn't . . .

I hope people won't . . .

I wish we could . . .

I wish more people would . . .

B **Group work** Discuss your sentences. Decide on the three most pressing problems, and figure out some possible solutions. Present your ideas to the class.

A I wish we could do something like eradicate all the diseases in the world.
B Oh, definitely. Maybe if wealthy countries made cheaper vaccines, it would help.

In conversation . . .

You can use *Absolutely* or *Definitely* to agree strongly with someone.

4 Speaking naturally Shifting word stress *See page 140.*

Lesson C *What if . . . ?*

1 Conversation strategy Imagining possible scenarios

A Would you consider doing any of these things for charity? Why? Why not?

plant a tree   adopt a polar bear   sponsor a child

B ◀ꁫ CD 2.18 **Listen. What does Lucia think about buying gifts? What does Jim think?**

Lucia	I wish I knew what to get my nephew for his birthday. I should have thought about it earlier, and I wouldn't be in this last-minute panic now.
Jim	I suppose there's no point in getting him just another toy.
Lucia	Yeah. You know, the average kid here has 150 toys, which is unbelievable. It's just ridiculous . . .
Jim	I suppose it is.
Lucia	. . . especially when there's so much poverty in the world. I mean, suppose everybody gave to charity instead of buying useless gifts.
Jim	But just imagine you were five years old and you got this card from your aunt that said she planted a tree for you somewhere. I mean, how disappointed would *you* feel?
Lucia	I suppose. Well, what if I adopted a polar bear for him?

C **Notice** how Lucia and Jim use *what if . . . ?* and the imperatives *suppose* and *imagine* to suggest possible scenarios or ideas. Find the examples in the conversation.

> *I mean, suppose everybody gave to charity . . .*
>
> **In conversation . . .**
>
> *What if . . . ?* is the most common of these expressions. It is mostly used in follow-up questions. It doesn't usually start a conversation.

About you

D **Complete the conversations with *suppose, what if,* or *imagine*. There may be more than one answer. Then practice with a partner. Practice again, giving your own answers.**

1. *A* _____ you wanted to buy an unusual gift for a kid. What would you get? A microscope?
   B Maybe, but _____ you didn't really know the kid? It would be hard to choose, huh?
2. *A* _____ a friend planted a tree for your birthday. How would you feel?
   B Good question. I'm not sure. Yeah, . . . or _____ they adopted an animal or something?
3. *A* _____ you had to buy a last-minute gift for a friend. What would you do?
   B Oh, I'd probably just get a gift card. Something easy.
4. *A* _____ a friend wanted to give to a charity in your name. Which one would you choose?
   B Oh, um, . . . maybe a children's hospital or something. But _____ I really wanted a gift?

2 Strategy plus *I suppose*

◀))CD 2.19 You can use *I suppose* when you're not 100 percent sure or don't want to sound 100 percent sure.

I suppose there's no point in getting him just another toy.

I suppose can also be a response, to show the other person is right or has a good point.

A *It's just ridiculous.*

B *I suppose (it is).*

In conversation . . .

I suppose is more common in a full sentence than as a response.

I suppose (that) . . . ■■■■■■■■ *I suppose.* ■

A ◀))CD 2.20 **Match each question with two answers. Write the letters a–f. Then listen and check. Practice with a partner.**

1. Don't you think it's hard shopping for gifts? _____ _____
2. Do you always buy birthday cards for people? _____ _____
3. Do you ever "re-gift" unwanted presents? You know, pass them on to other people? _____ _____

   a. I suppose I do. But I'll often just send an e-mail if it's last minute.
   b. No, never. I suppose I'd worry that someone would find out!
   c. Usually. I do it because I like to get lots on my own birthday, I suppose.
   d. Actually, I enjoy it. Though I suppose it's not easy if you don't know what people want.
   e. Sometimes. I suppose it's better than keeping something you don't want.
   f. I suppose. Usually, I buy gift cards so people can choose what they want.

About you **B** **Pair work** **Take turns asking the questions above. Give your own answers using *I suppose*.**

3 Strategies Make the world a fairer place.

About you **A** **Group work** **Discuss the ideas for making the world a fairer place. How many other ideas can you add? Which could you do easily?**

* Buy fair trade products from companies that pay farmers or workers a fair price.
* Join a campaign for clean drinking water for everyone.
* Participate in a sponsored walk, run, or other event to raise money for a charity.
* Sign a petition to support women's rights.
* Volunteer to help disadvantaged children learn to read.

A *Suppose we only bought fair trade coffee. Then farmers would get a fair price.*

B *That's true. I suppose we could do that for other foods, too.*

B **Pair work** **Agree on one idea that you would like the class to adopt. Prepare a presentation to "sell" your idea to the class. Vote on the best idea.**

Lesson D *Mercy Ships*

1 Reading

A Prepare Look at the photos and the title. Can you guess what the article is about?

B Read for main ideas Read the exclusive interview. What does the Mercy Ships organization do? How is Dr. Cheng involved?

ON THE *Mercy Ships*

An interview with Dr. Leo Cheng

Q: Can you tell us what the Mercy Ships are and what kind of work they do?

Dr. Cheng: Mercy Ships run a hospital ship that brings world-class surgical and medical services to people in countries where there is a need. The organization Mercy Ships was started by Don and Deyon Stephens. Don and Deyon were caught in the Caribbean during a huge tropical storm, which caused a lot of devastation. There was a girl sitting beside them, and she was shaking – very cold – and praying for a ship to come and help the injured and sick, and to bring supplies to rebuild the hospitals and schools and so on. That gave them their vision, and since 1978, Mercy Ships has been doing just that – bringing hope and healing and rebuilding lives. If Don and Deyon hadn't been caught in that storm, they might not have had the idea for the Mercy Ships.

Q: So, what do you do on the Mercy Ships? Can you tell us about your work?

Dr. Cheng: I trained as a dentist, then a doctor, and then a general surgeon. I specialize in the head and neck areas, and I remove benign lumps or tumors. Here in the UK, it takes half an hour to treat a patient, but the problem in many developing countries is that a small lump doesn't get treated, so it grows into something enormous. That's something that we don't see here.

Q: If you hadn't worked on the Mercy Ships, do you think you'd be a different person today?

Dr. Cheng: Definitely. I would be a very different person. When I first went to work for Mercy Ships, my life changed. Everybody is there to offer service to others. We do not get a salary. We do not have a pension. We have to pay our own expenses to travel out there, which is not cheap.

Q: How does your work change people's lives? Can you give me an example?

Dr. Cheng: Well, let me tell you about a grandmother who came to the ship, and then you'll understand how the surgery changed her life. This woman had a large growth on her neck. She realized that her grandchildren were no longer sitting on her lap, and she was devastated and spent all her time alone. Her only wish was that her grandchildren would sit on her lap again. The night before surgery, she said, "I'm so looking forward to hugging my grandchildren and to putting them on my knee again." And obviously, to her, that was her pride and joy. The surgery brought joy back into her life. There are a lot of stories like that.

> **Mercy Ships is an international charity that provides free medical care and humanitarian aid. Over the last 30 years, it has worked in more than 70 countries, performed over 56,000 surgeries, and completed more than 1,000 community-development projects focusing on water, sanitation, and agriculture and impacting about 2.9 million people.**

C Read for detail Complete the sentences about the article. Then compare with a partner.

1. If Don and Deyon Stephens hadn't been in the Caribbean, _____ .
2. If Dr. Cheng hadn't worked with Mercy Ships, he thinks _____ .
3. If the grandmother hadn't had surgery, _____ .
4. If Mercy Ships didn't exist, millions of people _____ .

② Focus on vocabulary Word building

A Look for these words in the article. Find . . .

1. two words with the root form *devastate*: _____ , _____
2. two words with the same meaning as *tumor*: _____ , _____
3. three words that mean the same as *big*: _____ , _____ , _____
4. a word that means the opposite of *harmful* or *malignant*: _____
5. three different professions: _____ , _____ , _____
6. three words that refer to people who need treatment: _____ , _____ , _____

B Pair work Take turns using the words in Exercise A to describe the work of Mercy Ships.

"Don and Deyon Stephens got their vision for Mercy Ships when they saw all the devastation in the Caribbean and . . ."

③ Listening and speaking Inspiring people

A ◀))CD 2.21 **Listen to another interview with Dr. Cheng. Check (✔) the things he talks about.**

☐ How to help Mercy Ships
☐ The jobs that are available with Mercy Ships
☐ How he spends his free time on the ships
☐ What he does during a typical surgery
☐ An ordinary woman who wanted to help
☐ What Dr. Cheng plans to do in retirement

B ◀))CD 2.22 **Listen again. Are the sentences true (T) or false (F)? Write T or F. Compare answers with a partner. Correct the false information.**

1. The only people who work on the ships are skilled doctors and nurses. _____
2. Dr. Cheng's daughter has also worked on the ships as a surgeon. _____
3. Dr. Cheng gives presentations and talks about his work with Mercy Ships. _____
4. One woman who was inspired by Dr. Cheng donated all her income. _____
5. Mercy Ships can only accept people who want to work long-term. _____

About you

C Group work **Discuss the questions.**

- If you had the opportunity to help Mercy Ships, what would you do? What skills could you offer?
- How do you think people benefit from working with the organization?
- What other programs do you know about that help people around the world?

"Well, I wish I could do something to help. If I hadn't just started a job, I'd volunteer to help in the kitchens or something."

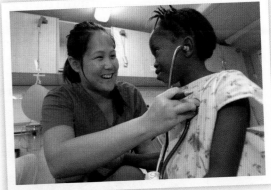

Writing *Volunteering*

In this lesson, you . . .
- make a polite inquiry.
- use *it* as a subject and an object.
- avoid errors with verb subjects.

Task | **Write an inquiry.**
Write an email inquiry to a volunteer program.

A **Look at a model** Read the email. Underline the sentences where Mary asks for information.

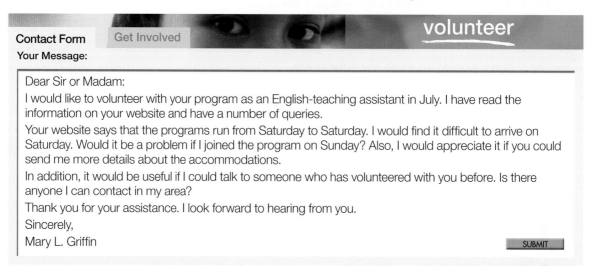

Contact Form   Get Involved   volunteer

Your Message:

> Dear Sir or Madam:
>
> I would like to volunteer with your program as an English-teaching assistant in July. I have read the information on your website and have a number of queries.
>
> Your website says that the programs run from Saturday to Saturday. I would find it difficult to arrive on Saturday. Would it be a problem if I joined the program on Sunday? Also, I would appreciate it if you could send me more details about the accommodations.
>
> In addition, it would be useful if I could talk to someone who has volunteered with you before. Is there anyone I can contact in my area?
>
> Thank you for your assistance. I look forward to hearing from you.
>
> Sincerely,
>
> Mary L. Griffin
>
> SUBMIT

B **Focus on language** Read the grammar chart. Then read sentences from the organization's reply below. Add *it* to the sentences where necessary.

Dummy *it* in writing

It can be a subject.	**It** would be **useful** if I could talk to someone in my area. Would **it** be **a problem** if I joined the program on Sunday?
Use *it* as an object after these verbs.	I would **appreciate it** if you could send details. I would **find it** difficult to arrive on Saturday.

In conversation . . .
People often use *love* in this way.
*I would **love it** if you could come over on Saturday.*

1. We would prefer if you could arrive on Saturday, because we do the training that evening.
2. We would appreciate if you could confirm your arrival time as soon as possible.
3. We would be grateful if you could send your payment for the accommodations.
4. You will find useful to talk to someone about volunteering.
5. There are volunteers in your town, so is not a problem to put you in touch with someone.

Common errors
Avoid using a form of *be* to start a statement.
***It** would be useful to talk to someone.* (NOT ~~Would be useful . . .~~)

C **Write and check** Write an inquiry with questions to a program below. Then check for errors.

Help build a home for a family.   Work in a wildlife sanctuary.   Help serve meals to the needy.

Vocabulary notebook *Wealthy = rich*

Learning tip Synonyms and paraphrases

To help you remember a new word, write down its synonyms – words with a similar meaning. If there isn't a synonym, write a paraphrase – an expression with a similar meaning.

wealthy = rich
to eradicate = to get rid of
poverty = being poor

A Match the words on the left with the synonyms and paraphrases on the right. Draw lines.

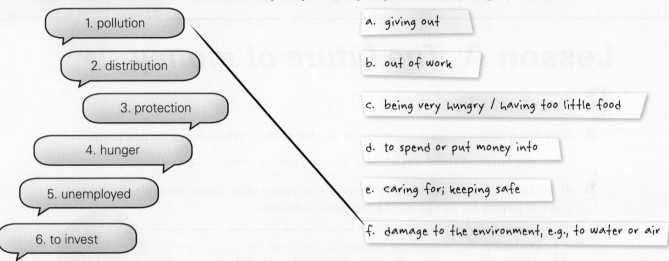

1. pollution
2. distribution
3. protection
4. hunger
5. unemployed
6. to invest

a. giving out
b. out of work
c. being very hungry / having too little food
d. to spend or put money into
e. caring for; keeping safe
f. damage to the environment, e.g., to water or air

B Now write synonyms or paraphrases for these words.

1. to protect _____
2. starving _____
3. to pollute _____
4. to distribute _____
5. to create _____

C Word builder Find the meanings of these words. Write synonyms or paraphrases to help you learn them.

1. abolish _____
2. conservation _____
3. destruction _____
4. population _____
5. resource _____

What do we want to *eradicate*?

These are the things people write most about eradicating: *poverty, disease (polio, malaria), drugs, racism, corruption, illiteracy,* and *homelessness.*

On your own

Make a list of the news stories you see or hear this week.

I saw / heard . . .
   a report on river pollution.
   a story about an
      unemployed father.

Into the future

In Unit 6, you . . .

- talk about money, technology, and future developments.
- describe future events.
- use modal verbs to express different meanings.
- soften your opinions with *would*.
- use *so* in responses like *I think so* to avoid repeating words.

Lesson A *The future of money*

① Grammar in context

A How many different ways are there to pay for things? Which ways do you prefer?

"Well, you can use a credit or debit card. I tend to use my credit card because . . ."

B ◀)) CD 2.23 **Listen to four students' comments from a class discussion. What different ways of paying for things do the students mention?**

Professor: So, imagine the headline 20 years from now: *Only one day left to turn in your old coins and bills.* Is this really going to happen? And if it does, what will it be like, do you think, to have a cashless society?

Amanda: Well, I mean, most people don't carry much cash now – I mostly use my debit card, and for bigger things, I use a credit card. So I think people are going to be using a lot less cash in the future. And in 20 years, we'll probably be doing all our shopping online, so there may not be a need for cash then.

Sam: I agree that everyone's going to use credit cards more. But the problem is, if we don't have better security, then there'll be more fraud and identity theft and everything. It's just a thought, but if paper money becomes obsolete, then our grandchildren might be looking at it in museums!

Oliver: But if we only use credit cards, then what are kids going to do? Will they have to carry prepaid debit cards? It just seems unlikely to me. I mean, we might see less cash in the future, but it won't be disappearing anytime soon. Though I have to say, it'll be good to get rid of those small coins.

Judith: I think in the future, every phone will have a chip that carries all our personal information – you know, our bank details and everything. We may not even need credit or debit cards. So you'll just use your cell phone when you buy things. It's already happening in some parts of the world, which is interesting.

C Answer the questions about the comments in Exercise B. Check (✓) the names.

Who thinks that in the future . . .	Amanda	Oliver	Sam	Judith
1. there could be problems with a cashless society?				
2. a cashless society is inevitable?				
3. credit cards are likely to become more popular?				
4. credit cards are likely to disappear?				
5. we're less likely to shop in stores?				

2 Grammar Describing future events

Figure it out

A Complete the summaries of the discussion on page 62 using the same verb forms that the students use. Then read the grammar chart.

1. Amanda thinks it's clear that people _____ (use) a lot less cash in the future.
2. Oliver says cash _____ (not disappear) anytime soon.
3. Sam thinks that his grandchildren _____ (look) at paper money in museums one day.
4. Judith says you _____ just _____ (use) a cell phone when you _____ (buy) things.

Future events with *be going to, will, may, might* ⬇

Grammar extra
See page 154.

Use a continuous form after *be going to, will, may,* and *might* for events you expect to be in progress at a future time.

You can use *be going to* when there's evidence now for a future event.	Everyone**'s going to use** cards more in the future. We**'re (not) going to be using** cash 20 years from now.
You can use *will, may,* or *might* in predictions. *Will* is more certain than *may* or *might*.	Every cell phone **will** (probably) **have** a chip. Cash (probably) **won't be disappearing** soon. There **may not be** a need for cash. We **might be using** phones.
Use the present form in *if* or time clauses that refer to the future.	If we only **use** cards, what are kids going to do? You'll use your cell phone when you **buy** things in the future.

In conversation . . .

The continuous form is mostly used after *will* and *be going to*. *Be going to be* + *-ing* is not common in writing.

B Circle the correct options to complete the sentences.

1. Coins and bills **disappear** / **might disappear** in the future.
2. One day we **won't be using** / **don't use** cash at all. But when cash **will become** / **becomes** obsolete, I think we **miss** / **'re going to miss** it.
3. If there**'s** / **'ll be** no cash in the future, we **won't need** / **don't need** wallets.
4. We may spend more if we **pay** / **'ll pay** with credit cards.
5. There probably **aren't** / **won't be** any real stores because we **shop** / **'re going to be shopping** online. You**'re not** / **won't be** able to try on clothes before you**'ll decide** / **decide** to buy them.
6. I think everyone**'s going to be using** / **uses** online banking in the future. We **don't have to** / **won't have to** go into actual banks anymore.

About you

C **Pair work** Do you share the opinions in Exercise B? Discuss your ideas.

"Well, I don't think coins and dollar bills are going to disappear, but they might become less common."

---

3 Listening Going cashless – the pros and cons!

A 🔊 CD 2.24 Listen. Rafael and Luana are talking about the pros and cons of a cashless society. Check (✓) the issues that they discuss.

☐ 1. convenience _____   ☐ 3. debt _____   ☐ 5. taxes _____
☐ 2. prices _____   ☐ 4. crime _____   ☐ 6. privacy _____

B 🔊 CD 2.25 Listen again. What do Rafael and Luana say about each checked issue above? Will it be: a) reduced, b) greater, c) the same? Write the letters a, b, or c above.

---

4 Speaking naturally Silent consonants *See page 140.*

Unit 6: Into the future   **63**

Lesson B *Presenting the future*

1 Vocabulary in context

A 🔊 CD 2.28 **Listen to these extracts from a presentation. What's the general topic of the presentation?**

1 "Hello, everybody. I'm just waiting for the projector – it won't connect. Oh, it must be warming up. It shouldn't take long. There. OK. **Can you all see the screen?** Let's see. I could make it a little bigger. Would somebody turn the lights off, please? Thanks. Um, **there should be a handout going around**, too. All right, **let's get started** . . ."

2 "So, today **I want to look at** the future of clothing. In particular, **I'll be talking about** the impact that technology will have on the clothes we wear. **I'll allow time for questions and comments at the end.** So, **I'd like to begin by** thinking about the question, 'What will our clothes be able to *do* in the future?' For example, we already have jackets that light up in the dark for road safety . . ."

3 "**As you'll see on the slide,** there are lots of other possibilities, too, such as clothes that use body energy to recharge cell phones and computers, and clothes that will be able to detect health problems. So, **let's move on** and **look at** ideas like these in more detail . . ."

4 "So as you can see, technology could have an impact on our lives in interesting ways – not least with self-cleaning fabrics. **Anyway, that's all I have time for**. So, **I'd better stop** there. Um, we should have time for one or two questions. **Does anyone have any questions or comments?**"

5 "If you're interested in reading more, you might want to check out some of the articles that are listed on the handout. **I'll just conclude by saying** thank you for listening. And now **I'll turn it over** to John, who's going to talk about clothes that heat or cool on demand . . ."

B Pair work **Cover the presentation and answer the questions. How much can you remember?**

   1. What does the speaker do before she starts her presentation?
   2. What topic does she specifically talk about?
   3. In what ways does she suggest clothing might be different in the future?
   4. Why does the speaker have to end her presentation?

Word sort **C** **Find expressions that the speaker uses in her presentation to do these things. Complete the chart. Compare with a partner.**

Start the presentation	
Introduce the topic	
Check that everyone can see or hear	Can you all see the screen?
Refer to a slide, a handout, or questions	
Go to a new topic or person	
End the presentation	

Vocabulary notebook
See page 71.

② Grammar Expectations, necessity, requests, etc.

Figure it out

A How does the speaker express the ideas below? Underline the sentences in the presentation. Then read the grammar chart.

1. I believe there's a handout going around.
2. The projector is unable to connect.
3. Can somebody turn the lights off?

Modal verbs 📥

Grammar extra
See page 155.

Modal verbs can express a range of meanings. Here are some.

Expectations	There **should / ought to** be a handout going around.
Guesses	The projector **must** be warming up. It **might / could / may** be broken.
Necessity	I **should / ought to / have to / need to / 'd better** stop. ('d = had)
Suggestions/advice	You **might want to** check out the articles on the handout.
Ability	**Can** you all see the screen?
Failure (to operate)	The projector **won't** connect to my laptop.
Requests	**Could / Would / Can** somebody turn the lights off, please?
Offers	I**'ll** make the screen bigger. I **can / could** turn it up.
Permission	**May* / Could / Can** I ask a question? Yes, you **may* / can**. (*More formal)

B 🔊 CD 2.29 Circle the best modal verbs to complete the extracts from a presentation. Then listen and check.

1. "OK, **can / would** you hear me at the back? Good. So, let's get started. You **could / should** all have a handout by now. Oh, wait – the projector **might not / won't** come on. It **might / ought to** be turned off. **May / Could** someone help me with it, please? Oh, it's not plugged in! Sorry. OK. So, **would / can** you see that clearly?"

2. "So, I'm sure you **need to / must** be wondering how clothes can have health benefits in the future. It **might / had better** be useful to play you something I heard on the radio. It's about hats that will turn hard when something hits them so they act like a helmet. So, I **need to / would** turn on the sound. Um, that **must / can** be the volume here. Oh, I'd **better / won't** turn it up. That's better. You **would / ought to** be able to hear at the back."

3. "So, let's move on. There are lots of fun possibilities, too. Simon, **may / would** I ask you to stand up, please? Thank you. Oh, you **might want to / would** turn around and face everyone. And **should / would** you show everyone your T-shirt? So, in the future, imagine T-shirts like this but with words or images that change color or react to music. Well, that's all I have time for. I **won't / have to** stop now. Does anyone have any questions or comments?"

C **Group work** Prepare and give a short presentation on one of the topics below. Use six of the expressions you learned from page 64. Share the best ideas with the class.

The future of . . .

 clothing   shopping   money

Lesson C *I would think . . .*

1 Conversation strategy Softening opinions

A Which do you enjoy more: going to the movies or watching movies at home?

B 🔊 CD 2.30 **Listen. What does Harry think about the future of movie theaters?**

Chris	Wow! There's almost no one here tonight.
Tina	Yeah. You know, I wonder if we'll still be going to the movies in ten years.
Harry	Oh, I think so.
Tina	I don't know. I'd say we probably won't. It's easier to watch movies at home – cheaper, too.
Harry	Yeah, but going to the movies is different. It's more social.
Chris	And it's a great first date. That's not going to change, is it?
Harry	I hope not. I would think that movie theaters will find ways to attract more people . . .
Tina	I guess so. But like what?
Harry	Well, things that make movies more realistic, like seats that move . . .
Tina	Ugh. I get motion sickness.
Chris	And gaming. And you'll be able to choose how the movie ends.
Harry	Yeah. I would imagine people will always want to go to the movies, but it'll be a different experience.

C **Notice** how Tina and Harry use *would* or *'d* to soften their opinions. Find examples in the conversation.

> I would say . . .   I'd say . . .
> I would think . . .   I'd think . . .
> I would imagine . . .

In conversation . . .

People mostly say: *I would say, I would think,* and *I'd say.*

About you

D 🔊 CD 2.31 **Listen to the opinions below. Complete each one with the softening expression you hear. Then discuss the opinions with a partner. Which do you agree with?**

1. _____ the whole experience is better at a theater. You get better sound, and the screen's bigger. At home I sometimes fall asleep during a movie.

2. _____ there'll be even more movies in 3D, because people like to feel part of the action.

3. _____ theaters will stay popular. People like to go out with their friends.

4. _____ theaters are not going to disappear anytime soon. But they're going to have to come up with some exciting innovations to stay in business.

5. _____ people would enjoy choosing the ending to a movie. It'd be fun.

6. _____ that we won't go to theaters in the future. We'll have the technology at home.

2 Strategy plus *I think so.*

CD 2.32 You can use *I think so* or *I don't think so* as a response. Don't use *I think* or *I don't think* as a response.

> I wonder if we'll still be going to the movies. . .

> Oh, **I think so.**

You can also use these responses.

I guess so or *I guess not.*
I hope so or *I hope not.*

In conversation . . .

I think so and *I don't think so* are the most common of these responses.

I (don't) think so.	▬▬▬▬▬▬▬▬▬
I guess so/not.	▬▬▬
I hope so/not.	▬

A Complete the conversations with appropriate responses from above. Then practice the conversations with a partner.

1. *A* Do you think going to the movies will be a very different experience in the future?
   B _____ . I mean, you'll still be watching a movie.

2. *A* Do you think that one day there'll be no actors at all, and they'll all be computer generated?
   B _____ . We'll always want to see real people in movies.

3. *A* Do people enjoy going to movie theaters just because it's something they can do with friends?
   B _____ . It's always fun to talk about the movie afterwards.

4. *A* Would you enjoy gaming in a movie theater?
   B _____ . It'd be fun to play with a theater full of people.

5. *A* Do you think people will stay home more to play virtual-reality games and stuff?
   B _____ . You don't always feel like going out to a theater in the evening.

About you

B Pair work Ask and answer the questions in Exercise A. Give your own answers.

3 Listening and strategies Future entertainment

A **CD 2.33** Listen to four conversations about entertainment in the future. What four topics do the people talk about? Number the topics below 1–4. There is one extra topic.

Topic	Agree	Disagree
_____ live music		
_____ reading		
_____ theater		
_____ travel		
_____ virtual-reality games		

B **CD 2.34** Listen again. Do the speakers agree? Check (✓) the correct columns in the chart above.

About you

C Group work Discuss the five topics above. What do you think will happen in the future?

A Well, I would think we'll still have books – even in 20 years. Don't you?
B Actually, I don't think so. I'd imagine we'll all be reading books on our computers or . . .

Lesson D *Future news*

1 Reading

A **Prepare** Look at these headings from an article. What do you think the article is about?

a. Miracle cures!

b. High-tech checkouts on the way!

c. Warmer, wetter, and more extremes!

d. More intelligent than a human!

B ⬇ **Read for main ideas** Read the article. Write the headings above the correct sections of the article.

What does the future look like?

1 _____

Buying groceries is going to be much more efficient in the near future, experts say. "Thank goodness," you might think, if you're one of the millions of consumers who hate to set foot in a supermarket. Retailers predict that computerized shopping carts will be directing us to different areas of a store, based on our shopping lists. (That's the shopping list you'll be downloading from your smartphone as you enter the store.) Touch-screen terminals in each section of the store will give you access to any information you need. If you want a recipe, you'll be able to print one out. If you want to find out where produce comes from or its nutritional value, you'll be able to get that information, too. Then when you get to the self-checkout, "smart scales" will recognize all your produce by sight, weigh it, and price it. These developments should eventually make shopping a much quicker and easier process.

2 _____

If scientists are correct, our weather is going to change dramatically in the next century, which will affect us in a number of ways. Climatologists say our climate will get warmer and wetter, and that we're going to experience flooding on a huge scale, as rising temperatures cause icecaps to melt and sea levels to rise. But what will the impact of climate change be? Islands and even whole countries might ultimately disappear under water, which could create millions of refugees and migrants, as people seek new homes. Economists say climate change will also affect coastal industries, such as tourism and fishing, while ecologists predict that thousands of plants and animals may well become extinct. The effects of climate change will likely be considerable.

3 _____

There's a much brighter future for the victims of accidents, and particularly those who have lost arms or legs. Inventors are already perfecting artificial limbs that can perform in much the same way as human limbs. Transplants might eventually become much more common than now. Already surgeons are attempting risky arm transplants. But imagine the more distant future, when scientists may not need to perform such surgeries and might, instead, be able to treat a patient with medicines that enable arms and legs to grow back. Accident victims in the future will certainly have more treatment options.

4 _____

The future of artificial intelligence is exciting. According to computer engineers, you won't need to type words into a search engine in the future. Instead, you'll be able to talk to your computer, ask it questions, and get immediate answers. It will also remember all your conversations so that it can give more precise help the next time you ask. One day your computer will even give you advice, or act as a therapist! Imagine that – everyone will have their own personal therapist right on their laptop! Speaking to computers will certainly change the relationship we have with them.

Reading tip

Writers use different ways to address the reader, including *you*, *we*, *everyone*, and *people*.

C React **Look back at the article, and write notes about the items below. Then compare with a partner.**

- two things you learned from the article
- something you already knew or had heard
- the development you think would be most useful
- the most interesting piece of news you read
- the change you feel is the least likely
- the best and the worst piece of news

② Focus on vocabulary Nouns for people

A **Find the words from the box in the article on page 68. Then use the words to complete the questions.**

✓ climatologists	inventors	retailers
consumers	migrants	therapists
ecologists	refugees	victims
economists		

How weather is REALLY predicted

Madame Futura

DONNELLY

1. What major changes do climatologists predict in the weather?
2. According to _____ , how will a change in climate affect plants and animals?
3. Why will climate change create millions of _____ and _____ ?
4. What industries might be affected by climate change, according to _____ ?
5. What kinds of changes might _____ make in their stores in the future?
6. How will that improve the shopping experience for _____ ?
7. What have _____ created to help _____ of accidents?
8. Do you think computers will make good _____ ? Would you take advice from one?

B Pair work **Ask and answer the questions in Exercise A. Use information from the article and any other information you know. Are there any areas where you do not agree?**
"One thing climatologists predict is that we're going to get more flooding. Actually, there have been some terrible floods this year."

③ Viewpoint Is it for the better or worse?

A Group work **Choose three topics from the list below. What changes might there be in these areas in the future? Will they be for the better or worse? Discuss your ideas.**

- education
- work
- technology in the home
- family life
- food

- the media
- medicine
- the climate
- computer software

> **In conversation . . .**
> You can use these expressions to quote information you've heard.
> *Apparently, / Evidently, . . .*
> *They say . . .*
> *I've heard / read . . .*

A *I would say that education will be very different. I mean, they say there might not even be school buildings in the future.*
B *Yes. Apparently, there are already some schools that exist only online.*

B Class activity **Take turns telling your ideas to the class. Vote on whether you think each idea will happen and if the change will be for the better.**

Writing *Future living*

In this lesson, you . . .
- structure a paragraph.
- use modal verbs with adverbs.
- avoid errors with adverbs.

Task **Write a short article.**
How will everyday life be different in the future?
Will it be better?

A **Look at a model** Read the paragraph. Do you agree with the writer? Underline the topic sentence, number the supporting sentences, and check (✓) the concluding sentence.

One aspect of life that will certainly be very different and better in the future is education. It will likely become more personalized, and students might well follow individual programs. Students will probably spend less time in class and more time studying online at their own pace. The traditional classroom will eventually disappear, and college buildings may well become obsolete because people will be able to study at home. As a result, education will undoubtedly be more motivating and effective. Studying will ultimately change and be a more rewarding experience for each individual student.

Paragraphs

Paragraphs sometimes have these parts:
- **a topic sentence,** which gives the main idea.
- **supporting sentences,** which give reasons, examples, or explanations to support the main idea.
- **a concluding sentence,** which summarizes the paragraph.

B **Focus on language** Circle seven more modal verbs with adverbs in the paragraph. Check the meaning of the adverbs. Then read the grammar chart.

Modal verbs + adverbs in writing

Writers use adverbs after *will* to show how certain they are.
Inevitably, certainly, and *undoubtedly* add certainty.
*Education will **certainly** be different.*
Inevitably is often used for negative events.
*It will **inevitably** be difficult for some.*
Ultimately and *eventually* mean "certain after some time."
*Schools will **eventually** disappear.*
Likely and *probably* mean "fairly certain."
*Students will **probably** not sit in class.*
Writers use *well* after *may, might,* and *could* to mean "more certain."
*Schools may **well** become obsolete.*

Writing vs. Conversation

People use *may well* in formal writing and speaking.

Conversation

Formal speaking

Academic writing

Common errors

Be careful with these adverbs.
Eventually does not mean "maybe."
Ultimately does not mean "recently."
Actually does not mean "now" – it means "in fact."
Currently means "now."

C **Rewrite the sentences using the adverbs given.**

1. Education will be more learner-oriented in the future. (certainly)
2. Students will study a wider range of subjects. (undoubtedly)
3. School buildings might become community centers. (well)
4. The idea of a school day will become obsolete. (eventually)
5. All college programs will be online. (likely)
6. Some students will have problems studying on their own. (inevitably)

D **Brainstorm and write** Look back at the task at the top of the page. Brainstorm and organize ideas for your article. Then write a paragraph with a topic sentence, supporting sentences, and a concluding sentence. Use the adverbs in Exercise B.

Vocabulary notebook *Present yourself!*

Learning tip Idea strings

When you learn a new expression, think of different ways you can use it. Create an "idea string" for it.

I'll be talking about . . .
the influence of television on young people. /
the use of technology in schools.

A Imagine you are giving a presentation. Use the expressions in the box to complete the "idea strings." Then add one more idea of your own.

> As you'll see . . .   I'll allow time for . . .   Let's . . .
> Can you see . . .   I want to look at . . .   There should be . . .

Let's . . .
The most common expressions with *Let's* in academic speaking are:
Let's see . . .
Let's say . . .
Let's look at . . .

1. _____ at the back? / the slide? / _____ ?
2. _____ a handout / a questionnaire / _____ going around.
3. _____ my research, / the future of transportation, / _____ .
4. _____ on the slide, / on your handout, / _____ , . . .
5. _____ questions / discussion / _____ at the end.
6. _____ get started, / move on, / _____ .

B Choose a topic for a presentation. Then complete these sentences with your own ideas.

1. In this presentation, I want to look at _____ .
2. I'd like to begin by _____ .
3. Let's move on and look at _____ .
4. I'd better stop there and _____ .
5. I'll just conclude by saying _____ .
6. I'll turn it over to _____ .

C Word builder Can you guess the meanings of these presentation expressions? Match each expression with its meaning. Write the letters a–h.

1. I'll also touch on . . . _____
2. I'd like to draw your attention to . . . _____
3. We'll come back to that later. _____
4. I'll just skip over this next slide. _____
5. I'd like to introduce (*name*) . . . _____
6. To sum up, . . . _____
7. The next issue I want to address is . . . _____
8. Please feel free to interrupt and ask questions. _____

a. The next thing I want to talk about is . . .
b. I'll also talk briefly about . . .
c. I won't talk about this next slide.
d. Here is (*name*) . . .
e. We'll look at or talk about that later.
f. You can stop me if you have a question.
g. I want you to look at . . .
h. To summarize, . . .

I'd like to begin by saying thank you for coming to my presentation today.

On your own

Choose a topic and prepare a short presentation. Record yourself. Then listen and count how many expressions you used from page 64.

Checkpoint 2 *Units 4–6*

1 Words for work

About you

A Complete the sentences with verbs. Which are the five most important pieces of advice? Discuss with a partner, using *would* / *'d* to soften your opinions.

How to get a promotion at work

1. __Follow__ your boss's advice.
2. _____ some training to _____ new skills.
3. _____ interest in getting a promotion.
4. Say how you can _____ the company money.
5. Always _____ the goals your manager sets.
6. _____ progress with projects and _____ deadlines.
7. _____ an application when there's a new position.
8. Don't be afraid to _____ competition from colleagues.

"I'd say it's important to follow your boss's advice – it might help you get a promotion."

About you

B Write sentences about your future career. Start your sentences with these expressions and a verb. Then compare ideas with a partner.

1. I think I'm going to be . . .
2. I'll probably be . . .
3. When I . . .
4. I might . . .
5. Before this class . . .
6. I may be . . .

"I think I'm going to be studying for another four years if I get accepted at grad school."

2 Wishes, hopes, and regrets

A Circle the correct verb forms to complete the conversations. Then practice with a partner.

1. *A* So, when you look back on last year, do you wish you **'d done** / **did** anything differently?
   B Yeah. I suppose. Like, I wish I **didn't spend** / **hadn't spent** so much last semester. You know, if I hadn't bought so many clothes and things, I **wouldn't be** / **wasn't** in debt now.

2. *A* What **would** / **will** you change about your city if you had the opportunity?
   B Well, I wish we **can** / **could** do something about the subway. I mean, I wish the trains **weren't** / **aren't** so crowded. And I wish people **don't** / **wouldn't** throw trash on them.

3. *A* If someone **had offered** / **would offer** you a job last year, would you **have taken** / **take** it?
   B As a matter of fact, I was offered a job. And I **might take** / **might have taken** it if it had been a really good job, but it wasn't. But if I had taken it, I **wouldn't be** / **weren't** in this class now. I just **wish** / **hope** I'll get a job next year.

4. *A* If you **can** / **could** raise money for a charity, which charity would you choose?
   B Well, if I **had to** / **would have to** choose a charity, I'd probably choose one for kids. In fact, I donated money to one last year. I hope it **made** / **would make** a difference.

About you

B Pair work Take turns asking and answering the questions in Exercise A. Use *as a matter of fact* or *in fact* to give or correct information.

A So, do you wish you'd done anything differently last year?
B I suppose. As a matter of fact, I wish I'd spent more time with my family.

3 The state of the world

A Fill in the blanks with the words in the box. Then circle the correct options to complete the sentences.

distribution	eradicate	polluted	protection	unemployment
environmental	✓ investment	poverty	starvation	wealth

1. _Investment_ in education is expensive, but it saves **the money /(money)** eventually. **Education /
   The education** is crucial because educated people are less likely to live below the _____ level.
2. Research **show / shows** that 10 percent of the population owns over 70 percent of the _____ .
3. People are more likely to be sick if there's **a pollution / pollution.** _____ air affects your health.
4. In areas of high _____ , over 25 percent of people don't have **a job / job.** You often find that
   people suffer from **the mental illnesses / mental illnesses** in these areas.
5. In **the / a** world today, 925 million people don't have enough to eat. We really need to do more
   to _____ hunger or _____ . The _____ of food should be more efficient.
6. If you are interested in the _____ of the environment, buy **the cotton / cotton** that is organic.
   There is **an / some** evidence that growing cotton causes serious _____ damage.

**About
you**

**B Pair work Discuss the information in Exercise A. What ideas do you have for solutions?
Use _I suppose_ when you're not 100 percent sure and adverbs to show your attitude toward
what you say.**

"I suppose investment in education is important. Clearly, it changes lives."

4 Prepare and present yourself

A Circle the best modal verbs. Then write in appropriate responses with *think*, *guess*, and *hope*
to complete the conversation.

A Hey, Bob. **Can /** **Will** I ask you a question? Do you have a minute?

B Um, _I guess so_ . I've got a class at ten, but I **should / need to** have a few minutes. What is it?

A Well, I have a second interview for a job tomorrow, and I really **will / should** get ready for it.
   I **need to / may** think about what to ask, you know, about salary or benefits and stuff.

B Yeah. You **can / ought to** think about what you want. You **might want to / 'll** make a list.

A OK. **Would / May** you help me? I've got my laptop. Oh, it **won't / shouldn't** turn on.

B You**'d better / won't** plug it in. OK, so let's see . . . Do they provide health insurance?

A Oh, _____ . They **must / might want to** have it. Don't all companies offer some help with insurance?

B _____ . Not all of them do. And ask, "**Can / Might** I work from home?" Do they allow it?

A _____ . I know some people do. Oh, and they **should / had better** offer training.

B How many presentation expressions can you add to the word webs?

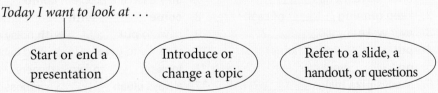

Today I want to look at . . .

(Start or end a
presentation)   (Introduce or
change a topic)   (Refer to a slide, a
handout, or questions)

**C Pair work Prepare a presentation on the ideal company. What benefits would it offer?
Use _what if . . . ?_, _suppose_, and _imagine_ to suggest possible ideas.**

"Today I want to look at the ideal employer. Imagine a company that gives you 12 weeks vacation."

Getting along

In Unit 7, you . . .

- talk about getting along with people.
- use phrasal verbs.
- use infinitives and *-ing* forms.
- learn how to make your point clear.
- use *I have to say* to make a strong point.

Lesson A *House rules*

1 Vocabulary in context

A ◀》CD 3.02 **What are house rules? Why do people have them? Think of one rule. Then read the article. Is your rule mentioned?**

Living with roommates

▶ You're **looking forward to** living with a roommate, but will you get along? Before you move in together, **come up with** some house rules about what you both expect. For example:

- If you **have** friends **over** for dinner, ask if it's OK *before* they show up.
- If you get back late, come in quietly – don't **wake** anyone **up**.
- If you're the last one to go to bed, turn off the TV and lights.
- If you borrow something, ask first and *always* **give** it **back**.

▶ Roommates often argue about chores. Instead of **putting up with** your roommate's mess, figure out some rules that work for you, like these:

- If you make a mess, **clean** it **up**.
- If you drop it, pick it up.
- If you take it out, put it back.

▶ If your roommate's bad habits still drive you crazy and you **run out of** patience, don't **put off** talking about it. When a problem **comes up, go over** things right away. Of course you might find out that you have to **give up** a few bad habits of your own! But with a little good humor, you'll get over any problems and things should work out.

About you

B Pair work Complete the expressions in the questions with words from the article. Then take turns asking and answering the questions.

Do you . . .

1. often **have** friends _____ ?
2. keep **running** _____ of cash?
3. ever **wake** anyone _____ ?
4. **put** _____ doing chores?
5. **go** _____ your bills?
6. always **give** things _____ ?
7. stay calm if a problem **comes** _____ ?
8. **come** _____ with ideas for meals?
9. have to **put** _____ **with** noisy neighbors?
10. ever try to **give** _____ bad habits?
11. **look** _____ **to** family dinners?
12. always **clean** _____ your mess?

Word sort

C Complete a chart like this with the ideas in Exercise B. Then compare charts with a new partner.

I . . .	I don't . . .
often have friends over.	have to put up with noisy neighbors.

Vocabulary notebook

See page 83.

2 Grammar Using phrasal verbs

Figure it out

A How does the article express the ideas in bold? Rewrite the sentences. Then read the grammar chart.

1. If you **arrive home** late, come in quietly.
2. If you're the last to go to bed, **don't leave** the lights **on**.
3. If you borrow a book, **return** it.
4. Don't **tolerate** your roommate's mess.

Grammar extra
See page 156.

Phrasal verbs 📩

Intransitive phrasal verbs have no object. *come in, come up, get back, show up, work out*	*If you **get back** late, **come in** quietly.*
Some transitive phrasal verbs are separable. *clean up, give back, give up, put off, turn on/off, wake up*	**Turn off** the TV. OR **Turn** the TV **off**. **Turn** it **off**. (NOT ~~Turn off it~~.)
Some transitive phrasal verbs have a fixed word order. *get through, get over, go over + sb / sthg; have sb over*	*You'll **get over** the problem / it.* *I often **have** friends **over**.*
Some phrasal verbs also take a preposition. <u>3-word phrasal verbs</u> *come up with, look forward to, put up with, run out of*	*If you **run out of** patience, **come up with** some rules.*

About you

B Write the words in parentheses in the correct place in the sentences. If there is more than one possible answer, write both answers. Then ask and answer the questions with a partner.

1. Are you looking to having your own place? (forward) Do you plan to move with anyone? (in)
2. Have you come any rules for your home? (up with) What are they?
3. Do you always clean any mess right away? (up)
4. What problems come in your home? (up) Do things usually work? (out)
5. Has a friend ever shown early or late and woken your family? (up, up)
6. If you had a problem with your neighbors, would you put it? (up with) Or would you have them and go things? (over, over)
7. Do you borrow things from neighbors if you run them? (out of) Do you give them right away? (back)

C Pair work Agree on the six best house rules to have. Use a phrasal verb in each rule.

"How about – if you want to listen to music at 3:00 a.m., please turn it down so you don't wake me up."

3 Listening and speaking My worst roommate

A Pair work Imagine you had a roommate who did the things in the chart. Which problems would be the worst?

	The problem with my roommate was that he/she . . .		He/She didn't . . .
1. Marc	☐ a. got up late every day.	☐ b. used my things without asking.	
2. Hana	☐ a. didn't share the chores.	☐ b. had friends over all the time.	
3. Emilio	☐ a. woke me up early.	☐ b. didn't put things away.	
4. Cassie	☐ a. never cleaned up.	☐ b. always turned off my music.	

B 🔊 CD 3.03 Listen to four people talk about roommates. What was each person's problem? Check (✔) a or b. Then listen again and write one thing each roommate didn't do.

About you

C Group work Agree on a way to solve each problem. Share your ideas with the class.

Lesson B *Does family size matter?*

1 Grammar in context

A 🔊 CD 3.04 **Listen. Who is from a big family? Who is from a small family? Which two people were "only children"? Can you figure it out? Then read and check.**

"Only children" and siblings compare experiences growing up.

1 OSMAN

People often say, "It must be stressful to live like that." But it wasn't. There was always somebody to play with and share secrets with and everything. I think it's important for kids to be around other kids. I guess the only thing was, I used to long for somewhere quiet to study.

3 LILLI

Looking back, I don't know how my mom did it as a single parent. It was impossible for her to have time for herself. Still, we always had enough to eat, nice clothes to wear, books to read, etc. We were very close, maybe because it was just the three of us.

2 SOPHIA

I suppose I was a bit lonely being by myself all the time – I was always having to find ways to occupy myself. And like, there was no one else to blame if I got into trouble – I couldn't get away with anything! It's hard to tell how it affected me, but . . . it's not worth worrying about now, though.

4 SEAN

Personally, I had no real problems growing up. I got lots of attention, but I guess there was a lot of pressure on me to do well in school. I mean, I don't feel I missed out on anything. I had lots of opportunities to socialize with other kids in school.

B **Check (✔) the columns to give your personal answers to the questions. Then compare with a partner. Give reasons for your views.**

Which of the people above do you think . . .	Osman	Sophia	Lilli	Sean	None
had a very happy childhood?					
had an unhappy childhood?					
missed having siblings (= brothers and sisters)?					
sometimes found family life stressful?					
enjoyed being with their siblings?					

2 Grammar Describing experiences

Figure
it out

A Circle the correct verb forms to complete the sentences. Use the article to help you. Then read the grammar chart.

1. Osman thinks it's important for children **to grow up / growing up** with other children.
2. Sophia says that she was sometimes a little lonely **to play / playing** by herself.
3. Lilli says she always had enough **to eat / eating** as a child.
4. Sean feels that he had no real problems **to be / being** an only child.

Infinitives (*to* + verb)	-*ing* forms (verb + -*ing*)
After adjectives, you can use infinitives, especially in *It* clauses. This is common in generalizations.	You can also use -*ing* forms. This is common when people describe an actual experience.
It was **impossible** for her **to have** time for herself.	I was a bit **lonely being** by myself all the time.
After nouns or pronouns, use infinitives to add more details or say how you use them.	After these expressions, use -*ing* forms: *have fun, have (no) trouble / problem(s); be worth.*
We always had nice **clothes to wear**. There was always **someone to play with**.	I **had fun / no problems growing up** in my family. It**'s** not **worth worrying** about.

Grammar extra
See page 157.

Common errors

Don't add *for* or use *for* instead of *to*.
We had **books to read**. (NOT ~~for to read, for read~~)

In conversation . . .

After adjectives, infinitives are far more common.

About
you

B Complete the comments with a correct form of the verbs. Sometimes there is more than one answer. Then discuss the views with a partner. Do you agree with each other?

1. It's hard _____ (imagine) growing up as an only child. I had six sisters, and we had lots of fun _____ (make up) games together. The advantage of a big family is that it's impossible _____ (be) lonely.
2. One disadvantage of being an only child is that I never had anybody _____ (share) problems with. I had no trouble _____ (find) kids _____ (play) with, though. I guess it makes you more independent.
3. I was the oldest, so it was my job _____ (take care of) my brothers. There were a lot of things _____ (do). Big families are OK, but parents don't have much time _____ (spend) with each kid.
4. My sister and I fought all the time. It was hard _____ (sit) in the same room without arguing. After she left home, it was easier _____ (be) together. Families don't always get along.

3 Viewpoint A big or small family?

A Pair work Is it better to grow up in a small family or in a big family? Discuss the advantages and disadvantages of each situation, and agree on an answer.

"Basically, it's better to be in a small family because you get more time with your parents, you know, one-on-one."

In conversation . . .

You can use *Basically, . . .* to give your main opinion.

B Class activity Present your argument for a big family or a small family to the class. Then take a class vote.

Lesson C *What I mean is . . .*

① Conversation strategy Making your meaning clear

A Which of these things should parents expect their children to do? At what point in their lives? In high school? In college? After college?

contribute to household bills	do household chores	move out	pay rent
cook their own meals	do their own laundry	pay for food	observe the house rules

B ◀))CD 3.05 **Listen. What is Franco's problem? What is Sarah's view?**

Sarah   So how are things going, now that you've graduated?

Franco   OK, but it was hard moving back in with my parents. I'm not saying we don't get along, but frankly there's a bit of friction. You know, they have all these rules.

Sarah   Well, I have to say, it *is* their house. What I mean is, it's probably not easy for them, either.

Franco   I know. I'm just saying it's hard to get used to. And they've even asked me to pay rent now.

Sarah   Well, . . . you'd have to pay rent if you had your own place.

Franco   I know. I don't mean that they should support me completely, but I could use some help till I get on my feet. In other words, I just wish they'd give me a break.

Sarah   Well, you could always work more hours if you need to.

C   **Notice** how Sarah and Franco make their meaning clear by adding to or repeating their ideas. They use expressions like these. Find examples in the conversation.

> *What I'm saying is, . . .*   *I'm (just) saying . . .*
> *What I mean is, . . .*   *I'm not saying . . .*
> *I mean, . . .*   *I don't mean . . .*
> *In other words, . . .*

About you

D   **Match the comments. Write the letters a–f. Then discuss with a partner. Are any of the situations true for you?**

1. I can't wait to get my own place. _d_
2. You can save money when you live at home. ____
3. I guess you have to live by your parents' rules. ____
4. My mom says I have to move out when I get a job. ____
5. I've always had to do my own laundry and stuff. ____
6. If you don't pay rent at home, you should still contribute somehow. ____

a. I'm just saying I can take care of myself and do that kind of thing.
b. What I mean is, you could help redecorate a room or something.
c. I don't mean that you shouldn't contribute toward rent, though.
✔ d. I'm not saying living with my parents is bad. But it'll be fun fixing up my own apartment.
e. What I'm saying is, you're really a guest in their home.
f. In other words, she just wants me to be independent, which is fine.

2 Strategy plus *I have to say . . .*

🔊 CD 3.06 You can use *I have to say* to show that you want to make a strong statement, often to say something controversial.

> Well, **I have to say,** it *is* their house.

In conversation . . .

You can use these expressions to say what you really feel.

Honestly	▬▬▬▬▬▬▬▬▬
I have to say	▬▬▬▬▬
(Quite) frankly	▬▬▬▬
To be honest (with you)	▬▬▬
To tell you the truth	▬▬

A 🔊 CD 3.07 **Listen. Write the expressions you hear. Then practice with a partner.**

1. *A* Do you think it's hard for adult children to live with their parents?
   B I _____ don't think it is. Some of my friends complain about their parents. But _____ I think they're lucky to have a free place to live.

2. *A* Is it reasonable for parents to ask their kids to pay rent to live at home?
   B I don't really know, _____ . I know some parents who pay all their kids' expenses, and _____ I think that's a bad idea.

3. *A* When do you think is the best time for kids to move out and be independent?
   B _____ , I think it depends. I suppose after they get their first real job. Though my sister's working, and _____ , she couldn't afford to move out right now.

About you

B Pair work **Take turns asking the questions above and giving your own answers. Use expressions like *Honestly* to make strong statements and to say how you feel.**

3 Listening and strategies "Boomerang" kids

A **Read the advice for parents. Do you know any parents who have done these things?**

How to deal with your "boomerang" kids

- ☐ Set up a work-for-rent arrangement. _____
- ☐ Refuse to lend money. _____
- ☐ Don't buy clothes or personal items. _____
- ☐ Remove the TV from his/her bedroom. _____
- ☐ Insist he/she has to apply for a job every day. _____
- ☐ Insist he/she has to be home by 11:00 p.m. _____
- ☐ Set a move-out date. _____
- ☐ Have a no friends / no parties rule. _____

B 🔊 CD 3.08 **Listen to two parents talk about "boomerang" children. Check (✔) the rules in Exercise A that Karen advises Steve to set.**

C 🔊 CD 3.09 **Listen again. Does Steve think he can set each rule that Karen advises? Write Yes or No next to each rule in Exercise A.**

About you

D Group work **Which advice in Exercise A do you think is reasonable? Which is not? Can you think of other rules parents should make?**

"To be honest, I think it's reasonable to set up a work-for-rent arrangement. What I mean is, . . ."

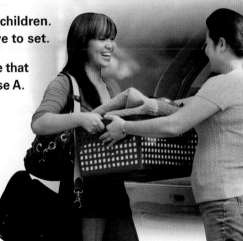

4 Speaking naturally Conversational expressions *See page 141.*

Lesson D *How <u>not</u> to get along!*

1 Reading

A **Prepare** What do satirical articles do? Check (✔) the boxes below. Do you enjoy reading satire? Explain what you like or don't like about it.

Satirical articles . . .

☐ make fun of people.
☐ give a balanced view of an issue.
☐ use humor to criticize people.

☐ exaggerate or say the opposite of what's true.
☐ show respect for people or organizations.
☐ joke about social or political trends.

B ⬇ **Read for style** Read this satirical article. Which of the things in Exercise A does it do? Give examples.

How to lose friends

| THE CITY WEEKLY | **community voices**

Now That I've Driven All My Friends Away, *I Finally Have Time For Me!*

by Bradley Crouch

¹ Who needs friends? You work hard all day, and then they expect you to give up your evenings to hang out with them at movies and restaurants. That's exhausting, as well as expensive. You can't even take weekends off because there are parties, nightclubs, bike rides, beach trips, and more. Some friends will even try to tag along on your vacation! With friends like these, you won't have a moment to yourself.

² Luckily, I've found ways to get people like this off my back. Just follow the five steps below, and you, too, will finally have time to do lots of important things, like playing online games for hours on end, heating up microwave dinners, and watching late-night TV infomercials alone in the dark.

³ **Step 1: Don't get around to calling them back**.
Don't feel guilty about not returning friends' calls. Just think of it this way. If a telemarketer left you a message, would you call back? Of course not! They just waste your time. Well, in the same way, your friends probably just want you to waste your time listening to their tedious stories. Just put off making those calls, or better still, ignore them completely!

⁴ **Step 2: If you must talk, make it painful**.
Despite your best efforts to shake them all off, you may still end up talking to a friend. If this happens, talk about yourself – constantly. Friends hate this! Focus on topics that are boring, gross, or both, such as what time you woke up or an embarrassing medical

problem. Just make sure you don't ask your friends any questions about themselves!

⁵ **Step 3: Don't show up on time**.
Let's say you followed Steps 1 and 2, but your friends still managed to come up with plans for you. Maybe you agreed to see a movie together. What I would do in a case like this is arrive 30 minutes after the movie starts. That way you annoy your friends, but you still get to see most of the film. Or simply let them down and don't show up at all.

⁶ **Step 4: Always be short of cash**.
Never bring money when you're out with friends. Let them pay! That will make your time with them less painful. After all, it's fun spending other people's money, especially when you have no intention of paying them back.

⁷ **Step 5: Sit back and do nothing**.
As a result of taking the steps above, you should notice a growing emptiness in your calendar, inbox, and life. Congratulations! Now you can sit back and enjoy your freedom. Just think. The next time everyone else is stuck at another backyard barbecue, on a ski trip, or on a night out, you'll be at home alone, staring at your cell phone, which will never ring.

⁸ So, I hope this all made sense and that you now have time for yourself – for a change.

Reading tip

Writers often start with a question that sets the scene for the topic or problem they are going to address.

C Understanding reference Find the expressions in the article. What do the underlined words refer to? Do they refer to ideas that come before or after them in the article? Complete the chart.

Expression	Paragraph	Refers to	Before?	After?
1. hang out with <u>them</u>	1	your friends	✔	
2. <u>That's</u> exhausting	1			
3. people like <u>this</u>	2			
4. the five steps <u>below</u>	2			
5. important <u>things</u>	2			
6. think of it <u>this way</u>	3			
7. If <u>this</u> happens	4			
8. Friends hate <u>this</u>	4			
9. <u>That way</u> you	5			

About you

D React Pair work Discuss the questions.

- Did you find the article humorous? Which parts did you find most amusing?
- Does the article make any serious points? What is the main message of the article?
- Which step would be most effective in getting rid of your friends?
- Have you ever done any of the things in the article? What happened?

2 Focus on vocabulary Idiomatic expressions

A Find the expressions in bold in the article. Figure out their meanings. Then match the two parts of the sentences to check your answers. Write the letters a–f.

1. If you **drive** your friends **away**, _____
2. If you **tag along** with someone, _____
3. If you **get** someone **off your back**, _____
4. If you don't **get around to** something, _____
5. If you **let** people **down**, _____
6. If you are **short of** or **on** something, _____

a. you don't find the time to do it.
b. you stop that person from annoying you.
c. you don't have enough of it.
d. you disappoint them.
e. you do things so they won't be your friends.
f. you go along even if you're not needed or invited.

B Pair work Take turns using the expressions in Exercise A to give advice on friendships.

"If you don't want to drive away your friends, it's a good idea to listen to them and . . ."

3 Viewpoint Who needs friends like these?

Group work Do you have problems like these with people you know? What other problems do people have with their friends? Discuss suggestions for solving the problems.

He never shows up on time.

He keeps letting me down at the last minute!

In conversation . . .
You can use these expressions to suggest solutions.
You could always tell her . . .
You might want to . . .
It's a good idea to . . .

She always tags along with us – even if we don't invite her.

She's always short of money when it's time to pay the bill.

He talks about himself all the time.

He never gets around to returning my calls.

"If people are always showing up late, it's a good idea to meet them at a café. I started doing that with a friend of mine, and now I don't feel so bad waiting for him anymore."

Unit 7: Getting along **81**

Writing *Friends or family?*

In this lesson, you . . .
- use a thesis statement.
- use *What* clauses for key points.
- avoid errors with subjects.

Task | Write an introduction to an essay.

The saying "Blood is thicker than water" suggests that family relationships are more important than friendships. Do you agree?

A **Brainstorm** Discuss the essay question above with a partner, and take notes. Do you agree with the saying? Give three reasons for your opinion.

B **Look at a model** Read the introduction to an essay below. Underline the thesis statement.

> **Thesis statements**
>
> A thesis statement in your introduction tells the reader the main point or argument you will make.

The expression "Blood is thicker than water" suggests that our relationships with family members are closer than the relationships we have with our friends. It implies that friendships are less important. On the one hand, it is fair to say that our family is an important part of our lives. Family members often put up with our annoying habits or support us when problems come up. On the other hand, our friends are the people that we choose to be in our lives and that choose us to be in theirs. Families do not have this choice. What is more important than being part of a family, in my view, is having a strong network of friends.

C **Focus on language** Read the grammar chart. Then rewrite the sentences below as *What* clauses. There is sometimes more than one way to rewrite them.

> ### *What* clauses in writing ⬇
>
> You can use a *What* clause in a sentence to give the most important information in a paragraph. *What* clauses are often the subject of the verb *be*. Notice that the verb is singular.
>
> | ADJECTIVE | NOUN | TO + VERB | THAT CLAUSE |
> | --- | --- | --- | --- |
>
> *What is **important** is **a network of friends**. / **to have** close friends. / **that you have friends**.*
>
> | VERB | NOUN | TO + VERB |
> | --- | --- | --- |
>
> *What we all **want** is **good friends**. / **to have** good friends.*
>
> | VERB | THAT CLAUSE |
> | --- | --- |
>
> *What this **implies** is **that you should respect your friends**.*
>
> **In writing . . .**
>
> You can write a thesis statement with other structures, but a *What* clause is a good choice.

1. It's essential to have a good relationship with your family. _____
2. Everyone needs the support of their family. _____
3. It's important to show respect to your family members. _____
4. It's clear – family relationships are stronger than friendships. _____
5. This means that blood really is thicker than water. _____

D **Write and check** Look back at the Task at the top of the page. Write an introduction to an essay. Use a *What* clause in your thesis statement. Then check for errors.

> **Common errors**
>
> Sentences need a subject.
>
> ***What is important*** *is to have good friends.*
> ***It*** *is important to have good friends.*
> (NOT ~~*Is important . . .*~~)

Vocabulary notebook *Look forward to it!*

Learning tip	Personalize

When you learn a new expression, such as a phrasal verb, use it in a true sentence about someone you know. Describe the person or your relationship with him or her. Write notes next to a photograph.

My sister is great. I always <u>look</u> <u>forward</u> to spend<u>ing</u> time with her.

A Write the names of people you know to make these sentences true.

1. _____ has never run out of money.
2. _____ puts off everything until the last minute.
3. I always look forward to seeing _____ .
4. _____ gave up a job one time.
5. I like to have _____ over for dinner.

We're running out of . . .
The things people talk about *running out* of most are:
time
money
space
breath

B Now write the name of someone you know in a photo frame. Add a photo if you can. How many of the phrasal verbs in the box can you use about the person?

clean up	come up with	give up	look forward to	run out of
come up	give back	go over	put up with	wake up

Magdi

We always go over our homework together.

C **Word builder** Find the meanings of the phrasal verbs below. Can you use them to write about the person in Exercise B?

1. get around to (doing) something _____
2. come across (as) _____
3. go along with _____
4. go through _____
5. look out for someone _____
6. look up to someone _____

This is my mom, who puts up with me and my sister.

On your own
Make an online photo album of your friends and family. Write a caption for each photo, using a phrasal verb.

Food science

In Unit 8, you . . .

- talk about food, farming, and nutrition.
- use the passive to talk about the past, present, and future.
- use verb complements.
- use rhetorical questions to make a point.
- add examples as part of your argument.

Lesson A *Vertical farming*

1 Grammar in context

A What kinds of farms are there in your country? What do they grow or produce? Which foods does your country import and export?

B ◀))CD 3.12 Listen to the radio interview. Which photo best illustrates the topic?

IS (17)

Anchor By the year 2025, the world population is expected to rise to 8 billion. In order to grow enough food, it is estimated that 1 billion hectares (almost 2.5 billion acres) of new land will be needed – that is, if the farming methods that are practiced today continue. Environmentalists say something must be done if food shortages are going to be avoided. That's why the idea of "vertical farming" is being discussed at an eco-conference this week. Celia Hernandez, our environmental correspondent, joins me. Celia, what is vertical farming? And where did the idea come from?

Celia The idea was developed by Dickson Despommier, a professor at Columbia University, back in 1999. Vertical farms are basically high-rise greenhouses that can be built in cities. So crops will be grown indoors – and in water, instead of in soil.

Anchor And what are the advantages of growing food in this way?

Celia Well, supporters say it's more reliable because crops won't be affected by weather conditions like drought or cold. It's also more environmentally friendly, because waste can be composted and water will be recycled. And because crops will be grown, harvested, and consumed in the same urban area, transportation costs will be greatly reduced. So in theory, food should be cheaper, too.

[sidebar tabs: HOME | LISTEN LIVE | PROGRAMS | PODCASTS]

C Pair work **Answer the questions about the interview.**

- Why is vertical farming an important topic?
- What will vertical farms look like? Where will they be?
- In what ways are vertical farms different from conventional farms?
- Why will vertical farming probably make food cheaper?

2 **Grammar** Information focus

Figure
it out

A **How might the journalists say the sentences below? Rewrite the sentences, starting with the words given. Use the interview to help you. Then read the grammar chart.**

1. Some people expect the population to rise by 3 billion. *The population . . .*
2. Dickson Despommier invented the idea. *The idea . . .*
3. The weather won't affect crops. *Crops . . .*

The passive 📥

Grammar extra
See page 158.

You can use the passive to make the "receiver" of an action the focus, when you don't know the "doer," or if you feel the "doer" is not important. You can introduce the "doer" with *by*.

Active sentences	Passive sentences
Experts **expect** the population to rise.	The population **is expected** to rise.
A professor **developed** the idea.	The idea **was developed by** a professor.
They **haven't built** vertical farms.	Vertical farms **haven't been built**.
They**'re going to discuss** the issue.	The issue **is going to be discussed**.
They**'ll grow** crops in water.	Crops **will be grown** in water.
The weather **won't affect** crops.	Crops **won't be affected by** the weather.
Someone **must do** something.	Something **must be done**.

B 🔊 CD 3.13 **Rewrite the underlined parts of the sentences from the rest of the interview. Use the passive and add *by* where it is needed. Then listen and check your answers.**

crops will be grown

1. *A* So they will grow crops in water? I know they do this *this is done* already, but how does it work?

   B Well, they add nutrients to the water. So the plants use less energy to get the nutrients. And plants that they grow in this way grow faster and bigger.

2. *A* People often say that they use too many pesticides in farming. Do vertical farms use them?

   B Um, no, they won't need pesticides. This is because they'll protect the crops inside the building. So they will reduce the use of pesticides. And groundwater, which pesticides have contaminated for years, will be cleaner.

3. *A* Now, reports say that we are going to see vertical farms in our cities soon. Is that true?

   B Well, they can't build them without more research. They carried out some trials last year and they wrote a report, but they haven't published it yet. I'd say they're not going to build them anytime soon. But environmentalists say we must not ignore the situation and should take action soon because we're going to need more food with the population increasing by 5,000 a day. They say that we need to find a solution soon.

C Group work **Discuss the advantages and disadvantages of vertical farming.**

A One of the biggest advantages is that food will be grown and sold in the same area.
B So transportation costs will be reduced and foods won't need to be packaged.
C Yes, but the only thing is that jobs will be lost and . . .

Lesson B *Food for health*

1 Vocabulary in context

A ◀)) CD 3.14 **How many foods can you think of that are good for your health? Make a list. Read the website article below. Which of your foods are mentioned?**

Top foods for health . . .

Don't let your diet make you unhealthy. The right foods can help you stay fit, boost your energy levels, and make you feel great.

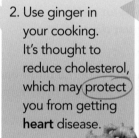

1. Blueberries are said to be good for your **brain**. They can help you concentrate and improve your memory. Have a headache? Try cherries to make the pain go away.

10. Both kiwis and mangoes are said to keep your **eyesight** from deteriorating.

9. You may know that milk helps strengthen **bones** and **teeth**, but did you know that soybeans and tofu do, too?

2. Use ginger in your cooking. It's thought to reduce cholesterol, which may protect you from getting **heart** disease.

3. Eating too much salt may cause your **blood pressure** to rise. But did you know that hibiscus tea is believed to lower it?

8. Snack on pineapple. It benefits the **digestive system** and might keep you from getting an upset stomach.

4. Avocados are good for your **skin**. But don't just eat them! Applying avocado to your skin may prevent it from aging.

7. Apples are thought to help to remove toxins from your **liver**. Raisins can help you build strong **muscles**.

6. In studies in South Korea, chili peppers have been shown to increase your **metabolism**, which may contribute to weight loss.

5. Mushrooms are said to boost your **immune system**, which can protect you from getting colds or the flu.

Word sort | **B** **Make a chart like this with words from the website.**

Food	What it may be good for	The benefit
blueberries cherries	your brain headaches	can help you concentrate make pain go away

Vocabulary notebook

See page 93.

2 Grammar Describing causes and results

Figure it out

A Circle the correct option in each question. Use the article to help you. Then read the grammar chart.

1. Which fruits are said to help you **keep / keeping** your eyesight in good condition?
2. What might cause your blood pressure **rise / to rise** if you have too much of it?
3. What might mushrooms prevent you **from getting / to get**?

Find the verbs in the article.

Verb complements ⬇

Grammar extra
See page 159.

Verb + object + verb (base form) | Blueberries are said to **help** you **concentrate**.
help*, let, make | **Make** the pain **go away** with cherries.
*Can also be used with an infinitive.

Verb + object + infinitive | Eating too much salt may **cause** your blood pressure **to rise**.
allow, cause, enable, help | Researchers say chili peppers **enable** you **to lose** weight.

Verb + object + from + -ing form | Avocado may **prevent / stop** your skin **(from) aging**.
keep, prevent*, protect, stop* | Kiwis are said to **keep** your eyesight **from deteriorating**.
*Can also be used without *from*.

In conversation . . .
The pattern *help* + object + verb is more common than *help* + object + infinitive.

B Complete the sentences with a correct form of the verbs given. Add *from* if necessary. Sometimes there is more than one answer.

1. The sugar in soda can cause your blood pressure <u>to rise</u> (rise). Fruits like watermelon and tomatoes are said to help you <u>lower</u> (lower) it.
2. Don't let dinner with friends <u>make</u> (make) you heavier. Research shows that eating with friends makes you <u>eat</u> (eat) up to 33 percent more food.
3. Asparagus may stop you <u>from having</u> (have) mood swings. It's thought to help some people <u>cope</u> (cope) with depression.
4. Chocolate may enable you <u>to concentrate</u> (concentrate) better. Some studies have also found that it protects your skin <u>from aging</u> (age).
5. Some studies seem to show that green tea contains chemicals which may prevent you <u>from getting</u> (get) certain types of cancer.
6. People who allow themselves <u>to eat</u> (eat) treats occasionally generally stay thinner.
7. If kids don't eat breakfast regularly, it may keep them <u>from performing</u> (perform) well on tests. However, too many sugary breakfast foods may make kids <u>behave</u> (behave) badly.
8. One possible way to keep your skin <u>from getting</u> (get) dry is to drink lots of water!

About you

C Pair work Which of the ideas in Exercise B did you know about? Which ideas will make you change your eating habits? How?

"I didn't know the sugar in soda makes your blood pressure rise. That might make me drink less."

3 Viewpoint Top tips for eating well

Pair work Decide on your top ten tips for eating well to put on a health website. Then share ideas with another pair.

A OK. How about, "Drink water. It stops your skin from getting dry."
B All right. And we could add, "It may prevent your skin from aging."

In conversation . . .
You can use *All right* and *OK* to start a new topic or to agree.

Unit 8: Food science   87

Lesson C *Why do they do that?*

1 Conversation strategy Using questions to make a point

A Read the three research findings. Are you like these average consumers?

- Only 50 percent of young adult consumers read the ingredients on food labels.
- U.S. consumers spend about 90 percent of their food budget on processed foods that contain additives like food coloring and artificial flavors.
- Many people believe the marketing claims that manufacturers make, even though some of them may be misleading.

B ◀))CD 3.15 **Listen. What's the problem with food, according to Edward and Debra?**

Edward	I think the main problem with our diet these days is that we eat too much processed food. Take cereal, for instance. If you look at the list of ingredients, you can't even pronounce most of them.
Debra	Oh, I know.
Edward	I mean, can all those additives be good for you?
Debra	Yeah, and look at food coloring and artificial flavors. I mean, why do they need to add that stuff?
Edward	I know. I imagine most people don't read the labels.
Debra	And then the manufacturers make all those claims such as "Lowers your cholesterol." I mean, do most people really believe that stuff? I think a lot of those claims are misleading.
Edward	Yeah, I have to say, we're not very well-informed about food, generally.

C **Notice** how Edward and Debra use rhetorical questions to make their point. They don't expect each other to answer these questions. Find two more examples in the conversation.

> *. . . can all those additives be good for you?*

D ◀))CD 3.16 **Complete the rest of Edward and Debra's conversation with the rhetorical questions in the box. Listen and check. Then practice the whole conversation.**

Debra Yeah, I guess. My parents taught me about food when I was growing up. _____c_____ It's so important.

Edward It is. But part of the problem is that healthy food costs so much more. I mean, _____a_____

Debra And the trouble is, most people have forgotten how to prepare food properly. _____c_____ Everyone just lives on fast food.

Edward I know. I think we've just forgotten what real food is. _____b_____

a. why is it so expensive?

b. Isn't it a shame?

c. Why don't people cook anymore?

d. Why don't they educate kids about these issues?

About you | **E** **Pair work** **Discuss the points that Edward and Debra make. Which points do you agree or disagree with? Use rhetorical questions to make your point.**

2 Strategy plus Giving examples

Take cereal, **for instance.**

🔊 CD 3.17 You can use these expressions to give examples.

They make claims **such as / like** "Lowers your cholesterol."
Some claims are misleading – **for instance,** / **for example,** "low fat."
Take cereal, **for instance.**
Look at food coloring.

About you

Complete the sentences with your own ideas. Then compare with your group. How many different ideas did you think of?

1. A lot of <u>fast foods</u> make you gain weight. Take <u>milkshakes</u>, for instance. They're <u>full of fat</u>.
2. Snack foods often have <u>too much salt</u> in them. Look at <u>potato chips</u>, for example.
3. Manufacturers make a lot of claims on food packages. I've seen <u>claims</u> like <u>fat free</u>, (high in calcium) for example.
4. They say the healthiest foods are <u>fresh fruits and vegetables</u>. Things such as <u>beets</u> and <u>berries</u>.
5. Lots of things are added to processed food, you know, things like <u>coloring</u> (additive) food.

3 Listening and strategies A food revolution!

A **Look at the photos of Jamie Oliver, a famous British chef. What do you think he's doing in each picture? Discuss with a partner.**

a. ☐

b. ☐

c. ☐ PETITION

d. ☐

e. ☐ IT'S IRISH FOR TITLE   BONDS TRIAL

B 🔊 CD 3.18 **Listen to two radio show hosts talk about Jamie Oliver. Number the photos in Exercise A in the correct order 1–5.**

C 🔊 CD 3.19 **Listen again. Answer the questions. Then compare with a partner.**

1. Why did Jamie Oliver start a TV series in the United States?
2. Why did Jamie start a petition?
3. What did the school chefs think about him at first?
4. What kind of impact has Jamie had?

About you

D 🔊 CD 3.20 **Pair work** **Listen to five people talk about Jamie Oliver. Discuss each reaction. Give your views and use rhetorical questions to make your point.**

A I agree. I mean, who has time to cook without using some processed foods? And some are probably fine.
B Yeah, take frozen vegetables. They're processed and they're OK.

4 Speaking naturally Strong and weak prepositions *See page 141.*

Lesson D *Where did all the bees go?*

1 Reading

A **Prepare** What do you know about bees? How many facts can you think of?

Bees live in hives.

B ⬇ **Read for main ideas** Read the article. What problem does the article describe? Why is it serious? What are the possible causes?

Where did all the bees go?

[1] The majority of people probably don't pay much attention to bees, except perhaps on the rare occasion that they're stung by one. However, that all changed with the publication of numerous articles several years ago, which reported a strange phenomenon called "colony-collapse disorder" (CCD). Beekeepers had been opening their hives, only to discover that many of their bees had mysteriously disappeared – and suddenly beekeeping became a hot news topic.

[2] According to the reports, some beekeepers had lost more than 70 percent of their bee colonies, and commercial beekeepers even reported losses of up to 90 percent. It was an alarming discovery, considering that bees pollinate over 90 of America's flowering crops – including avocados, cucumbers, and soybeans – as well as a range of fruit crops from apples to cranberries and kiwis.

[3] "This is the biggest general threat to our food supply," said agricultural scientist Kevin Hackett. He has a point. According to the U.S. Department of Agriculture, approximately one-third of our diet comes from plants that are pollinated by insects, and the honeybee is responsible for about 80 percent of that pollination. A Cornell University study estimated that bees pollinate more than $14 billion worth of U.S. seeds and crops annually.

[4] One example is the lucrative billion-dollar U.S. almond crop, which accounts for over 70 percent of the world's commercial production of almonds, and which is entirely dependent on honeybees. It is estimated that the almond crop alone would need about 1.5 million hives – roughly two-thirds of the colonies in the U.S. – to produce a successful harvest.

[5] U.S. farmers were not the only ones facing this problem. A similar decline in the bee population was reported in Canada, Brazil, and parts of Europe. Researchers worldwide started looking for answers, and a range of theories for the losses soon emerged. One theory was that the bees were dying from a virus, a parasite, or a fungus infection. Other theories blamed poor bee nutrition, pesticides, and cell phone radiation. It was also suggested that bees are simply stressed, because they are now raised to survive a shorter off-season and work more intensively than ever before.

[6] Since the total number of beehives has dropped by a quarter and the number of beekeepers has fallen by half, demand for beekeeping services has pushed up farmers' costs. The cost of renting a hive rose from $55 to $135 in three years. Many more beekeepers now travel across the country with their colonies, trucking some tens of billions of bees with them to pollinate crops. Others have started importing bees to keep up with demand. None of these solutions, however, really addresses the underlying problem. A solution needs to be found because without bees our food supply is threatened and our very survival is at stake. So the critical question remains not only, "What caused the disappearance of the bees?" but "What can we do about this terrible loss?"

C Understanding statistics **Are the statistics true (T) or false (F)? Write T or F. Correct the false statistics.**

1. Some beekeepers lost more than 70 percent of their bee colonies. _____
2. For others, only about 10 percent of their bees survived. _____
3. Bees pollinate all the flowering crops in the United States. _____
4. Two-thirds of what we eat comes from plants that are pollinated by insects. _____
5. Bees pollinate up to $14 billion worth of U.S. seeds and crops each year. _____
6. The United States grows less than half of the world's almonds. _____
7. It would take exactly two-thirds of the bees in the U.S. to pollinate the almond crop. _____
8. There are 50 percent fewer beekeepers now. _____

About you **D** Pair work **Discuss the information in Exercise C. Which facts did you find surprising?**

2 Focus on vocabulary Nouns and verbs

A **Complete the questions with the noun forms of the verbs given. Use the article to help you. The paragraph numbers are in parentheses.**

1. Who made the _____ (discover) that bees were disappearing? How? (para. 2)
2. Why is _____ (pollinate) so important? (para. 3)
3. What _____ (threaten) does colony-collapse disorder pose? (para. 3)
4. How important are honeybees in the _____ (produce) of almonds? (para. 4)
5. What theories are there to explain the _____ (disappear) of so many bees? (para. 6)
6. Do you think our _____ (survive) is really at stake? (para. 6)
7. How would the _____ (lose) of the bee population affect your life, do you think? (para. 6)

B Pair work **Ask and answer the questions in Exercise A. Refer back to the article on page 90 to support your answers.**

3 Listening and speaking Backyard beekeeping

A CD 3.23 **Listen to a radio interview with a beekeeper. Check (✔) the topics he talks about.**

☐ How he became interested in bees   ☐ How to care for a hive
☐ How bees actually pollinate flowers   ☐ The dangers of beekeeping

B CD 3.24 **Listen to more of the interview, and complete the statistics.**

1. A hive can produce about _____ pounds of honey a week.
2. Bees visit something like _____ flowers to produce a pound of honey.
3. The beekeeper has over _____ bees.
4. There are roughly _____ bees in a hive.
5. Bees travel up to _____ miles to pollinate crops.

C CD 3.25 **Listen to the last part of the interview. Write two advantages and two disadvantages of backyard beekeeping.**

About you **D** Pair work **Discuss the advantages and disadvantages of beekeeping. Would you ever keep bees? Why? Why not?**

"I think backyard beekeeping is a good idea for several reasons. Firstly, it can help . . ."

You know what they say... busy as bees!

HONEY

DONNELLY

Writing *Ups and downs*

In this lesson, you . . .

- write about graphs, charts, and trends.
- use prepositions and approximate numbers.
- avoid errors with *fall, rise* and *grow*.

Task   **Write a report for a science class.**

What's happening to bees?

A   **Look at a model** Match each graph or chart with two sentences below. Write the letters a–d next to the sentences.

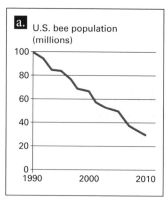

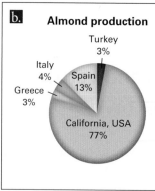

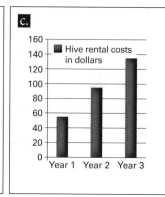

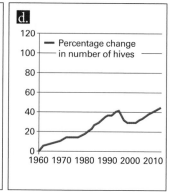

1. The cost of renting a hive rose from $55 to $135 in three years. ___c___
2. There was a decline in the U.S. bee population of approximately 70 percent. _____
3. The majority of almonds are grown in the United States. _____
4. The number of bee colonies in the U.S. fell by more than 70 percent. _____
5. There was an increase in the number of hives worldwide of about 45 percent. _____
6. The U.S. accounted for over 70 percent of global almond production. _____
7. Globally, the number of hives increased by roughly 45 percent. _____
8. There was a rise of just over 145 percent in the cost of hives. _____

B   **Focus on language** Read the grammar chart. Then circle the correct preposition, and add an appropriate expression to give an approximate number in the news report below.

Prepositions in writing ⬇	Approximate numbers	
The bee population **declined by** *more than 70%.*	**+/–**	*about / approximately / roughly*
Globally, the number of hives **increased by** *about 45%.*	**+**	*over / more than*
There was a **decline in** *the bee population* **of** *over 70%.*	**–**	*under / less than*
A **rise of** *145%* **in** *the cost of hives affected farmers.*	**>|**	*nearly / almost / up to*

Researchers are concerned about the decline **in / by** bee colonies. Some blame hard winters. In a normal winter, the number of bees in a hive drops **by / for** _____ (+/–) 10 percent. However, in recent years, beekeepers have seen an annual fall **in / of** _____ (+/–) 30 percent **in / of** the number of bees in their hives. Some had losses **by / of** _____ (+/–) 50 percent, and some even lost _____ (>\|) 90 percent of their bees. Overall, the U.S. experienced a decline **of / in** _____ (+) 70% **in / by** its total bee population. However, this problem does not exist everywhere. In fact, globally, there has been an increase **by / of** _____ (+) 45 percent **from / in** _____ the number of hives, and honey production has also risen **by / in** _____ (+/–) 100 percent in the last 50 years.

C   **Write and check** Look at the Task at the top of the page. Write your report. Then check for errors.

Common errors

Don't add *down* and *up* to the verbs *fall, rise,* and *grow* to describe trends.
The bee population **fell,** *then* **rose/grew.**
(NOT . . . *fell down / rose up / grew up*)

Vocabulary notebook *Picture this!*

Learning tip   A picture dictionary

Create a picture dictionary on your computer. Find pictures that show words and expressions you want to learn. Copy and paste the pictures into a document, and write notes about each one.

Respect the copyright of pictures that are on the Internet!

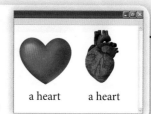

a heart   a heart

A   Label the pictures below with the words in the box. Then write health tips for each picture.

blood pressure	digestive system	eyesight	✓ immune system	teeth

1.

immune system

Mushrooms boost your immune system.

2.

_____

_____

3.

_____

_____

4.

_____

_____

5.

_____

_____

> ### On the other hand . . .
>
> *Hand* is the body part that is used the most in expressions in conversation. The most common are:
> *on the one hand*
> *on the other hand*
> *(get) out of hand*
> *(do something) by hand*

B   Now create a document on your computer for these words. Use an Internet search engine, and find pictures for each one. Write a health tip for each picture.

1. skin	2. bones	3. muscles	4. brain	5. liver

C   **Word builder** Find the meanings of the words in the box. Then find and label pictures like the one above.

circulation	joints	kidneys	lungs	sinuses

Eat blueberries – they're good for your brain.

On your own

Make a food chart for your kitchen wall. Use pictures from magazines and add health tips. See how many of the items you can eat or drink in one week!

Success and happiness

In Unit 9, you . . .

- talk about success and happiness.
- use *all*, *both*, *each*, *every*, *neither*, *none of*, *no*.
- learn more uses of *-ing* forms.
- use expressions like *in terms of* to focus in on your ideas.
- give opinions with expressions like *As far as I'm concerned, . . .*

Lesson A *Successful people*

1 Vocabulary in context

A 🔊 CD 3.26 **Make a list of well-known successful people. What makes them successful? Then read the article. Do the people on your list have the qualities described in the article?**

Three characteristics of successful people

1. Vision All successful people know they won't **get anywhere** without a vision. Fred Smith's vision was for an overnight package-delivery company. One of his college professors reportedly didn't think the idea would **get off the ground.** Nevertheless, Fred pursued his vision, and today FedEx is one of the world's largest delivery companies.

Mark Zuckerberg had a vision for a social networking website and dropped out of college to **get** it **under way.** How Facebook **got to be** one of the most widely used networking sites is considered a marketing phenomenon. Both men became billionaires.

Mark Zuckerberg

2. Persistence No success comes easily. Akio Morita, founder of Sony, sold fewer than 100 of his first rice cookers. Harland Sanders's Kentucky Fried Chicken recipe was rejected 1,009 times before a restaurant accepted it. Neither product **got off to a good start**, but neither of the entrepreneurs let failure **get them down** or **get in their way**. In fact, it's rare to find successful people who *haven't* experienced any setbacks. However, they tend to learn from their failures and **get on with** the job of rebuilding their businesses.

3. Passion Every successful person **gets ahead** in life because they simply love what they do. Celebrity chef Rachael Ray had no formal training in culinary arts, but loved creating recipes and built a career around it. In fact, history is full of people who **got to the top** by doing things they loved – Andre Agassi, Ralph Lauren, Sir Richard Branson. Each one was successful, and none of them graduated from college.

Rachael Ray

About you

B Pair work **Find expressions in the article to replace the words in bold below. Do you agree with the sentences? Discuss with a partner.**

1. You won't **succeed** in life or **go as far as you can** in your career if you don't like what you do.
2. It's not hard to **start** a business, but only businesses that **start out well** will be successful.
3. You won't **make any progress** in life if you don't have a passion.
4. Failure only **becomes** a problem if you let it **make you unhappy.**
5. Successful people don't let anything **stop them.** They **continue** building their businesses.

Word sort

C Complete the chart with *get* expressions from the article.

starting things	problems	making progress
		(not) get anywhere

Vocabulary notebook

See page 103.

2 Grammar Talking about *all* and *none*

Figure it out

A Rewrite the sentences below, replacing the underlined words with phrases from the article. Then read the grammar chart.

1. <u>Every successful person knows</u> you need a vision.
2. <u>The two men</u> became billionaires.
3. <u>The two products didn't sell</u> at first.
4. <u>Not one of these people</u> graduated from college.
5. <u>Success doesn't come</u> easily.

Determiners ⬇

Grammar extra
See page 160.

Singular nouns	*Each entrepreneur was successful.* *Every restaurant rejected the recipe.*	*No entrepreneur wants to fail.* *No restaurant accepted the recipe.*
Both (= two)	*Both products got off to a good start.* *Both (of) these men became billionaires.*	*Neither product was a success at first.* *Neither of the men let failure get them down.*
Plural nouns	*All successful people have a vision.* *All (of) these people were successful.*	*No successful people get ahead easily.* *None of these people graduated from college.*
Uncountable nouns	*All (of) their hard work paid off.*	*None of their hard work was wasted.*

About you

B Circle the correct determiners in the conversations. Then practice with a partner. Practice again, this time giving your own answers and ideas.

1. *A* Do you know any successful people?
   B Yes. **Each / All** my close friends are successful. They worked hard, and **all of / every** their efforts paid off. **None / No** success is easy. **None of / No** my friends had it easy, anyhow.

2. *A* In what way are the people you know successful?
   B Well, **both / each** person is successful in a different way. One's happily married with kids. One's a nurse. Another's very wealthy. But **all of / every** friend I have is doing what they love.

3. *A* What do you think successful people have in common?
   B Well, they take risks. Two businesspeople I know got off to a bad start, but **neither of / neither** their companies failed in the end. They didn't let fear of failure get in their way.

4. *A* What successes have you had in life so far? How did they make you feel?
   B Well, I graduated from college. I'm sure **every / all** student is happy to graduate, but for me college wasn't easy. **Each / Both of** my roommates thought I would quit.

3 Viewpoint The five laws of success

A 🔊 CD 3.27 Listen. Take notes on what each person says is most important about success.

B **Pair work** Now discuss the ideas. Do you agree? Decide on your top five laws of success, and share them with another pair.

A It seems to me that every successful person has a positive outlook.
B Absolutely. You can get anywhere in life with a positive outlook.

> **In conversation . . .**
> You can say *It seems to me* to give an opinion.

Lesson B *Happy moments*

❶ Grammar in context

A What are some of the happiest moments in life? Share your ideas as a class.

"Well, one of the happiest moments in life is when you graduate from college."

B ◀))) CD 3.28 **Listen. What were some of the happiest moments in Anna's and Wesley's lives? Practice the conversation.**

Anna	I think some of the happiest moments in my life were playing on this beach as a kid.
Wesley	Yeah? My happiest moment was graduating from college, when all that hard work finally paid off.
Anna	You know, college really wasn't my thing. I mean, I tried to make the most of it. But I got so stressed, taking exams all the time. I remember sitting outside on the last night, talking. My friends were out there with me, crying. And I was sitting there, thinking, "Gosh, I'm glad it's all over!"
Wesley	And look at you now – with a successful career and everything.
Anna	I know. There are so many things going on in my life. And being successful feels good. But it's not everything. Remember when we were kids and we'd run around, playing in the sand, not caring about anything?
Wesley	Yeah. Hey, look – there are some people digging for clams over there. Want to look for some?
Anna	Sure. Come on. I'll race you!

C Pair work **Discuss the questions. Do you share the same interpretation?**

1. What do you think Anna and Wesley's relationship is?
2. Who do you think is more successful? Why?
3. Who do you think sounds happier? Why?

About you

D Pair work **Find the expressions in bold in the conversation and check their meaning. Then ask and answer the questions.**

1. Do you think hard work always **pays off**?
2. Have you ever done anything that wasn't **your thing**?
3. Are you **making the most** of your classes?
4. Will you be glad when your studies are **all over**?
5. What good things **are going on** in your life?
6. Do you believe that success **isn't everything**?

"I think hard work always pays off. You won't get anywhere if you're lazy."

2 Grammar Adding information

A **How do Anna and Wesley say these things? Find the sentences. Then read the grammar chart.**

1. There are so many things that are going on.
2. I got so stressed when I took exams.

3. My happiest moment was when I graduated.
4. When you're successful, it feels good.

-ing forms

Grammar extra
See page 161.

An -ing form can be a reduced relative clause.	There are some people **digging** for clams. I've got so many things **going on** in my life.
An -ing form can describe one event that happens at the same time as another. Notice the commas.	We'd run around, **playing** in the sand, **not caring** . . . I was sitting there, **thinking**.
An -ing form can come before or after *be*. It can be the subject or object of a verb.	My happiest moments were **playing** on this beach. **Being** successful is/feels good. I remember **sitting** outside.

B CD 3.29 **Rewrite the anecdotes so that each sentence uses an -ing form from the grammar chart. You will need to cross out words, change verbs, or do both. Then listen and check.**

having

1. **One of the happiest moments in my life was** ~~when I had~~ dinner in Italy with my husband. We were on a little island on a lake, and we were eating outside at a restaurant. And there were these musicians who were playing music. The moment when we watched the sunset was so romantic. I can't remember when I felt happier.
2. **I think the happiest day in my life was** the day I celebrated my 18th birthday and played volleyball on the beach. There were some other guys there who were playing a game, too, and we played against them. They were really good, so the fact that we won felt really great. We've all stayed friends ever since, and when we get together, it always reminds me of that day.
3. **My earliest happy memory was** when I won the school spelling bee. I felt so proud as I stood there. Everyone in the audience stood up and clapped. And when I saw my parents' faces, it was the best moment. I stood on the stage for ages and didn't want it all to end.

C **Pair work** **Talk about happy moments in your life. Use the words in bold in Exercise B to start.**

3 Listening and speaking Happy moments gone wrong!

A CD 3.30 **Listen to three people talk about moments that went wrong. Number the topics 1–3. There are three extra topics.**

_____ a graduation ceremony _____ a birthday _____ moving into a new home
_____ opening night at a play _____ a marriage proposal _____ a dream vacation

B CD 3.31 **Listen again. Answer the questions in the chart for each person.**

	What went wrong?	How did each person feel?
1. José		☐ a. annoyed ☐ b. worried
2. Cho Hee		☐ a. angry ☐ b. embarrassed
3. Katy		☐ a. disappointed ☐ b. confused

C **Group work** **Discuss the situations in Exercises A and B. How would you have felt? Tell your group any stories you know about when things went wrong.**

Lesson C *As far as happiness goes, . . .*

1 Conversation strategy Focusing in on a topic

A Do you agree with this statement? Why or why not?

"The best way to define happiness is in terms of success."

B 🔊 CD 3.32 Listen to a group discussion in a psychology class. Which comments do you agree with?

Professor	So, how do you define happiness and success? Are they the same thing?
Marta	As far as I can tell, they're not necessarily the same thing. I mean, according to a recent job-satisfaction survey, accountants are the most unhappy. But as far as careers go, accounting is considered one of the best.
Frank	Yeah. I mean, we're brought up to believe that happiness means having lots of money – a big house and everything. But as far as I'm concerned, you can't define happiness in terms of what you own. No possession in the world can make you truly happy.
Juliette	I agree. When it comes to being truly happy, it's about doing things that have meaning. You can't just sit around, waiting to be happy.
Marta	As far as happiness is concerned, it's all about relationships, I think. You know, you *need* strong social networks. There's a lot of research that shows people who are lonely aren't just unhappy, but their health is affected, too.

C **Notice** how the students use expressions like these to focus in on a topic. Find the examples in the conversation.

> As far as (success) is concerned, . . .
> As far as (careers) go, . . .
> When it comes to happiness / being happy, . . .
> . . . in terms of . . .

In conversation . . .

These expressions are more common in formal speaking.

	Conversation	Formal speaking
in terms of	▪	▪ ▪ ▪ ▪ ▪ ▪
As far as . . . concerned	▪	▪ ▪ ▪
When it comes to	▪	▪ ▪

About you

D Complete the sentences with your own ideas. Then compare with a partner.

1. When it comes to being truly happy, _____ is/are more important than _____ .

2. As far as true happiness is concerned, it has nothing to do with _____ .

3. As far as having a successful career goes, you _____ .

4. You can't define success just in terms of _____ .

5. As far as relationships are concerned, it's important _____ .

"When it comes to being truly happy, good relationships are more important than anything."

2 Strategy plus *As far as I . . .*

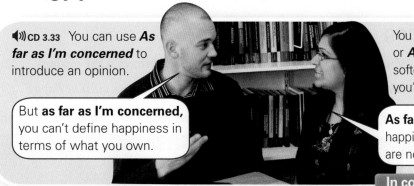

🔊 CD 3.33 You can use *As far as I'm concerned* to introduce an opinion.

> But **as far as I'm concerned,** you can't define happiness in terms of what you own.

You can use *As far as I know* or *As far as I can tell* to soften an opinion, or when you're not 100 percent sure.

> **As far as I can tell,** happiness and success are not the same thing.

In conversation . . .

As far as I'm concerned is the most frequent expression.

As far as I'm concerned	■ ■ ■ ■
As far as I know	■ ■
As far as I can tell	■

About you

Complete the conversations with your own ideas. Then take turns asking and answering the questions with a partner.

1. *A* Do you think people spend too much time worrying about being happy?
   B Well, as far as I'm concerned, _____ .

2. *A* Do you think people believe having lots of money will make them happy?
   B Good question. As far as I know, _____ .

3. *A* Do you think having a successful career is overrated?
   B You know, as far as I can tell, _____ .

3 Strategies What makes people unhappy?

A 🔊 CD 3.34 **Listen to the conversations. Write the expressions you hear. Then practice with a partner.**

1. *A* Would having a long commute make you unhappy, do you think?
   B Maybe. Sitting in traffic is the worst thing, _____ .
   A Because I read that _____ commuting, people who have to travel one hour to work each day need to earn 40 percent more to be as happy as people who walk to work.

2. *A* Is it true that people are less happy when there's an economic recession?
   B I'd say so. I mean, _____ jobs, there's less work going around, and people get laid off.
   A Right. But there are fewer divorces during a recession, _____ . Why is that?
   B Well, _____ , it's because people can't afford to get divorced!

3. *A* Do you think that people who live in big cities are happy? _____ , it's stressful to live with like, 15 million other people.
   B Yeah. _____ , living in a small town is better. I mean, _____ stress.
   A Though _____ culture _____ , there are a lot more things going on in a big city, I guess.

About you

B Pair work **Take turns asking and answering the questions in Exercise A. Give your own answers.**

C Group work **What other things make people unhappy, do you think? Discuss your ideas. Can you agree on the five most common things that make people unhappy?**

"As far as I can tell, there are lots of things that make people unhappy, like having no friends."

4 Speaking naturally Stress in expressions *See page 142.*

Lesson D *The politics of happiness*

1 Reading

A **Prepare** **What factors make a country "happy"? Brainstorm a list of ideas.**

"I would think that wealth is one factor. People in rich countries must be happy."

B **Read for main ideas** **Read the article. How many of your ideas are mentioned?**

Unhappy?
Maybe you're not in the right country!

China

Bhutan

India

1 If you're not feeling as happy as you'd like, maybe you should consider moving to another country – like Denmark, for example. According to social psychologist Adrian White, who analyzed data and surveys of 80,000 people in 178 countries, Denmark is the happiest nation in the world, closely followed by its northern European neighbors Finland, Norway, and the Netherlands.

2 Not surprisingly, perhaps, the happiest countries are also the healthiest and wealthiest and those that provide their citizens with a good level of education. People may pay high taxes in these countries, but they are rewarded with other benefits such as shorter work weeks, as well as more vacation time. All of these contribute to a general sense of well-being. Size also matters. Smaller countries, which have a strong sense of national identity and social cohesion, rate better in terms of happiness than countries with larger populations.

3 While the governments of many countries seek to increase wealth and prosperity for their citizens, at least one government has made its citizens' happiness a priority. In Bhutan, a tiny country between China and India, happiness is part of government policy. Instead of measuring GNP (Gross National Product), Bhutan measures GNH (Gross National Happiness). Their rationale is that by putting a high value on health, education, and general well-being, citizens' lives will be improved in ways that enrich their nation's environment and culture. The program seems to be working: 19 percent of Bhutan's inhabitants live below the poverty level, yet only 4 percent of the population claim to be unhappy.

4 There could well be lessons here for other governments hoping to improve both their GNP and GNH. Happier people tend to be more productive, leading to greater economic wealth. Moreover, they are often healthier, resulting in lower spending on health care. Ideas for producing happier citizens might include reducing unemployment – a major cause of unhappiness – improving parenting skills to create happier families, and finding ways to stimulate kindness toward others, which is known to make both the givers and receivers happier. In Japan, for example, "community credit" programs encourage couples who live too far from their aging parents to "adopt" an elderly person locally to care for. By doing this, they can earn credits that their own parents can use to "buy" similar volunteer care in their own neighborhoods. Governments adopting such programs might well see both the happiness and wealth of their nations improve.

5 Of course, neither relocating to a new country nor waiting for new government policies may be the best way to guarantee your future happiness. Fortunately, however, researchers are coming to the conclusion that the main ingredient for a happy life is love. And that's something that no government can help you with.

C **Reading for detail** Do the statements below agree with the information in the article? Write Y (Yes), N (No), or NG (Information not given).

1. All European countries are happy. _____
2. Education contributes to a nation's well-being. _____
3. Most of Bhutan's population lives above the poverty level. _____
4. Wealth makes people happy, according to the research. _____
5. There are good economic reasons for governments to make citizens happier. _____
6. In Japan, there are programs to help people become better parents. _____

About you

D **Pair work** **React** **Discuss the questions.**

- What do you think of the idea that governments can be responsible for your happiness? Whose responsibility is it to make people happy, do you think?
- Do you think you live in a happy country? Why? Why not?
- What could be changed in your country to make people happier?

2 Focus on vocabulary Synonyms

A **Find a word in the article with a similar meaning to replace each word or expression in bold. Change its form, if necessary. The paragraph numbers are given.**

What do governments do?

Analyze

1. **Study** economic trends. (para. 1)
2. Collect taxes from the country's **people**. (3 possible answers) (para. 2, 3)
3. Decide the **most important things** for the **country**. (para. 3, 1)
4. Develop **plans** for how the country operates. (para. 3)
5. **Try to find** ways to make the country **richer**. (para. 3, 2)
6. **Encourage** economic growth. (para. 4)

About you

B **Pair work** **Use each word from Exercise A to describe other things that governments do.**

"One thing the government is doing at the moment is analyzing the banking industry."

3 Listening and speaking Happiness and the community

A CD 3.37 **Read the sentences from a handout for a sociology class. Guess the missing words. Then listen to part of a lecture, and complete each sentence with no more than three words.**

1. There's evidence that people in richer areas are _____ people in poorer areas.
2. Furthermore, research suggests that in _____ people are less happy.
3. Happiness is a good thing. Happy people _____ , and they are also healthier.
4. In addition, happy people tend to be good citizens and _____ to their communities.

B CD 3.38 **Listen to more of the lecture. Write the three proposals that the lecturer suggests can make communities happier.**

1. _____
2. _____
3. _____

About you

C **Pair work** **What do you think of the ideas in Exercise B? Can you agree on three policies that would make your community a happier place?**

Writing *Policies for happiness*

In this lesson, you . . .
- answer an essay question.
- add ideas with *as well as*, etc.
- avoid errors with *in addition to*, etc.

Task   Write a paragraph in an essay.

Should a government try to make its citizens happy? How? Give specific reasons and examples.

A   Look at a model Read this paragraph from an essay. What is the student's answer to the first question above? What reasons does the student give? What other reasons can you think of?

> As far as governments are concerned, there are several good economic reasons for having policies that make citizens happy. First, happiness is important to the economy because happy workers are more effective, as well as more productive. In addition, research shows that happy people contribute more to their community in terms of volunteering. Furthermore, happy people tend to be healthier, which means that they cost less in terms of health care. Every government should try to increase citizens' happiness in addition to stimulating economic growth in other ways.

B   Focus on language Look at the paragraph again. How does the student add ideas? Circle three more expressions (not including *and*). Then read the grammar chart.

Adding ideas in writing

You can use *as well as* and *in addition to* to add ideas within a sentence.
As well as mostly connects noun phrases and adjectives.
*Happy workers are more effective, **as well as** more productive.*

In addition to mostly connects noun phrases. Use an *-ing* form to add a verb.
*Governments can increase happiness **in addition to** (stimulating) economic growth.*

In addition, furthermore, and *moreover* add ideas to a previous sentence.
*Happy people are productive. **In addition**, they contribute more to their community.*

Writing vs. Conversation

Moreover and *furthermore* are mostly used in formal writing and formal speaking.

C   Rewrite the sentences, replacing the words in bold with the expressions given. Make any necessary changes to punctuation or grammar. Then compare with a partner.

1. Governments can have an effect on people's health. **Also**, they can affect their well-being. (In addition)
2. Some governments measure their nation's happiness **and** their GNP. (as well as)
3. Happy people take fewer sick days. **Also**, they tend to be more productive at work. (Furthermore)
4. An economic recession is bad for a country. It makes people unhappy, **too.** (Moreover)
5. People in happier countries have a shorter work week **and** they get more vacation time. (in addition to)
6. People are responsible for their own health **and** for creating their own happiness. (in addition to)

D   Write and check Now write your own paragraph for the essay question. Then check for errors.

Common errors

Remember to use an *-ing* form after a preposition.
*It makes us happier in addition to **making** us richer.* (NOT . . . *in addition to* ~~make~~ . . .)
Don't use *as well as* to connect a clause with a new subject.
*This increases happiness as well as **stimulating** wealth.* (NOT . . . ~~it stimulates . . .~~)

Vocabulary notebook *Get started!*

Learning tip   Formal or informal?

When you learn a new expression, imagine using it in an everyday situation. Write the situation and what you would say.

I have a lot of homework, and a friend calls and asks me to go out. "I'm sorry. I can't go out with you tonight. I really need to <u>get started on</u> my homework."

A   Read the situations below. Complete the things you can say using the expressions in the box. Write the correct forms of *get*.

get (me) down	get anywhere	get in the way	get it off the ground	get on with	get to be

1. My friend and I just started a small business, but it's not easy.
   "*It's not easy _____.*"

2. I just finished practicing my violin, and I managed to play a more difficult piece.
   "*It's definitely _____ easier.*"

Dictionary tip

Look up all the main words in an expression, not just the first word.
For example, for *get off the ground*, look up *ground*.

3. I had a lot of problems with my ex-girlfriend last year.
   "*It was really _____ . I often felt very depressed.*"

4. I have a lot of homework, and it's affecting my free time.
   "*All this work is _____ of my social life!*"

5. I'm trying to write a paper, and I'm not making any progress.
   "*I'm not _____ with this!*"

6. My best friend just got divorced.
   "*He just wants to _____ his life.*"

B   Now write your own situations and things you can say for these expressions.

1. get ahead _____
   " _____ ."

2. get off to a good start _____
   " _____ ."

3. get under way _____
   " _____ ."

4. get to the top _____
   " _____ ."

C   **Word builder** What do these *get* expressions mean? Write a situation and something you can say for each one.

1. I like to **get my own way**.   4. I wanted to **get involved** in the project.
2. I didn't **get a lot out of** it.   5. I just **got carried away**.
3. I couldn't **get through to** him.   6. I can't **get it together**.

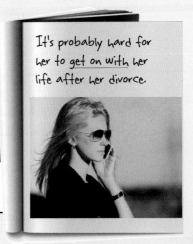

It's probably hard for her to get on with her life after her divorce.

On your own

Find a celebrity magazine. What can you say about each celebrity?
Annotate the photos using *get* expressions from the lesson.

Checkpoint 3 *Units 7–9*

1 Childhood memories

A Rewrite these memories in your notebook. Use an *-ing* form to rewrite the underlined sentences. Replace the words in parentheses with a correct form of a phrasal verb in the box.

clean up	come up with	give up	have over	put off	run out of
come up	give back	go over	✓ look forward to	put up with	wake up

1. I was always the first person home after school. <u>I used to sit by the window and wait for my mom to get home from work.</u> I (couldn't wait) seeing her car in the driveway.

   I was always the first person home after school. I used to sit by the window, waiting for my mom to get home from work. I looked forward to seeing her car in the driveway.

2. During summer vacations, I'd (invite . . . over) my friends for play dates. <u>There were always kids who played at our house.</u> If we made a big mess, my mom always (tolerated) it. She (made it clean) afterward, too!

3. I always found homework difficult. I'd (postpone) doing it. Or I'd just (stop). My dad would always (check, read) it with me. He helped me with any problems that (appeared). <u>I used to listen to him and think he was the smartest guy.</u>

4. My grandma was always (thinking of) fun things to do. She never (stopped having) ideas! <u>I remember that I played with her for hours.</u>

5. My sister was always taking my things. She never (returned them), either! And she'd (stop me sleeping) early. <u>The fact that I had to get up early was the worst.</u>

About you

B **Pair work** Take turns telling stories from your childhood. Use expressions like *honestly, frankly, to be honest,* and *to tell you the truth* to make your statements stronger.

"When I came home after school, my mom was always there. I have to say, I loved that."

2 Happiness and politics

A Complete the comments with *all, both, each, every, neither, no,* and *none*. Use *of* when necessary. Sometimes there is more than one correct answer.

1. In some countries, ___all___ college education is free. _____ student should get that, so they don't have huge college bills to pay off.
2. _____ country should have a policy to make _____ their citizens happy. Unfortunately, _____ the countries in this region do that.
3. _____ family should pay for their own health care. It's your own responsibility.
4. Many people have _____ formal job training. _____ employee should get training.
5. _____ government wants its economy to fail. When there are _____ jobs, the priority should be to stimulate the economy and create new jobs.
6. Denmark and Finland are two of the happiest nations. _____ countries spend a lot on education. _____ country has good health care, too. However, _____ these countries has low taxes!

About you

B **Pair work** Discuss the views in Exercise A. Do you agree with each other? Use expressions like *in other words, what I mean is,* and *I'm not saying* to make your meaning clear.

3 Healthy living

A Complete the sentences with a correct form of the verbs given. Use *from* when necessary. Then circle the correct words to complete the comments.

1. It's probably good for you __to drink__ (drink) milk. It may strengthen your **teeth / metabolism**. It might also prevent your **bones / liver** _____ (break).

2. It can be bad for some people _____ (eat) too much meat. But fish may stop you _____ (get) **heart disease / immune system**. It may also be good for your **brain / muscles** because it helps your memory.

3. It's probably not healthy _____ (eat) too much salt. In some cases it might cause your **blood pressure / digestive system** _____ (rise).

4. Make sure there's always fruit _____ (snack on) in the fridge. Fruit like blueberries can help you _____ (concentrate). And some research shows kiwis can keep your **skin / eyesight** _____ (deteriorate).

5. We always had vegetables _____ (eat) at school. And I've always enjoyed _____ (eat) them, actually, which is good. I mean, they can protect you _____ (get) all kinds of diseases. And putting avocados on your **skin / muscles** can make it _____ (feel) really soft.

6. It's worth _____ (teach) kids about food. My family always has fun _____ (cook) together.

7. I've never had any trouble _____ (watch) my weight. I eat chili peppers, and I read they enable some people _____ (lose) weight. I think they increase your **metabolism / liver**.

About you

B Pair work Discuss the comments in Exercise A. Use the expressions in the box.

> When it comes to . . . ,   in terms of . . .   As far as I know,   As far as I can tell,
> As far as . . . go / goes *or* is / are concerned,   As far as I'm concerned,

"As far as milk is concerned, I know it's good for you, but it's not a big part of my diet."

4 Expectations

A Circle the correct *get* expressions in the conversation. Then rewrite the sentences, changing the verbs in *italics* to the passive form.

Young people are expected . . .

A We *expect* young people to achieve so much. They need a good degree to get (ahead) / **down**.

B I know. They feel they have to get **to be / to the top** in their careers. Or they think people *won't see* them as successful. They*'ve done* a lot of research on the pressure this causes. It gets people **down / off** to a bad start. It's really getting **off the ground / to be** a national problem.

A Yeah. Over 20 companies *rejected* one of my friends. She couldn't get **in the way / anywhere** with her career. She just wanted to get a job and to get **on with / under way** her life.

B Yeah. They *should do* something about unemployment. I mean, parents *are going to support* their adult children a lot more. Parents just want their kids to get **under way / off** to a good start.

About you

B Pair work Discuss the topic in Exercise A. Use expressions like *take*, *like*, and *for instance* to give examples from your life. Use rhetorical questions to make a point.

"I think we are expected to achieve a lot. For instance, you have to get work experience and a degree. I mean, why do we have to have work experience before we get a job?"

Going places

In Unit 10, you . . .

- talk about travel and vacations.
- learn more about reported speech and reported thought.
- draw conclusions from things people say.
- use *In what way?* to ask for details.

Lesson A *Travel blog*

1 Vocabulary in context

A ◀)) CD 4.02 **Look at the pictures. What can you guess about Rob's trip? Then read the blog and check your guesses.**

Rob's *Amazon* travel blog

<u>Days 21 and 22:</u> Bolivia – to Rurrenabaque via La Paz

The first views of La Paz were **amazing** – **impressive** downtown buildings surrounded by vast suburbs climbing up breathtaking mountains; the trip was **fascinating** but **tiring**. I slept well that night. The next morning, I asked about travel to Rurrenabaque, gateway to the Amazon Basin. The tour agent informed me that the last bus had left. She also said the trip would take an **exhausting** 18 hours or more by bus – a **depressing** thought – so I opted to fly despite the cost. I called the airport; they said all the flights that day were full. They told me there were seats on the 6:00 a.m. flight the next day, which meant getting up at 4:00 a.m.! So I went to the airport the following

morning. I was **puzzled** that only a handful of people were checking in, which was **surprising**, since Rurrenabaque is a popular destination. I soon discovered why. The check-in agent explained that the plane was just a 16-seater – a **frightening** prospect. Then she said there might be a delay because of bad weather, which wasn't very **encouraging**. In the end, the flight was on time, though I have to say it was pretty **challenging**. The pilot warned us that the landing would be really bumpy – and it was! Actually, it was **terrifying**. I was just happy to get there safely, and I felt much more **relaxed** in the evening. It was the start of my Amazon adventure!

B **Answer the questions. Underline the words in the blog that give you the answers.**

When did Rob feel . . . a. tired? b. depressed? c. surprised? d. terrified?

Word sort   **C** **Make a chart like this of the adjectives in bold in the blog. Add the other adjective and verb forms.**

You feel . . .	because something is . . .	The verb is . . .
amazed	amazing	amaze

Vocabulary notebook
See page 115.

About you   **D** **Pair work** **Talk about travel experiences you have had. Take turns using words from your charts.**

"I flew in bad weather once. It was pretty frightening. Actually, I was terrified."

2 Grammar Reporting what people say

Figure it out

A Read the things below that people said to Rob. Write how he reports them in his blog. How are the reports different from the words the people actually used? Then read the grammar chart.

1. "There are seats on the 6:00 a.m. flight tomorrow."   2. "There may be a delay."

Reported speech: statements 📥

Grammar extra
See page 162.

When you report things people said in the past, the verb tense often "shifts back."

"The plane's just a 16-seater." ➔ The agent explained (that) the plane **was** just a 16-seater.
"The last bus **has left**." ➔ She informed me (that) the last bus **had left**.

These modal verbs change in reported speech:	These modal verbs don't change:
can ➔ could; will ➔ would; may ➔ might; must ➔ had to.	could, should, would, might, used to.
"There **may** be a delay." ➔ She said (that) there **might** be a delay.	

Time expressions often change, too.

"The flights are full **today** and **tomorrow**."
➔ He said the flights were full **that day** and **the next day**.

Common errors

Use an indirect object after *tell*, but not after *explain* or *say*.
He told **me** the flight was full. (NOT ~~He told the . . .~~)
He explained/said the flight was full. (NOT ~~He explained/said me . . .~~)

B In Rurrenabaque Rob met up with Conrad, who had been there before. Complete the reported speech from the rest of Rob's blog. Add *me* where necessary.

1. "We can take a boat trip on the Beni River tomorrow." *Conrad said . . .*
2. "We'll see some amazing wildlife." *He told . . .*
3. "We must make a reservation today." *He explained . . .*
4. "I saw some monkeys, and we may even see pink dolphins." *He said . . .*
5. "People used to leave trash in the forests." *He explained . . .*
6. "Tour companies have become more aware of the environment." *He told . . .*
7. "We should go on a guided tour today so we can learn all about the rain forest." *He said . . .*

C **Pair work** Close your books. Take turns remembering the things that Conrad said.

"Conrad said they could take a boat trip on the Beni River the next day."

3 Listening and speaking More adventures in Bolivia

A 🔊 CD 4.03 Listen. Natalie talks about things you can do in Bolivia. Number the photos 1–5.

Eduardo Avaroa National Park

Oruro

Lake Titicaca

La Paz

Huayna Potosí

B 🔊 CD 4.04 Listen again. Describe what you can do in each place, using no more than four words.

About you

C **Group work** What interesting travel destinations have you been told about? Tell your group.

"My friend José told me Cairo was a great place to go. He said the museums were fascinating."

Lesson B *I never travel without it!*

① Grammar in context

A **Look at the pictures. Why do you think people might take these things on a trip?**

"Well, an eye mask and earplugs would be useful on a long flight. Otherwise, it's hard to sleep."

an eye mask and earplugs

a flashlight

shampoo and conditioner

a scented candle

family photos

green tea

B 🔊 CD 4.05 **Read the article. Complete each comment with one of the items above.**

We asked six experienced travelers what special items they take with them on a trip.

"People I meet often ask me whether I'm married or have any kids, so I always have a few _____ to show them." **Carl, Los Angeles**

"People often ask me why I always take _____ with me when I travel. It makes a hotel room feel more like home." **Hae-won, Seoul**

"I find traveling so exhausting. A friend told me to try _____ . It energizes you. I always take some with me now."
Hugo, Mexico City

"My sister asked me to lend her _____ for a road trip she was taking. Up until then, it had never occurred to me how useful it could be – especially if you go out at night and there are no streetlights. So now I always take one with me." **Erkan, Istanbul**

"My co-worker wanted to know if I had any tips for sleeping better in hotel rooms. I advised her to take _____ . I always carry them with me." **Teri, New York**

"My own favorite _____ . A friend of mine who's a hairstylist told me not to use the ones that you find in cheap hotels. They can damage your hair." **Raquel, San Juan**

About you

C **Pair work** **What would you never travel without? Why? Tell a partner.**

A I'd never go away without music to listen to. Traveling can be so boring, even on a short bus trip.
B Me neither. And I would never travel without my e-reader.

2 Grammar Reporting what people ask and instruct

Figure it out

A How do the speakers in the article report the things that people said to them? Underline the places in the article that give you the answers. Then read the grammar chart.

1. "Are you married?"
2. "Why do you always take a scented candle?"
3. "Try green tea."

Grammar extra
See page 163.

Reported speech: questions and instructions

Reported questions use the word order of statements. They do not have question marks.
"Are you married?" → People often ask me **whether/if I'm** married.
"What do you take with you?" → We asked people **what they take/took** with them.
"Why shouldn't I use hotel shampoo?" → She asked me **why she shouldn't use** hotel shampoo.

You do not need to "shift back" the verb tense when you report information about the present or future that is still true or relevant.
"Do you have any kids?" "I have two." → A woman asked me if I **have** kids. I told her I **have** two.
"Where are you going on your next trip?" → He wanted to know where I **'m going** on my next trip.

Use an infinitive after *ask, tell, order, advise* to report a request, a suggestion, or an instruction.
"Can you lend me a flashlight?" → My sister asked me **to lend** her a flashlight.
"Don't use hotel shampoo." → A friend told/advised me **not to use** hotel shampoo.

In conversation . . .

Ask . . . if is more common in conversation than *ask . . . whether.*

B Lucy and her friend Sally are packing for a trip. Look at what Sally says, and complete the reports. Which reports might be different after they get back?

1. "Are you taking your running shoes?" Sally asked Lucy _____ .
2. "Put the shoes in a plastic bag." She told her _____ .
3. "Why do you always take a pillow?" Sally wanted to know _____ .
4. "Does it have to be that pillow?" She asked Lucy _____ .
5. "Don't pack too much stuff." Sally advised her _____ .
6. "How many bags are you taking?" Sally wanted to know _____ .

3 Viewpoint Get ready for a trip.

A **Pair work** Imagine you are going on a bus tour. Ask about six things that your partner plans to take. Ask your partner to do three things for you.

A Are you taking something to read?
B Yeah. I think I might download some new books.
A Can you recommend a book in English that's not too hard?

The tour company said they would provide everything but the kitchen sink.

TOUR BUS

DONNELLY

B **Pair work** Tell another classmate the questions your first partner asked, and what he or she asked you to do.

"Nela asked me if I was taking something to read. I said I might download some new books. She asked me to recommend a book for her."

4 Speaking naturally Silent vowels *See page 142.*

Lesson C *So what you're saying is . . .*

1 Conversation strategy Drawing conclusions

A Look at the advertisement from a website. Do you think space tourism will ever become popular? Would it appeal to you? Why? Why not?

Book your place in space, and go on the voyage of a lifetime . . .

- Travel at three times the speed of sound (2,500 mph / 4,000 kph).
- Experience the sensation of total silence 68 miles (110 km) above the earth.
- Feel the freedom of being weightless as you float in the air.

B 🔊 CD 4.08 **Listen. What does Wen think about going into space? How about Hai-Fang?**

Wen	I read this article that said people would be taking vacations in space within a couple of decades. Can you imagine going into space? It would be such a weird sensation.
Hai-Fang	Weird in what way? Isn't it just like being on a plane, only higher up?
Wen	Yeah, but imagine being weightless and floating around.
Hai-Fang	Oh, you mean eating your lunch upside down? Yeah, that would be weird.
Wen	But it'd be fascinating – like the trip of a lifetime. A voyage into the unknown.
Hai-Fang	So what you're saying is you could live out your *Star Trek* fantasy. Hmm. I think I'd prefer to keep my feet on the ground.
Wen	So I guess you won't be coming, then, when I blast off into outer space?
Hai-Fang	I doubt it. You know I don't even like roller coasters!

C **Notice** how Hai-Fang and Wen draw conclusions from what the other one says using expressions like these. Find examples in the conversation.

> *you mean . . .*
> *(so) you're saying (that) . . .*
> *(so) what you're saying is . . .*
> *(so) I guess . . . (then)*

D Complete the rest of the conversation with the expressions above. Then practice. Do you agree with the views? Discuss with a partner.

Hai-Fang	. . . Yeah, I just don't think going into space would be my thing.
Wen	_____ you'd find it too scary?
Hai-Fang	Yeah. Imagine being in a tiny cabin with no chance of escaping in an emergency!
Wen	_____ it's just not worth the risk, then.
Hai-Fang	Exactly.
Wen	_____ you'd never go bungee jumping or skydiving?
Hai-Fang	No way.

② Strategy plus *In what way?*

It'd be such a weird experience.

Weird **in what way?**

🔊 CD 4.09 You can use **In what way?** to ask for more details about someone's ideas or opinions.

A 🔊 CD 4.10 **Listen to the start of five conversations. How does each one continue? Write the letters a–e.**

1. Eating meals in space would be so weird. _____
2. Space travel must be bad for the environment. _____
3. Going into space would be terrifying. _____
4. Sitting in a tiny cabin would be frustrating. _____
5. A space vacation would be life-changing. _____

a. I'd want to be outside doing a space walk.
b. You can't escape if something goes wrong.
c. You'd never look at things in the same way again.
d. Well, for one thing, it pollutes the atmosphere.
e. Well, imagine your pizza floating around!

B 🔊 CD 4.11 **Now listen to the complete conversations, and check your answers. Then practice with a partner. Can you continue the conversations?**

③ Strategies A different travel experience

A **Fill in the first two blanks in each conversation with expressions from the lesson. Then choose a comment in the box to complete each conversation. Practice.**

> You'd have to trust the pilot and hope you landed safely!
> It would be like spending your vacation in prison.
> An adventure is something that just *happens*. Nobody organizes it.

1. *A* Some scuba divers did an underwater vacation for two weeks! Wouldn't that be just terrifying?
   B Terrifying _____ ?
   A Well, I think I would just panic all the time. I wouldn't enjoy one minute of it.
   B _____ you'd be scared?
   A Exactly. _____

2. *A* You know, I think adventure travel must be a bit boring.
   B I'm not sure what you mean. Boring _____ ?
   A Well, someone else organizing your vacation isn't really an *adventure*, is it?
   B _____ an adventure is something you organize yourself?
   A No. _____

3. *A* I think going up in a hot-air balloon would be quite challenging.
   B _____ it would be an unpleasant experience?
   A No, I just mean it would be . . . well . . . challenging.
   B But challenging _____ ?
   A _____

About you

B **Pair work Practice the conversations in Exercise A again, giving your opinions. Then take turns starting conversations about different kinds of unusual trips.**

A *My friend said she'd been on safari. She said it was a bit scary.*
B *Scary in what way?*

Lesson D *Global tourism*

❶ Reading

A Prepare Is tourism a big industry in your country? If so, in which areas?

"We get a lot of tourists here. One of the most popular places is . . ."

B ⬇ **Read for main ideas** Read the article. How big is the tourist industry? What are the challenges for the agencies that manage tourism?

The tourist threat

1 Tourism is one of the world's largest industries. According to the World Travel and Tourism Council, it's a $2 trillion business that directly accounts for almost 1 in 11 jobs globally. Worldwide, many countries have come to rely heavily on tourism as an important part of their economy, while other countries – such as some of the smaller Caribbean island nations – are almost completely dependent on tourism for their survival.

2 Despite its economic benefits, tourism has a downside, too. While countries eagerly spend millions attracting tourists to their shores, they are also struggling with the negative impacts that tourism brings with it.

3 One of the biggest threats is environmental. The building of roads, hotels, and resorts can quickly destroy those very beautiful landscapes on which tourism depends in the first place. Development on wetlands, for example, impacts wildlife; forests disappear as they are cleared to make way for buildings and to provide fuel.

4 In addition, the tourist industry also puts a huge pressure on scarce water supplies. In dry Mediterranean areas, tourists using leisure facilities like swimming pools and golf courses consume almost twice as much water as local residents.

5 Tourism accounts for about 60 percent of air travel and creates noise and air pollution, which have negative effects on the environment. In Yosemite National Park, in the U.S., the number of roads and parking lots has increased so much to keep pace with the growing number of visitors that smog is now adversely affecting the wildlife and vegetation.

6 Tourism is also responsible for producing huge amounts of waste. Cruise ships in the Caribbean generate a lot of trash – more than 70,000 tons each year. It even affects remote regions like the Himalayas, where Everest, the world's highest mountain, has more than 100 tons of trash sitting on its slopes and peaks.

7 In spite of these problems, responsibly managed tourism can bring many positive benefits to communities and the environment. Revenues from park-entrance fees pay for the protection of sensitive areas – or in Borneo for the care of young orangutans. Income from departure taxes in Belize covers some of the costs of conserving the reefs.

8 Furthermore, tourism brings people into close contact with natural areas like rain forests, and can give them a better understanding of the environment and the consequences of destroying it. This awareness can lead to pressure on local governments to preserve these beautiful areas, and can result in the protection of endangered plants and animals.

9 A further positive effect of tourism is that it can lead to alternate employment opportunities. In Guatemala, Spanish-language schools for tourists now hire local people who were previously employed in industries such as hunting and deforestation.

10 Although tourism has many positive benefits, it clearly has a negative impact as well. The challenge for local and national agencies is to manage tourism so that communities can benefit economically, and yet at the same time, make sure that the tourist areas are preserved for all to enjoy.

Reading tip

The final paragraph of a long article often gives a short summary of the whole article.

C Read for topic The writer of the article mentions a number of effects that tourism has. Which four of these effects are mentioned? Check (✔) the boxes.

- ☑ Deforestation to provide fuel *pgh 3*
- ☑ Stress on water resources *pgh 4*
- ☐ Poor planning of buildings and facilities
- ☑ Atmospheric pollution from transportation *pgh 5*
- ☐ Damage to plants from hikers
- ☑ Littering of tourist areas *pgh 6*

D Read for evidence Read the article again to find these things. Then discuss your own views on tourism with a partner, using the information to help you build your argument.

- three <u>statistics</u> that show the <u>economic importance</u> of tourism *pgh 1 (2) ; pghs 5 (1)*
- <u>five</u> specific examples of how <u>tourism has affected places negatively</u> *3, 4, 5, 6 (2)*
- <u>two</u> examples of how tourist dollars can help a country *7*
- an example of how <u>tourism stops people harming the environment</u> *pgh 8*

"Tourism is important in terms of employment, and it says here that about 10 percent of the global workforce works in tourism somehow."

2 Focus on vocabulary Synonyms

A Find the words in bold in the article. Then find words with similar meanings in the same paragraph. Use them to rewrite the sentences below, making any changes necessary.

1. Tourism is one of the biggest **industries** here. *businesses*
2. Some areas **are almost completely dependent on** tourism. *rely heavily on*
3. The **building** of tourist resorts has had a huge impact on the environment. *development*
4. Air pollution and noise have **negative effects on** the wildlife. *adversely affected*
5. Tourists **generate a lot of trash.** *produce huge . . .*
6. **Income** from tourism has helped protect endangered plants and animals. *revenue*
7. People have a greater **awareness** of environmental issues, which can **result in** better protection of the environment. *understanding* *lead to*
8. Hotels and other businesses **hire** local people, which benefits local communities. *employ*

About you **B Pair work** Which sentences are true for your country? Discuss and give examples.

"Tourism is definitely one of the biggest businesses here. It's an important industry in . . ."

3 Listening and speaking Responsible tourism

A Pair work Look at the tourist pamphlet on the right. Think of different ways to complete the sentences.

B ◀)) CD 4.12 Listen to a short presentation by an eco-tour guide. Complete the sentences in the pamphlet.

C ◀)) CD 4.13 Listen again. Answer the questions.

1. What two reasons does the guide give for shopping at local markets?
2. Why does the guide encourage people not to bargain?
3. What story does the guide tell about a tourist who bought coral?

About you **D Pair work** Agree on the five most important things that people can do to be responsible tourists. Prepare a short presentation for tourists. Take turns presenting to the class.

> ### How to be a responsible tourist . . .
>
> 1. Choose a tour company that does not _____ .
> 2. Stay in a place that _____ .
> 3. Save _____ .
> 4. Buy _____ .
> 5. When you buy things, pay _____ .
> 6. Ask before _____ .

Writing *Are tourists welcome?*

In this lesson, you . . .
- write up your survey notes.
- contrast ideas with *although,* etc.
- avoid errors with *although.*

Task **Write a survey article.**

Are tourists a good or bad thing?

A **Brainstorm** Ask your classmates the question above, and take notes on their views. Then compare with a partner.

"Maria thinks tourism is a bad thing. She said she'd left a museum once because of all the tourists."

B **Look at the models** Read the extracts from two articles in a student magazine. Complete the last sentence in each extract with one of your own ideas.

Tourists are a nuisance!

Tourism brings a number of benefits to our community. It creates employment and strengthens the local economy. However, my survey shows that residents have mixed feelings about its impact. Although tourism has its advantages, many people feel that large groups of tourists are a nuisance. In fact, most people said they would prefer the tourists to stay away despite the jobs that tourism creates. When I asked one person why he held this view, he said . . .

Tourists are a good thing . . .

With the growth in tourism, I asked local students whether tourism brought problems or benefits. Interestingly enough, even though many people find tourists annoying, the view of most is that the advantages of tourism outweigh the disadvantages. It is true that tourists leave litter and crowd the streets. Nevertheless, most people welcome tourists to the region. We need them in spite of the problems they create. One person said . . .

C **Focus on language** Circle five more expressions in the extracts in Exercise B that contrast ideas. Then read the grammar chart.

Contrasting ideas in writing

Use *although* and *even though* to connect clauses.
Although / Even though *tourism creates jobs, it has disadvantages.*
Tourism is a good thing, ***although / even though*** *it brings problems.*

Use *despite* and *in spite of* before noun phrases or *-ing* forms.
Despite / In spite of *(causing) problems, tourists are welcome.*
Tourism can be good ***despite / in spite of*** *the problems it causes.*

Nevertheless, like *however,* contrasts an idea in a previous sentence.
Tourists may bring problems. ***Nevertheless****, people welcome them.*

Writing vs. Conversation

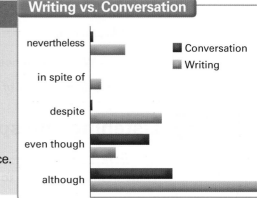

D Circle the correct expressions to complete the sentences.

1. **Although / Despite** groups of tourists can be annoying, tourism is important to the local economy.
2. You can still enjoy the sights in the city, **in spite of / although** the crowds of tourists.
3. Tourism creates employment, **even though / despite** many of the jobs are low paid.
4. Tourism can damage the environment. **Despite / Nevertheless**, resorts are still being developed.

E **Write and check** Write your article. Include your classmates' views. Then check for errors.

Common errors

Use *despite / in spite of* before a noun phrase. Avoid *although.*
Despite *the problems, tourism has benefits.* (NOT ~~Although~~ *the problems, tourism . . .*)

Vocabulary notebook *So amazing!*

Learning tip   Word forks

When you learn a new word, find other words in the same word family – for example, the noun(s), verb(s), adjective(s). Make word forks. You can add example sentences.

frighten	verb **to frighten** *Flying frightens me.*
	adj **frightening** *The flight was frightening.*
	adj **frightened** *I felt frightened during takeoff.*
	noun **fright** *I had a terrible fright.*

A   Complete the word forks with verb and adjective forms.

1.

amaze
- | verb   When I arrived, the city ___amazed___ me.
- | ____   The architecture was _____ .
- | adj   I was _____ when I saw the buildings.

2.

fascinate
- | verb   Rome has always _____ me.
- | adj   Rome is a _____ city.
- | ____   I'm always _____ just to watch the people there.

Dictionary tip

Read the example sentences in a dictionary to see how each form of a word is used.

surprise
noun [C/U]

*I want the party to be **a surprise**. **To my great surprise,** they gave us what we asked for.*

3.

impress
- | ____   What _____ me most was the beach.
- | ____   The beach was _____ .
- | ____   The beach was clean, which _____ me.

4.

terrify
- | ____   What _____ me is sailing.
- | ____   I think the ocean is _____ .
- | ____   I'm _____ when I get on a boat.

B   Think of trips you have made. Use your own ideas to create word forks for these verbs.

1.

depress
- | ____ _____
- | ____ _____
- | ____ _____

3.

exhaust
- | ____ _____
- | ____ _____
- | ____ _____

2.

encourage
- | ____ _____
- | ____ _____
- | ____ _____

4.

relax
- | ____ _____
- | ____ _____
- | ____ _____

C   Word builder What are the noun forms of the verbs in Exercises A and B? Add them to the word forks. Use a dictionary to help you write example sentences.

Travel Blog

The museums are fascinating.

On your own

Write a travel blog for a place that you have visited or know well. Add photos.

11 Culture

In Unit 11, you . . .

- talk about weddings, gifts, and traditions.
- use relative clauses with *when, where, whose*.
- use verbs with two objects.
- soften comments with expressions like *a little*.
- say *Yeah, no* to agree and make a comment.

Lesson A *Weddings*

1 Vocabulary in context

A ◀)) CD 4.14 **Think of ten words associated with weddings. Then read the postings on this web page. How many of your words are mentioned?**

Write a new post   *Analyze for relative clauses.*

▶ **When is a good time to get married?**

Björn   The best time here in Sweden is the summer, when it stays light all night.

Ming Wei   It depends. Here it's often decided by a fortune-teller, whose job is to choose the best day.

Alex   Any weekend when you can get off work. :-)

▶ **What's your favorite part of the wedding?**

Rodrigo   There's a very touching moment when the bride **walks down the aisle** with her **bridesmaids**, and the **groom** turns and sees her in her wedding dress for the first time.

Gosia   My favorite part is when they **go to the reception**, where the couple is met by their parents. The parents give the newlyweds a gift of bread and salt, which in Poland symbolize the prosperity and hardship of life.

Manuel   It's when the bride and groom **exchange vows**.

▶ **How have weddings changed in recent years?**

Kumiko   There was a time when weddings were very traditional in Japan, but that changed in the 1980s, when **Western-style ceremonies** became more popular.

Jun Ho   Here in South Korea, marriages were traditionally arranged by a **matchmaker**, whose responsibility was to find the right partner for you. I have lots of friends whose parents met that way, but **arranged marriages** aren't as common nowadays.

Cassidy   There aren't as many **religious ceremonies**. Some people go to Hawaii, where they get married on the beach, or there are actually places in the States where a celebrity look-alike, like Elvis, **performs a civil ceremony**.

Chris   They go on longer. They have all these **bachelor and bachelorette parties** now, where you celebrate with your friends. Sometimes they go on all night, and some last the whole weekend. Then there's the **rehearsal dinner**, where the **parents of the groom host a dinner** for everybody who's involved – the bridesmaids, the **best man**, and **groomsmen**.

Word sort

B **Make a chart like the one below. Use the words in bold from the postings.**

Types of weddings	People involved	Things people do
Western-style ceremony	bride	walk down the aisle

Vocabulary notebook
See page 125.

About you

C **Pair work Take turns using the words in the chart to ask questions about the postings. How much do you remember? Are any of the postings true for your culture?**

A Where were matchmakers used traditionally?

B I think it says in South Korea. It's interesting because my friend's mother had a matchmaker . . .

2 Grammar Adding information: time, place, possession

Figure it out

A Rewrite each pair of sentences as one sentence. Replace the words in bold with one word. Use the web page on page 116 to help you. Then read the grammar chart.

1. Things changed in the 1980s. **At that time**, people started to choose Western-style weddings.
2. After a wedding ceremony, the guests go to a reception. **There** they have a meal.
3. We used to use matchmakers. **Their** responsibility was to find the right husband or wife for you.

Relative clauses with *when*, *where*, and *whose* ⬇

Grammar extra
See page 164.

When, *where*, and *whose* can introduce defining and non-defining relative clauses.

Time – *when*	There's a touching moment **when** the bride walks down the aisle. The best time to get married is the summer, **when** it stays light all night.
Place – *where*	There are places in the U.S. **where** a celebrity look-alike performs the ceremony. Some people go to Hawaii, **where** they get married on the beach.
Possession – *whose*	I have lots of friends **whose** parents used a matchmaker. Some couples use a fortune-teller, **whose** job is to choose the best day.

Common errors

Don't confuse *whose* with *who's* (= *who is* or *who has*).

About you

B Complete the postings with *when*, *where*, or *whose*. Often *when* and *where* are both correct. Then work with a partner. Compare traditions in your country with the ones below.

1. A week before the wedding, the bride and groom go to a photographer's studio, _____ the wedding photos are taken. The bride wears her wedding dress and everything.
2. Couples often marry at half past the hour, _____ the hands of the clock are moving up instead of down. It's believed that the marriage will get off to a good start.
3. After the bride and groom have exchanged rings, there's a ceremony _____ the bride and groom each light a candle.
4. At the reception, there's a dance _____ the guests pin money onto the bride's dress. There are some weddings _____ guests "pay" to dance with the bride or groom.
5. The best man, _____ job is to take care of the rings, also makes a speech at the reception.
6. My favorite part is the event _____ the bride is painted with henna. It's called the *Mehndi*.

3 Viewpoint Views on weddings

Group work Discuss the questions. Do you have similar experiences and views?

- Have you ever been to a wedding? If so, what kind of ceremony was it?
- Was it a traditional wedding, or was there something different about it?
- How important is it to keep wedding traditions?
- How much do people spend on average on weddings? Is it a waste of money?
- What's your idea of a perfect wedding?
- Which wedding traditions would you like to change?

In conversation . . .

You can repeat words or ask *Did you say . . .?* to show interest or surprise.

A I went to a wedding last year where the reception was at a theme park.
B A theme park? OR Did you say a theme park?

Lesson B *Gift giving*

1 Grammar in context

A What gifts have you bought or given on the occasions below? On what other occasions do people give presents?

an engagement party

a retirement party

a housewarming party

a baby shower

B 🔊 CD 4.15 Listen and take the quiz. Check (✔) a, b, or c. If you check c, write your own answer.

Breakout Rooms (Complete after grammar explanation p119)

Gift giving is an important part of every culture, but customs and attitudes can vary even within one culture. Take this quiz and then compare answers with a friend.

① When someone gives me a gift, I usually . . .
- ◯ a) open it immediately.
- ◯ b) open it later when I'm alone.
- ◯ c) other _____

② When someone gives me a present to open, I tend to . . .
- ◯ a) tear off the wrapping paper and throw it away.
- ◯ b) unwrap it carefully and save the paper.
- ◯ c) other _____

③ I give money or gift cards to friends on their birthdays . . .
- ◯ a) all the time or often.
- ◯ b) occasionally or very rarely.
- ◯ c) other _____

④ If someone bought me a gift that I didn't like, I would . . .
- ◯ a) "re-gift" it and give it to someone else.
- ◯ b) take it back to the store and exchange it.
- ◯ c) other _____

⑤ If a friend bought a birthday gift for my mother, . . .
- ◯ a) I'd buy something similar for his or her mother.
- ◯ b) I wouldn't buy his or her mother one in return.
- ◯ c) other _____

⑥ If a co-worker complimented me on something I was wearing (for example, jewelry), I'd . . .
- ◯ a) offer it to him or her as a gift.
- ◯ b) simply say "thank you."
- ◯ c) other _____

⑦ If a friend bought me a gift for my home and I hated it, I would . . .
- ◯ a) put it in a closet.
- ◯ b) feel obliged to display it.
- ◯ c) other _____

⑧ If a friend made a gift for me, I would . . .
- ◯ a) appreciate it more than a gift from a store.
- ◯ b) feel disappointed that it wasn't a real gift.
- ◯ c) other _____

About you | **C** Pair work Compare your answers. Do you share the same views?

A When someone gives me a gift, I open it immediately. It seems impolite to wait.

B I suppose. But if I get a gift before my birthday, I'll usually wait and open it on the day.

2 Grammar Giving things to people

Figure
it out

A Complete the second sentence so it means the same as the first. Use the quiz to help you. Then read the grammar chart.

1. When someone gives a present to me, I open it. *When someone gives me* _____ .
2. I give my friends money or gift cards all the time. *I give money or gift cards* _____ .
3. If someone made me a gift, I'd love it. *If someone made a gift,* _____ .

Verbs with two objects ⬇

Grammar extra
See page 165.

Notice the patterns with verbs like *bring*, *buy*, *give*, *lend*, *make*, *offer*, *send*.

	indirect object	direct object		direct object	prepositional phrase
I never give	my friends / them	money.	*I never give*	money	**to** my friends / them.
She lent	someone	her book.	*She lent*	her book / it	**to** someone.
A friend sent	my mother	a gift.	*A friend sent*	a gift	**to** my mother.
I bought / made	his mother	something / one.	*I bought / made*	something / one	**for** his mother.

The pattern above is more common in general conversation, especially with *give*.

Use the pattern above when the direct object is *it* or *them*.

She lent **it** *to* **a friend.** (NOT *She lent a friend it.*)

Common errors

I bought a gift **for** *my sister.* (NOT *. . . to my sister.*)

B Rewrite the questions using the alternate pattern in the chart. If it's not possible, write X.

1. Would you ever buy a gift for your neighbor?   *Would you ever buy your neighbor a gift?*
2. When would you give a gift card to somebody?
3. When would you buy someone flowers? Would you give them to a teacher?
4. What would you think if someone sent you red roses out of the blue?
5. Imagine someone really liked a vase in your home. Would you offer it to that person?
6. Have you ever made someone a gift or a card? Did you make it for a friend?

About
you

C Pair work Take turns asking and answering the questions. Give your own answers.

3 Listening and speaking Gift giving around the world

A What rules are there about these things in your culture? What do some gifts symbolize?

1. wrapping gifts   2. offering gifts   3. accepting gifts   4. inappropriate gifts

B ◀)) CD 4.16 Listen to a radio interview about gift giving. What gifts are inappropriate in each country, according to the guest on the show? Write them in the chart. Then listen again and write the reason.

Country	Inappropriate gifts	Reason	Other advice
1. Japan			
2. Russia			
3. Chile			
4. Korea			
5. Mexico			

C ◀)) CD 4.17 Listen to the rest of the interview. Write one more piece of advice for each country.

About
you

D Pair work Prepare an interview on gift giving in your country.

"So, Fernando, when would you give flowers to someone in Brazil?"

Lesson C *It's kind of bizarre!*

1 Conversation strategy Softening comments

A What do people do at birthday parties in your culture? What interesting traditions are there? Do people ever do bizarre things?

B ◀))) CD 4.18 Listen. What do Guy and Ann think about birthday traditions in different cultures?

Guy So that was interesting at your birthday party – when everyone sang "Happy Birthday" out of tune. It was kind of unusual.

Ann Yeah. It's a tradition here. It's weird, huh?

Guy Well, yeah, it's a little strange. Though I guess we have some odd traditions, too. Like where your friends pull your ear – once for every year of your age, which is also sort of silly.

Ann Yeah, no. A lot of traditions are a bit odd like that. Here people punch you! I'm not quite sure why we do that.

Guy Yeah? And I heard there are some countries where they throw flour all over you.

Ann Which is definitely weird.

Guy Yeah, no. I guess traditions can seem slightly bizarre if they're not from your own culture.

Ann Actually, they can seem kind of bizarre even if they are!

C **Notice** how Guy and Ann soften their comments using expressions like these. Find examples in the conversation.

kind of	a (little) bit	not really
sort of	slightly	not quite
a little	somewhat	

In conversation . . .

Kind of, *a little*, and *sort of* are the most common expressions. *Somewhat* and *slightly* are more common in formal speaking. People often use *not quite* with *sure*, *right*, *true*, *clear*, and *certain*.

D ◀))) CD 4.19 Listen. Complete the conversations with the expressions you hear. Then practice with a partner. Practice again, this time giving your own responses.

1. *A* We have a tradition here where we put butter on kids' noses to avoid bad luck.
   B Which sounds _____ bizarre. I mean, it's _____ strange, huh?

2. *A* Here we turn people upside down and bang them on their head, which is crazy. I mean, it's _____ a good idea, is it?
   B No. It seems _____ dangerous to me. I mean, you could get hurt.

3. *A* On friends' birthdays, we used to pull their hair, which was _____ weird, I guess.
   B Yeah. It sounds _____ irritating. Well, _____ annoying, anyway.

4. *A* I think I'd be really upset if people threw flour all over me.
   B Me, too. It sounds _____ mean to me. It's _____ odd, anyway.

5. *A* At our kids' birthday parties, we throw them up in the air. I wonder why.
   B I'm _____ sure, but I guess it's _____ a fun thing to do!

2 Strategy plus *Yeah, no.*

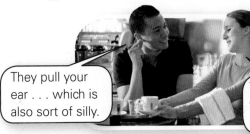

They pull your ear . . . which is also sort of silly.

Yeah, no. A lot of traditions are a bit odd like that.

◀))) CD 4.20 You can use *Yeah, no* to agree with someone and then make a comment of your own.

In conversation . . .

People almost always say *Yeah, no* rather than *Yes, no.*

A ◀))) CD 4.21 **Listen to the start of five conversations. How does each one continue? Number the responses 1–5.**

_____ Yeah, no. It's good that people carry on traditions.

_____ Yeah, no. It's nice to do fun stuff with your friends on your birthday.

_____ Yeah, no. Society needs to recognize birthdays like 80 or 100.

_____ Yeah, no. It's good to celebrate special birthdays. Here it's when you're 18.

_____ Yeah, no. It's nice to celebrate with your family and have family memories.

About you

B ◀))) CD 4.22 **Pair work Listen and check. Then discuss each of the views in Exercise A. Do you agree?**

3 Strategies Funny family traditions

A **Complete the conversations. Add expressions to soften A's comments, and choose an appropriate response from the box. Then practice the conversations with a partner.**

> Kids can be kind of mean.
>
> It's bizarre how things like that get started.
>
> It can be a little embarrassing.
>
> Kids love fun things like that.

1. **A** When my sister and I were little, my grandmother always gave us money on New Year's Day. But she didn't hand it to us. She put it in our shoes the night before, so we found it when we woke up the next morning. It was _____ unusual, but it was fun.

   B Yeah, no. _____

2. **A** We have a tradition on birthdays that's _____ silly, where we see who can buy the worst gift. It's _____ stupid, really, I guess. I'm _____ sure now why we do it.

   B Yeah, no. _____

3. **A** My family has a tradition of giving names to new babies by just picking places from a map, which is _____ bizarre! My sister wants to call her new baby Orinoco if it's a boy and Amazon if it's a girl. It's _____ unfair to the kids if you ask me.

   B Yeah, no. _____

4. **A** So every year on Halloween, we'd make this homemade candy with chili peppers in it. And we'd give it to friends like it was some nice gift. It was _____ mean, really.

   B Yeah, no. _____

About you

B **Group work Think of two family traditions you have. Take turns telling the group about them. What are the most unusual traditions?**

"In my family, we have kind of a funny tradition on New Year's Day where we all have a big pillow fight. It's a little crazy, but it's always fun."

4 Speaking naturally Consonant groups *See page 143.*

Lesson D *Threats to culture*

1 Reading

A **Prepare** What things in your everyday life come from different cultures? Make a list.

"We get a lot of Chinese movies, and let's see, . . . there are lots of . . ."

B ⬇ **Read for main ideas** Read the article. What are some different aspects of culture? What can threaten culture?

Are we losing our culture?

1 The word *culture* refers not only to the beliefs and customs of our society, to its art, literature, and music, but also to basic everyday activities, such as our eating habits, how we greet people, and how we dress. Cultures give us a sense of identity and belonging in society. Therefore, the loss of one's culture is, for many, alarming. In 46 out of 47 countries where opinion polls were taken, many people believe their traditional ways of life are under threat and that something should be done to ensure the preservation of their culture. Yet for some, the loss of culture is a natural result of globalization and progress, and an opportunity to embrace other cultures. So is the globalization of culture a threat or an opportunity?

2 Those who see globalization as a threat argue that societies are losing unique aspects of their cultures. As an example, they cite the growing number of endangered languages, as English, Chinese, and Spanish, the main languages of business, spread globally. Omotik, a language spoken in East Africa, has only 50 surviving speakers. Consequently, it is in danger of extinction. There are also increasing fears in China, where the loss of musical and dance traditions, as well as traditional crafts, is causing concern to many.

3 Some who stress the downside of globalization complain that it is becoming increasingly difficult to distinguish Tokyo or Seoul from London or New York. The same chain restaurants and coffee shops exist worldwide, with identical logos and brands. Young people, whose ideas are often influenced by Western or other popular cultures, wear the same fashions, tend to watch the same movies, and adopt similar ideas – often neglecting or even rejecting the traditions their parents grew up with.

4 Others dismiss such concerns and instead focus on the benefits of globalization. They accept that Western culture is spreading, but they also point to how Western countries and many other parts of the world are being exposed to world cultures. Young Americans enjoy Japanese manga magazines and watch Korean movies. British youth are familiar with Brazilian martial arts. Thai teenagers download pop music from Hong Kong, while young French students take on internships in Shanghai. Many argue there are benefits to these cross-cultural exchanges and that they lead to better understanding between cultures. They say world traditions are celebrated more widely because of this. Chinese New Year, now celebrated in most big cities around the world, is just one of the many festivals that are recognized internationally.

5 Nevertheless, many grass-roots organizations and governments are making efforts to guarantee the protection of their cultures. One successful example is Wales. There was a time when social pressures were killing off the Welsh language, but after decades of effort, it is now a vibrant part of Welsh life again. Around the world, there are similar efforts to revive local languages, music, foods, crafts, and traditional sports. Ironically, it might well be that the threat of losing a culture will ultimately lead to its rejuvenation.

Ysgol School

Reading tip

Those, many, some, and *others* often refer to groups of peo
*The loss of one's culture is, for **many**, alarming.*
(= for many people)

C Understanding viewpoints Would the writer of the article agree (A) or disagree (D) with the statements below? Write A or D.

1. Many people say they are worried about threats to culture. _A_
2. Most big cities are unique and have their own identity. _D_
3. English is the only business language. _D_
4. Increasingly, young people are continuing the traditions of their parents. _D_
5. Young people are rarely exposed to cross-cultural exchanges. _D_
6. Many festivals that were once local now take place around the world. _A_

About you **D** React Pair work Are the sentences in Exercise C true for your society? Discuss.

"I think people worry about losing our culture. You rarely hear traditional music anymore."

② Focus on vocabulary Opposites

A Find words in the article that are opposite in meaning to the words in bold. Paragraph numbers where you can find the words are in parentheses. Use the words to complete the questions below.

1. What do you think about the **loss** of culture? Is the _preservation_ of culture important? (para. 1)
2. In what ways is globalization a **threat**? In what ways is it an _opportunity_? (para. 1)
3. What is the **downside** of global brands and chain restaurants? What are the _benefits_ ? (para. 4)
4. Why do some _dismiss_ the view that loss of culture is bad, even though others **accept** it? (para. 4)
5. Is modern life **killing off** any traditions in your culture? Which could you _revive_ ? (para. 5)
6. What are some of the _local_ traditions in your area? What **global** celebrations are observed? (para. 5)

B Pair work Discuss the questions in Exercise A. Do you have the same views?

"I think the loss of culture matters. Countries where culture is under threat will lose their identity."

③ Listening and speaking Reviving a dying language

About you **A** 🔊 CD 4.25 Read the list of things that can be done to revive a dying language. Add other ideas. Then listen to a seminar discussion. Check (✔) the ideas the students discuss.

- ☑ teach it in elementary school
- ☐ make it mandatory in college
- ☑ offer homestays in areas where it's spoken
- ☑ translate public signs and notices
- ☐ pay higher salaries to people who speak it
- ☑ use it on TV and radio, and in other media

About you **B** 🔊 CD 4.26 Listen again. Underline the two ideas that the students agree might work.

About you **C** 🔊 CD 4.27 The students repeat some of the ideas in the article on page 122, but use different forms of the words. Listen again and write the missing words.

1. Is language _revival_ possible? (revive)
2. A language may become _extinct_ . (extinction)
3. We need to _preserve_ our culture, too. (preservation)
4. Can this _exposure_ to a language help? (exposed)
5. The _growth_ of English is inevitable. (growing)
6. Globalization _threatens_ languages. (threat)

About you **D** Group work Discuss the advantages and disadvantages of the various ways to revive a language. Agree on the best three ways. Can they help with learning English?

Writing *Are we losing it?*

In this lesson, you . . .

- structure a conclusion.
- explain cause and effect with *due to*, etc.
- avoid errors with *due to*.

Task **Write a conclusion to an essay.**

Are we in danger of losing our culture as a result of globalization?

A **Look at the models** Read the thesis statements and the two concluding paragraphs below. Which statement appeared in the introduction to each essay? Write a, b, or c above each paragraph. There is one extra option.

a. It is not possible to tell if our culture is in danger, **because** (it is too early.) Only history will tell us.

b. In this essay, I will argue that we are in danger of losing our culture **as a result of** globalization.

c. In my view, it is **because of** globalization that we have opportunities to learn about other cultures.

> **Concluding paragraphs in an essay . . .**
> - restate the thesis statement.
> - summarize the arguments.
> - give a clear opinion.
> - can start with *In summary* or *In conclusion*.

1. __b__

In conclusion, our culture is in danger **due to** globalization. We may not be able to preserve it **because** people are attracted by new ideas and ways of life. **Consequently**, we should take action now to show young people the value of our unique culture and encourage them to preserve it.

2. __a__

In summary, there are clearly positive and negative effects of globalization. However, it is difficult to know if it will damage our culture. **Therefore**, we need to wait for the judgment of future generations **since** they will be in a better position to see its impact.

B **Focus on language** The bold expressions in Exercise A link causes with effects or results. Circle the causes. Then read the grammar chart.

Expressing cause and effect in writing

	EFFECT	CAUSE (list)
Use *as a result of, because of,* and *due to* + a noun.	*Our culture is in danger* **due to** *globalization.*	
Use <u>because</u> or <u>since</u> + a clause.		**since** *we are attracted by new ideas.*

	CAUSE	EFFECT/RESULT
<u>Therefore</u> and <u>Consequently</u> often start sentences.	*Our culture is in danger.*	**Consequently**, *we should take action.*
Use *so* mid-sentence.	*Our culture is in danger,*	**so** *we should take action.*

C Complete the concluding paragraphs below with expressions from the chart.

1. In conclusion, our culture has changed __since / because__ globalization has brought us many new ideas and customs. These ideas are attractive, __so__ they are replacing some of our traditions. __Consequently__, we are in danger of losing our traditional values.

2. In summary, cultures are constantly changing __due to__ migration, trade, and tourism. We learn more about the world __because / since__ we are exposed to new people and ideas. __Consequently__ (Therefore), we should see globalization as positive.

D **Write and check** Write a concluding paragraph that gives your answer to the question in the Task above. Include (two arguments) to support your answer. Then check for errors.

> **Common errors**
> Use *due to* to give causes. Avoid using *due to* to say why people do things.
> Use *because (of)*.

Vocabulary notebook *Wedding bells!*

Learning tip   Word webs

You can write new vocabulary in word webs. Word webs are useful for writing down vocabulary about a topic. They can be as simple or as complex as you wish.

A   Complete the word web with the words in the box. Then add other vocabulary from page 116.

> arranged marriage   best man   bride   civil ceremony   ✓ groom

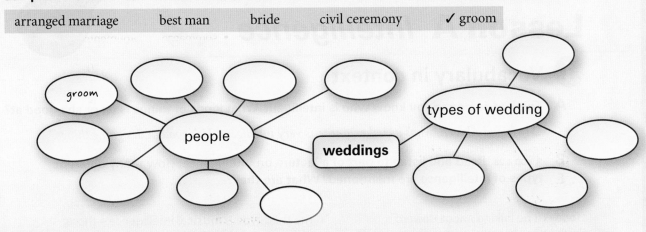

B   Now make your own word web for things people do at a wedding. Choose one more topic (for example, things people wear, eat, or say), and add other vocabulary you know.

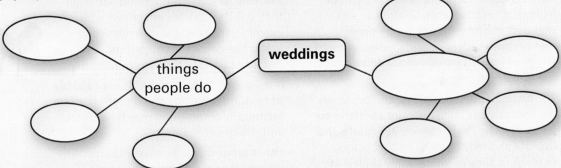

C   Word builder   Find the meanings of these expressions. Then add them to a word web.

> a bouquet   a veil   a wedding planner   to go on (a, your) honeymoon   to throw rice or confetti
> a maid of honor   a wedding band   a wedding registry   to propose (to someone)

On your own

Write a blog about a wedding you have been to or know about. Highlight key words and expressions. Find photos to illustrate the blog.

Deepak and Amrita got married on May 21. It was a traditional Indian ceremony.

What goes with *weddings*?

Here are the top ten words people use with the word *wedding* in writing and conversation: *wedding . . . present(s), anniversary, dress, ring(s), band(s), cake, gift(s), reception, vows, ceremony.*

Ability

In Unit 12, you . . .

- talk about intelligence, skills, and abilities.
- use adverbs and adjectives to describe and compare.
- use vague expressions when you don't need to be precise.
- agree with someone using responses like *No doubt.*

Lesson A *Intelligence*

1 Vocabulary in context

A   **Think of someone you know who is intelligent. What kinds of things is he or she good at?**

"My friend Ahmed, who's a civil engineer, is very intelligent. He's good at designing things."

B   ◀))CD 4.28   **Read and listen to part of a lecture on intelligence. How many different types of intelligence are mentioned? What are they?**

1   "Today I'll be talking about Howard Gardner, the highly respected professor of psychology at Harvard University. His work has been particularly important in terms of its impact on education. Gardner argues that defining intelligence as one single thing is both imprecise and inadequate, and suggests instead that there are different types of intelligences.

2   The first is **linguistic** intelligence. People who are linguistically intelligent **are sensitive to** language. They**'re** extremely **articulate** and **literate** and may become writers, actors, or lawyers. They**'re** often highly **skilled at** learning languages, too.

3   The second is **logical-mathematical** intelligence. These people **are scientifically minded** and **have a capacity for** investigating things. They're especially good at math and **are efficient at** solving problems – often incredibly quickly.

4   The third type is **musical** intelligence – those who **have a talent for** music. And the fourth is **bodily** intelligence. People with this **are able to** learn through movement; they use their bodies effectively – for example, they can balance relatively easily, like dancers or gymnasts.

5   The fifth intelligence is **spatial** intelligence. People with this **are capable of** creating drawings and designs that are technically correct, and may be architects and designers.

6   Other types of intelligence include **interpersonal** and **intrapersonal** intelligence. People with interpersonal intelligence **are** particularly **adept at** understanding others, while those with intrapersonal intelligence are remarkably good at understanding themselves.

7   These seven types make up Gardner's original theory. He later added . . ."

Word sort

C   **Make a chart like the one below for each type of intelligence. Use the words and expressions in bold from the lecture. Then complete the chart with your own ideas.**

Type of intelligence	People with it . . .	They would make good . . .
linguistic	are articulate	writers, actors, lawyers, teachers

Vocabulary notebook
See page 135.

About you

D   Pair work   Rate yourselves on a scale of 1–10 for each type of intelligence (1 = very bad at; 10 = very good at). Discuss your ideas.

"I'd say I'm good at languages and pretty articulate, so I'd give myself a 7 for linguistic intelligence."

2 Grammar Describing people and things

Figure it out

A How does the lecturer express the ideas in bold? Use the lecture to help you rewrite the sentences. Then read the grammar chart.

1. Some people are **very skilled** at learning languages.
2. These people **have scientific minds**.
3. Some people solve problems **quickly – I think it's incredible**.
4. These people are **adept at one thing that I want to focus on – they understand others**.

Adverbs ⬇

Grammar extra
See page 166.

You can use adverbs like these before adjectives and adverbs to introduce these ideas.

Degree – e.g., *extremely, highly, relatively*	They're **extremely** literate and **highly** skilled.
Type – e.g., *scientifically, linguistically*	**Linguistically** intelligent people are good at languages.
Opinion – e.g., *incredibly, remarkably*	They seem to solve problems **incredibly** easily.
Focus – e.g., *especially, particularly*	People with logical intelligence are **especially** good at math.

Common errors

Don't use an adjective to describe an adjective.   *I'm very **physically active**.* (NOT . . . *physical active*)

About you

B Unscramble the words to make questions. Then ask and answer the questions with a partner.

Do you know anyone who . . .

1. especially directions giving good at is?
2. well communicates with extremely other people?
3. is in interested himself or herself particularly?
4. any sports incapable of playing is completely?
5. clearly remarkably his or her ideas articulates?
6. quickly incredibly does mental math?
7. highly is maps drawing skilled at?
8. talented is musically?
9. well fairly chess plays?
10. easily languages relatively learns?

3 Listening and speaking Minds for the future

A Match the two parts of each sentence below. What are the five "minds" good at?

☐ A synthesizing mind
☐ An ethical mind
☐ A disciplined mind
☐ A respectful mind
☐ A creative mind

a. focuses particularly well on doing what is right.
b. works extremely hard.
c. takes other people's views and feelings very seriously.
d. is very adept at thinking in new and different ways.
e. can sort through facts to decide what is relevant.

Professor Howard Gardner

B 🔊 CD 4.29 Listen. José is telling Olga about an article on the five minds by Howard Gardner. Number 1–5 the five minds in Exercise A in the order he talks about them.

C 🔊 CD 4.29 Listen again. Circle the minds that Olga says she has.

About you

D Group work Which of the five minds do you have? Which do you still need to work on? How could schools and universities help students to develop in these five areas?

"I think I have a disciplined mind. I mean, I tend to work extremely hard and . . ."

4 Speaking naturally Stress and intonation See page 143.

Lesson B *Improving skills*

1 Grammar in context

A What unusual or interesting skills do you have? How good are you at each of them? Make a class list.

"Actually, I'm an extremely fast reader. I learned how to speed-read in high school."

B ◀))CD 4.32 Listen to the interviews. What skill has each person improved? How?

Have you improved any of your skills in the last year?

Linda Ho

"Actually, one thing I've gotten better at is speaking in public. I used to hate doing presentations at work – it was the worst thing. And you know, the more I thought about it, the worse I'd feel. I'd just get so nervous. But then I took a public-speaking course – it seemed the best and most sensible thing to do. And that helped, so, yeah, I definitely feel happier now. I'm more confident and less nervous than I used to be, which is good."

Nurdan Ozdag

"I took up the flute a year or so ago, and I *am* improving, . . . more slowly than I'd hoped, but hey – it's not an easy instrument. It's like anything, the harder you practice, the better you get. I probably don't play as often as I should. It's hard to find time with my job – work just gets busier and busier."

Bryan Jarvis

"I started mountain biking a few years back, and I just got really into it and decided to race competitively. It was actually much more difficult than I thought it would be. My biggest challenge will be a 50K* race next year. It'll be the furthest I've ever cycled. I've been training harder than ever – most often on weekends – so I'm cycling faster. I'm not as fast as I'd like to be, but I'm doing better."

(*50 kilometers or approximately 31 miles)

C Pair work Answer the questions about the interviews. Check (✔) the names.

Who . . .	Linda	Nurdan	Bryan
do you think has made the most progress?			
would benefit from more practice?			
had a fear of doing something?			
is most serious about improving his or her skills?			
got help to improve?			

2 Grammar Comparing

Figure it out

A How do the people in the interviews express the ideas below? Write the sentences they used. Then read the grammar chart.

1. Linda: I definitely feel happy now – I didn't before.
2. Nurdan: I *am* improving, but it's slower than I'd hoped.
3. Nurdan: I don't play very often. I should, though.
4. Bryan: I've never cycled further than this.

Grammar extra
See page 167.

Comparative and superlative adjectives and adverbs ⬇

	Comparatives and *as . . . as*	Superlatives
Adjectives	I feel **happier**, and I've gotten **better** at it. I'm **more confident** and **less nervous**. I'm not **as fast as** I'd like to be.	The race is my **biggest** and **best** challenge. Taking a course was **the most sensible** idea. I was **the least experienced** presenter.
Adverbs	I'm training **harder** than ever. I'm improving **more slowly** than I'd hoped. I practice **less often** than I should. I don't play **as often as** I should.	We all train hard, but I train **(the) hardest**. I train **(the) most often** on weekends. (Superlative adverbs with *least* are not common.)

Common errors

Use *in* for places and organizations. *I'm the fastest rider **in** the club.* (NOT . . . ~~of the club.~~)
Don't confuse *worse* and *worst*. *The **worst** thing is speaking . . .* (NOT ~~The worse thing~~ . . .)

About you

B 🔊 CD 4.33 **Circle the correct words to complete the conversations. Then listen and check. Practice the conversations with a partner, giving your own answers.**

1. *A* What do you do **better** / **well** now than a couple of years ago?
   B Well, I feel more **confidently** / **confident** about math. I'm better **that** / **than** I was. I'm not the best **in** / **of** my class, but I can do the problems **easy** / **more easily** now.

2. *A* Of all your skills, what do you do **better** / **the best**?
   B I'm a pretty good photographer. Though I don't take photos as **much** / **frequent** as I'd like.
   A Yeah? I'm the **worse** / **worst** photographer in the world.

3. *A* Are you good at sports? I mean, are you as good **as** / **than** you'd like to be?
   B I like baseball, but it's getting **harder** / **hardest** to find time to play.

4. *A* What's the **harder** / **hardest** thing you ever tried to learn to do?
   B Pottery. It looks **easier** / **more easily** than it is. But if you practice, you get **the best** / **better**.

3 Viewpoint I'm getting better and better . . .

Pair work **Discuss the questions below and ask questions of your own. Then prepare a one-minute presentation about your partner to give to the class.**

- Think of a skill you have. When did you start learning it?
- How did you learn the skill? Was it harder than you imagined?
- How long did it take to improve? How much better did you get?
- What advice do you have for someone who's improving a skill?

In conversation . . .

You can respond with *I bet* to show you understand what someone is talking about.

A *Well, one skill I've been working on is drawing cartoons. I'm getting better, but it's hard.*
B *I bet. How did you get interested in it?*

Lesson C . . . and all that.

1 Conversation strategy Using vague expressions

A Think of talented famous people. How are (or were) they gifted?

"Lang Lang is extremely talented. He started playing the piano at the age of three."

B 🔊 CD 4.34 Listen. What examples of talent do Jenna and Sam talk about?

Jenna Did you see that movie about that kid? She was three years old, and she did all these paintings and things and sold them for thousands of dollars.

Sam Yeah, I heard about that. Unbelievable, huh?

Jenna I mean, do you *learn* to paint and draw and stuff? Or are you just born with that kind of talent?

Sam Good question. It's the nature versus nurture thing. Her parents were probably always pushing her and everything.

Jenna It's like those six-year-old pianists that play classical concerts and that kind of thing. You have to be gifted.

Sam No doubt. But I'm sure they still have to do a lot of hard work and practice and all that.

Jenna True. But I still can't do paintings and that kind of thing.

Sam I know. Me neither. It's too bad when a six-year-old is more talented than you!

C **Notice** how Sam and Jenna use vague expressions like these. They don't need to be precise because the other person knows what they mean. Find the expressions they use in the conversation.

> . . . and things (like that) / and stuff (like that)
> . . . and all / and all that
> . . . and that kind of thing / and that sort of thing
> . . . and everything

In conversation . . .

Many vague expressions are less common in formal speaking. A more formal vague expression is *and so on*.

- and so on
- and all that
- and things
- and stuff

■ Formal speaking
■ Conversation

About you

D What do you think the expressions in bold mean? Write an idea for each one. Then compare with a partner. Do you agree with the statements?

– or born with talent

1. Anyone can play an instrument or learn a language. You don't have to be gifted **and all that**.
2. I think you can be good at most things – if you practice **and everything**.
3. I don't think artists just learn to draw **and stuff**. I think they're born with a talent for it.
4. I can't stand it when parents make their kids perform on stage **and that kind of thing**.
5. I think if parents push their kids **and that sort of thing**, the kids usually end up hating it.
6. I think anyone can learn to do practical jobs, like fix their own cars **and things like that**.

"I'm not sure. I think you have to have a special talent for music and things like that."

2 Strategy plus *No doubt.*

You have to be gifted.

No doubt.

🔊 CD 4.35 You can say **No doubt** to show that you strongly agree with someone.

In conversation . . .

(No) doubt is also used in these related expressions.
There's no doubt about it / that. ■■■■■■■■■
Without a doubt. ■■■
I don't doubt it. ■

A 🔊 CD 4.36 **Listen to things five people say. Choose the correct responses and number them 1–5.**

_____ I don't doubt it. I think it helps you learn languages, too.

_____ No doubt. They get all that pressure and everything.

_____ Oh, no doubt. Performing in public can be very scary.

_____ Oh, without a doubt. If you don't like doing something, you can't do it well.

_____ Oh, no doubt about it. My friend plays the piano remarkably well, and she never learned it formally.

B 🔊 CD 4.37 **Now listen to the full conversations and check. Do you agree with the views?**

3 Listening and strategies The genius in all of us

A 🔊 CD 4.38 **Listen to a radio show. According to the show, are the sentences true (T) or false (F)? Write T or F.**

1. The writer David Shenk thinks people are born with certain talents. _____

2. London cab drivers' brains are generally bigger than most people's. _____

3. Your home and school are the most important influences for developing a skill. _____

4. The composer Mozart was successful because he was taught by his father. _____

5. The basketball player Michael Jordan trained with players who were better than him. _____

B 🔊 CD 4.39 **Listen to the conversations below about the radio show. Complete each one with the expressions you hear. Then practice with a partner.**

1. *A* Do you believe we're born with talent, or do we develop it through practice?

   B Hmm. Probably both. I mean, if you're a natural athlete, you won't become *really* good if your parents and teachers don't encourage you _____ .

   A _____ . Yeah. It's the same for music _____ .

2. *A* Do you think children can succeed at anything if they're encouraged more?

   B _____ . My teacher gave me extra books to read _____ . I'm sure that helped me with my studies _____ .

3. *A* Do you think some parents push their kids too hard?

   B Yeah. My mom made my sister take ballet _____ . She hated it. It was a waste of money.

   A _____ . I mean, swimming and _____ are useful, but . . .

About you

C Class survey **Ask your classmates the questions in Exercise B. Then prepare a short report to give to the class. What do your classmates say about talent?**

Lesson D Ability, not disability

① Reading

A Prepare **Look at the photos and the title of the article. Can you guess what the article is about?**

B ⬇ **Read for main ideas Read the exclusive interview with Chris Waddell. What are some of Chris's achievements?**

Seeing things in a *completely* different way . . .

1 After sitting and talking with Chris Waddell for 20 minutes, you feel like anything is possible. Not so remarkable, perhaps, since he is a world-champion skier, and he has also climbed Mount Kilimanjaro – if it were not for the fact that Chris is sitting in a wheelchair and is paralyzed from the waist down. The ski accident that caused his paralysis happened when Chris was a college student. Nevertheless, just two years after his accident, he won a place on the U.S. Adaptive Ski Team. During the next 11 years, he won a total of 12 ski medals and, as a result, became the <u>most decorated</u> male skier in Paralympic history.

2 But Chris is not one to rest on past achievements. His mission to climb Mount Kilimanjaro, the highest mountain in Africa, was just another of the ways Chris is proving that we should change the way in which we view people with special needs. This is why I visited him at his Utah base – so that I could learn more about this incredibly difficult challenge and what inspired it.

3 **Q: So, Chris, what does being disabled actually mean to you? What is it that motivates you?**
A: I look at it this way. We all have certain shortcomings. It's just that some are more visible than others. I think I'm extremely fortunate. Through my disability, I've done things and met people – presidents even – that I would never have met otherwise.

4 **Q: What inspired the climb up Mount Kilimanjaro?**
A: Well, the date I chose to climb Mount Kilimanjaro was a halfway point in my life. I'd spent half of my life in a wheelchair. So it was a personal challenge – I am first and foremost an athlete – but I did it also in order to shine a light back on the disabled. To show that if you take the time to look, you might be surprised. People generally have a lot of preconceived ideas about disabled people. I wanted my climb to challenge those views, and so that people would start to see the 21-plus million disabled people in the world in a completely different light. It's about raising awareness.

5 **Q: How did you actually achieve it?**
A: I chose Mount Kilimanjaro because it's more readily accessible. You don't need ice picks and so on. But I used a specially adapted bicycle that I push with my arms. It was very physically challenging, and it took every last bit of my strength, but I had a team of friends, a doctor, and porters, who carried the supplies. Also a film crew, who made the documentary about the climb.

6 Chris Waddell has dedicated his life to defying the conventional wisdom of what a paraplegic can and cannot do. As a result, he has become a role model for all of us.

Visit Chris's website and be inspired!

C Read for detail **Circle the correct option to complete the sentences about the article.**

1. Before his accident, Chris Waddell was **a ski champion / a climber / <u>a student</u>**.
2. Compared to other male Paralympic skiers, he won **<u>more</u> / fewer / as many** medals.
3. Climbing Mount Kilimanjaro was an attempt to change **attitudes / his career / history**.
4. He chose Mount Kilimanjaro because it was **the most difficult / the closest / possible to climb**.
5. Chris found the climb **<u>difficult</u> / easy / not very challenging**.

D Paraphrase **Complete the paragraph with the expressions in the box.**

| completely different | physically challenging | special needs |
| extremely fortunate | readily accessible | specially adapted |

One of the things Chris believes is that everyone should see people with _special needs_ and disabilities in a _completely diff._ way. He feels he has been _extremely fortunate_ to have the chances he's had. But in reality, Chris has created his own opportunities. In order to highlight his cause, he has taken on a series of _physically challenging_ projects. Although Mount Kilimanjaro is _readily accessible_ to many people, Chris used a _specially adapted_ bicycle so that he could complete the climb. Chris proved yet again that anything is possible!

2 Focus on vocabulary Collocations

A **Find words in the article that are used with the words in bold. Use the words to complete the sentences below.**

1. Chris is a _world_-_champion_ **skier**. He's at the top of his sport. (para. 1)
2. He has _spent_ half his **life** paralyzed. (para. 4)
3. Chris hopes that his achievements will _shine_ a light on people with special needs. (para. 4)
4. People often **have** _preconceived_ **ideas** about being disabled and don't know what it means. (para. 4)
5. Chris likes to _challenge_ people's **views** and make them think. (para. 4)
6. His mission in life is _raising_ **awareness** about disabilities. (para. 4)
7. He has _dedicated_ his **life** to showing what people like him can do. (para. 6)
8. _Conventional_ **wisdom** says people like Chris can't climb a mountain. How wrong is that? (para. 6)

B Pair work **Take turns using the expressions in Exercise A to retell Chris's story. Which of his achievements do you find the most impressive?**

"Chris became a world-champion skier after his accident. It's incredible that he did that."

3 Viewpoint Disability and the community

Group work **Discuss the questions. Can you agree on one action point for the last two questions?**

- Do you know of any people who have overcome a disability to achieve something? How did they manage to do this?
- Do you personally know people who live with disabilities? What difficulties – if any – do they face?
- What views do people generally have of disabled people? Do any of these views need to be challenged?
- What facilities are there for people with special needs? What else could be provided?
- What do you think could be done to provide more opportunities for disabled people?

"One of our neighbors has Down Syndrome, and she's the most amazing athlete. She's incredibly motivated."

> **In conversation . . .**
> You can use a superlative adjective to make a description of someone or something stronger.

Writing *Extraordinary achievements*

In this lesson, you . . .
- brainstorm, then structure an essay.
- explain purpose with *so (that)*, etc.
- avoid errors with *so that*.

Task **Write an essay.**
Choose a person that you admire and say why you admire the person. Use specific reasons and details to support your answer.

A **Look at a model** Read part of an essay. Why did Gladys: a) leave home? b) go back to college? c) retire early? Circle the expressions the writer uses to introduce Gladys's purpose in doing things.

> One person that I admire is my mother, Gladys, because of her passion for life and for helping people. She left home at the age of 16 (so that) she could train as a nurse and then a midwife. After starting a family, she went back to college in order to qualify as a midwifery teacher. She suffered a serious illness in her fifties so she retired early to regain her health. Then, at the age of 69, she decided to enter local politics in order to give something back to her community. She ran for election and won a seat on the city council, where she worked tirelessly to help local citizens. Seven years later, she became mayor of the city.
>
> Her passion for life was evident at a young age. Leaving home was a big adventure for a teenage girl from a small village. She . . .

B **Focus on language** Read the grammar chart. Then complete the sentences below, using alternate expressions from the model.

Explaining purpose in writing ⬇

You can use *so (that)* + clause or *(in order) to* + verb to describe purpose.
She left home at the age of 16 **so (that)** *she could train as a nurse.*
She went back to college **(in order) to** *qualify as a midwifery teacher.*

> **Common errors**
>
> Use *so* or *so that* to introduce a purpose. Use *so* but not *so that* to introduce a result or an effect.
> *She suffered a serious illness,* **so** *she retired early.* (NOT . . . ~~so that she retired early.~~)

1. Gladys left school at the age of 16 <u>in order to train as a nurse</u>.
2. She went back to college _____.
3. She retired early _____.
4. She decided to enter local politics _____.

C **Brainstorm and plan** Brainstorm ideas for your essay, using the points below. Then use the model to plan your essay.

- Choose a person you admire.
- Say why you admire him or her.
- Give examples of things he or she did and why.

D **Write and check** Now write your essay. Then check for errors.

Introduction	→	Include a thesis statement.
Supporting paragraphs	→	Write a topic sentence and supporting sentences with examples, reasons, arguments.
Conclusion	→	Restate the thesis statement.

Vocabulary notebook *It's just the opposite!*

Learning tip   Opposite meanings

When you learn a new adjective or descriptive expression, find out how to express the opposite meaning. Sometimes you can use a prefix. Sometimes you have to use a different word.

> articulate ≠ inarticulate
> to be adept at ≠ to be bad at

Dictionary tip

Dictionaries and thesauruses often tell you the opposite meanings, or antonyms. Some adjectives have more than one meaning, so be sure to choose the correct opposite.

> hard: solid, firm ≠ soft
> hard: difficult, tough ≠ easy
> hard: cruel, severe ≠ kind

A Write the opposites of the words below. Use the prefixes *il, in,* or *un.*

1. articulate ≠ _inarticulate_
2. sensitive ≠ _____
3. literate ≠ _____
4. skilled ≠ _____
5. efficient ≠ _____

6. able ≠ _____
7. capable ≠ _____
8. important ≠ _____
9. correct ≠ _____
10. complete ≠ _____

B Now write opposites for these expressions.

1. be adept at ≠ _____
2. be bad at ≠ _____
3. have a capacity for ≠ _____
4. have a talent for ≠ _____

C Word builder Find and write the opposites of these adjectives. Use *il-, im-, in-, ir-,* or *un-.*

1. adequate
≠ _____
2. effective
≠ _____
3. convenient
≠ _____
4. legal
≠ _____
5. logical
≠ _____

6. likely
≠ _____
7. necessary
≠ _____
8. patient
≠ _____
9. precise
≠ _____
10. relevant
≠ _____

On your own

Make a word game. Write pairs of cards – one with a word and one with a prefix that can be used with that word. Then play a game with a friend. Shuffle the cards and place them face up. Take turns picking out matching cards.

im in un precise likely il literate correct

Checkpoint 4 *Units 10–12*

1 It's not as difficult as . . .

A How many words and expressions can you think of to describe weddings?

1. Western-style wedding

B Complete the TV interviews with the comparative or superlative form of the words given. Some use *less* or *least,* and some need *than.* Use *as . . . as* with the underlined words.

"In many countries, people are getting married _____ (late) in life. Many young people are thinking about marriage _____ (carefully), and some are not marrying at all. But why? Our reporter, Dan Browning, interviewed a bride at her wedding."

1. **Dan** Why did you decide to get married in your forties? Do you feel _____ (confident) you did when you were _____ (young)?

 Lisa Well, getting married was _____ (big) decision I've ever made – and obviously it's _____ (important). I waited because I was working _____ (hard) I could on my career. I might not have been _____ (successful) I am if I had gotten married _____ (early).

2. **Dan** Tell me, is staying single _____ (difficult) it used to be?

 Lisa I don't think so. People generally don't feel _____ (pressured) they used to to get married. It's _____ (good) to take your time. When I was young, I was _____ (sure) I am right now about life. My advice for young people is "Enjoy life and don't rush into marriage."

3. **Dan** Can you tell me: How much have you spent on your wedding?

 Lisa We're not sure. But we chose everything _____ (carefully) we could to keep the costs down. We even bought the _____ (expensive) dress we could find. But still, we'll be paying for the wedding for years! I guess we'll worry about that tomorrow.

C Report the interview in Exercise B, using the verbs *ask, explain, tell,* and *say* as in the sentence stems below. Sometimes there is more than one correct answer.

> The interviewer asked . . .   She explained . . .   She told him . . .   She also said . . .

The interviewer asked Lisa why she had decided to get married in her forties. She explained . . .

About you

D **Pair work** Discuss the interview in Exercise B. Use expressions with *no doubt* when you agree. Use expressions like *so what you're saying is* to draw conclusions.

A I think a lot of people are waiting longer before they get married.
B There's no doubt. OR So, what you're saying is people are older when they get married?

2 That's talent!

A Rewrite the sentences. Write complete expressions with the words in parentheses. Add words from the box. Rewrite the underlined sentences in a different way, if possible.

| articulate | ✓ interpersonal | literate | logical | musical | sensitive |

has a capacity for

1. My sister (capacity) understanding others. You know, she has great <u>interpersonal</u> skills. She's very
_____ to people's feelings and everything. <u>She always gives good advice to me.</u>

   She always gives me good advice.

2. My best friend is very _____ . She (able) pick up any instrument and play it. <u>A friend once lent her a guitar. She was playing it within three weeks!</u>

3. I love to talk, and I'm pretty _____ . I (pretty skilled) learning languages, too. <u>My parents bought me some Italian-language CDs when I was a kid. I listened to them all the time.</u>

4. <u>I sent my niece some calligraphy pens for her birthday.</u> She (talent) drawing and all that.

5. My sister (really good) singing and dancing. <u>She made a recording of her last show for us. My mom sent it to everyone!</u>

6. My brother has always read a lot since he was little. He's very _____ . You know he's very smart and he (capable) doing anything, really.

7. My dad (so efficient) solving problems and things. <u>I gave my math homework to him last week.</u> He did it in 20 minutes. He's just very _____ , I guess.

B **Pair work** Use the ideas in Exercise A to talk about people you know. Use *In what way?* to ask for details. Use expressions like *and all that* when you don't need to be precise.

A My English teacher has really good interpersonal skills and stuff.
B Yeah? In what way?

3 Traveling

A Rewrite the conversations. Use the correct adverb and adjective forms of the words in parentheses. Rewrite the underlined sentences as one sentence using *when, where,* or *whose*.

1. *A* What's the most (physical / challenge) thing you've ever done?
   B Well, the trek to Machu Picchu was kind of (exhaust). But it was worth it because it is an (incredible / impress) place. My friend did the climb (relative / easy), which was a little (depress) because he's ten years older than me. He was fine, but I was (total / exhaust) by the time we got there. But <u>I remember the first morning there. We got up early and watched the sunrise.</u> That was just (amaze).

   A What's the most physically challenging thing you've ever done?

2. *A* What's the most (frighten) thing you've ever done?
   B I'm not really sure. Maybe going on a roller coaster on my birthday. I was (absolutely / terrify). <u>There's a really great amusement park near here. Young people go to celebrate birthdays.</u> Anyway, I started off (complete / relax). <u>I was sort of OK, till we got to the top. I looked down and started screaming.</u> It was windy that day, so it was (particular / terrify).

B **Pair work** Take turns asking and answering the questions in Exercise A. Use softening comments if necessary. Use *Yeah, no* to agree and then make a comment of your own.

A I helped my friend move here last week, and that was kind of exhausting.
B Yeah, no. Moving is unbelievably tiring.

❸ Unit 1, Lesson B Questions with answers

Sometimes people ask an information question and then suggest one or more answers to it. Notice the intonation.

*How often do you tend to use **e**mail? Every **day**?*

*When do you update your **pro**file? At **night**? On the **week**ends?*

A ◀)) CD 1.05 **Read and listen to the information above. Repeat the example questions.**

About you **B** ◀)) CD 1.06 **Listen and repeat these questions. Then ask and answer the questions with a partner.**

1. Who do you generally text? Your family?
2. What topics do you avoid discussing online? Politics? Religion?
3. What personal information do you put online? Your phone number?
4. How much of your social life do you organize online? Like, all of it?
5. What do you think is the best way to end a relationship? Send a text?

About you **C** Pair work **Change partners and ask the questions in Exercise B again, suggesting a different answer. Continue each conversation.**

A Who do you generally text? Your friends?
B Um, yeah. I mostly text my friends. I guess I tend to call my family. How about you?

❹ Unit 2, Lesson A *which* clauses

Notice how a *which* clause has a slight pause before it. When a *which* clause ends what you say, it often has a falling intonation.

*I bet celebrities hate seeing bad photos of themselves, **which probably happens a lot**.*

*People always want to know everything about their lives, **which must be difficult**.*

A ◀)) CD 1.17 **Read and listen to the information above. Repeat the example sentences.**

B ◀)) CD 1.18 **Listen and repeat these sentences about celebrities.**

1. Photographers are always following celebrities around, which must be a pain.
2. The magazines make up all these stories about them, which is probably annoying.
3. People complain about them even when they do charity work, which is totally unfair.
4. They can't have a private life – even their breakups are in the news, which must be awkward.
5. People expect them to live perfect lives, which is impossible.
6. There are websites that tell you where celebrities are, which must be scary for them.

About you **C** Pair work **Discuss the sentences in Exercise B. Which ones do you agree with?**

A I agree with the first sentence. It seems like photographers are always taking pictures of celebrities, which must be annoying for them.
B I know. Some photographers will do anything to get good pictures, which really isn't right.

④ Unit 3, Lesson B Auxiliary verbs

Notice how the speakers reduce *Did you* and *Had you*.

Did you can be one or two syllables.

Did you struggle with any classes last semester?

What **did you** do about it?

Had you is always two syllables.

Had you heard the expression "Life's too short" before this class?

Where **had you** heard it?

A 🔊 CD 1.31 **Read and listen to the information above. Repeat the example questions.**

B 🔊 CD 1.32 **Listen and repeat these questions.**

1. Did you hear from anyone out of the blue last year? Who did you hear from?
2. Had you heard the expression "Truth is stranger than fiction" before this class? Where had you heard it?
3. Did you struggle with English when you first started learning it? Why did you find it difficult?
4. Had you been studying English for very long before you started this class? How long had you been studying?
5. Did you miss any classes last year? How many did you miss?
6. Did you learn anything from the life lessons you read about in this lesson? What did you learn?

About you

C **Class activity** **Ask your classmates the first question in each pair of questions in Exercise B. When you find someone who answers "yes," ask information questions to find out more details.**

A *Did you hear from anyone out of the blue last year?*
B *Actually, yeah I did.*
A *So, who did you hear from?*

④ Unit 4, Lesson A Word stress

Some words are stressed on the first syllable.

Some are stressed on the second or third syllable.

■ ▪   ■ ▪ ▪
deadline   *interview*

▪ ■   ▪ ■ ▪   ▪ ■ ▪ ▪   ▪ ▪ ■ ▪
advice   *employer*   *experience*   *information*

A 🔊 CD 2.03 **Read and listen to the information above. Repeat the example words.**

About you

B 🔊 CD 2.04 **Listen. Underline the stressed syllable in the words in bold. Then ask and answer the questions with a partner.**

1. Would you like to work in **management**? Do you have any **experience** in managing people?
2. How's your **knowledge** of English? Is there **evidence** you need English to get a job?
3. Have you ever submitted an **application** for a new job or a **promotion**?
4. Have you decided on a **career** yet? How much **competition** is there for jobs in that field?
5. Are you making **progress** in your studies or work? Have you had any **feedback**?
6. How much do you know about **computers**?
7. Do you have to meet **deadlines**? Is your **employer** or **professor** very strict about them?
8. What's the best way to prepare for an **interview**? What **information** should you know about the job?

❹ Unit 5, Lesson B   Shifting word stress

Notice that some words in the same word family are stressed on a different syllable.	Some words are stressed on the same syllable.
■ ■ environment environmental	■ ■ pollute pollution
■ ■ eradicate eradication	■ ■ invest investment

A ◀))CD 2.16   Read and listen to the information above. Repeat the example words.

B ◀))CD 2.17   Listen to these pairs of words. Are the words stressed on the same (S) or a different (D) syllable? Write S or D. Practice saying these words.

1. starving – starvation _____
2. create – creation _____
3. unemployed – unemployment _____
4. education – educate _____
5. distribute – distribution _____
6. economy – economic _____

About you

C Group work   If you represented a global charity, which of these issues would be your priorities? Discuss the ideas, then number the issues 1–7 (1 = highest priority, 7 = lowest priority).

- *End starvation.* Approximately one-third of the world's population is starving. _____
- *Educate every child.* Millions of kids don't go to school because they must work. _____
- *Stop polluting water, air, and soil.* Pollution causes 40 percent of world deaths. _____
- *Eradicate poverty.* Its eradication would give half the world's children better lives. _____
- *Invest in new jobs.* Investment in new jobs helps the economy and leads to economic growth. _____
- *Protect animals and plants.* Better environmental protection could save thousands of species. _____

❹ Unit 6, Lesson A   Silent consonants

Notice how some consonants are "silent" and not pronounced.

l →	could, walk, half	th →	clothes*	k →	know
gh →	ought, light	h →	hour, exhausted	p →	psychology
g →	design	t →	listen	n →	column
b →	debt				

* Some speakers pronounce the **th** in *clothes.*

A ◀))CD 2.26   Read and listen to the information above. Repeat the example words.

B ◀))CD 2.27   Read these sentences. Draw a line (/) through the silent consonants in the words in bold. Then listen, check, and repeat.

1. *A* **Could** you turn off the **lights**, please, so we can see the screen?
   B Oh, **right**. Hey, **listen**. Maybe we **should** close the blinds, too.

2. *A* Do you think **clothes** will be different in the future?
   B Oh, there's no **doubt** about that. We **might** even have clothes that heat up and everything.

3. *A* Are you interested in **design**? I mean, **could** you name any fashion **designers**?
   B I **know** a couple of **foreign** designers, but to be **honest**, I'm not really into fashion.

4. *A* Have you read anything about the **psychology** of shopping online?
   B Not much. **Though half** my friends spend **hours** shopping online. One even got into **debt** because of it. He **talks** about it a lot.

About you

C Pair work   Practice the conversations. Then practice again, giving your own answers.

4 *Unit 7, Lesson C* **Conversational expressions**

Notice how the speakers say the bold expressions quickly, in one breath.

■

What I'm saying is, most young people can't afford to live on their own.

■

To be honest, it's almost impossible to buy your own place.

A ◀)) CD 3.10 **Read and listen to the information above. Repeat the example sentences.**

B ◀)) CD 3.11 **Listen and repeat. Say the expressions in bold as quickly as you can.**

1. I like living with my parents. **I'm not saying** I won't move out one day. But for now it's fine.
2. **To be honest with you**, I feel sorry for people who live alone. **What I mean is**, they must get lonely sometimes. **I have to say,** I'd hate it.
3. **To tell you the truth**, it's hard to live far away from your relatives. **What I'm saying is**, it's just good to be near family. **I mean**, it just feels better somehow.
4. You can't do much about it if you don't like your college roommate. **In other words**, you're stuck.

About you
C Pair work **Discuss the views in Exercise B. Which ones do you agree with?**

4 *Unit 8, Lesson C* **Strong and weak forms of prepositions**

Notice how the speakers use strong forms of the prepositions *as, at, for, from, of,* and *to* at the end of a sentence. They use weak or reduced forms of these words in the middle of a sentence. However, *to* is strong before a word that starts with a vowel sound.

Strong forms	**Weak forms**
"Some foods make vague claims." "Such as?"	*"Claims such as 'improves digestion.'"*
On a menu, what's the first thing you look at?	*I look at the desserts first.*
If you read food labels, what do you look for?	*I look for additives – for instance, food coloring.*
Where do you get Vitamin D from?	*You can get it from the sun.*
What's chewing gum made of?	*It's often made of gum, sugar, and flavors.*
What do they add sugar to? To all foods?	*It's added to lots of foods, like cereals and . . .*

A ◀)) CD 3.21 **Read and listen to the information above. Repeat the example sentences.**

B ◀)) CD 3.22 **Listen. Circle the strong forms of the prepositions. Draw a line (/) through the weak forms. Then practice with a partner.**

1. *A* What foods can you get Vitamin C **(from)**? I mean, what foods should I look **for**?
   B Well, you can get it **from** vegetables such **as** broccoli and bell peppers.
   A So, do you think getting a lot **of** Vitamin C stops you **from** getting colds?
   B I'm not sure, but it is added **to** lots **of** foods.

2. *A* Which foods contain fat?
   B I'm not sure. I know some processed foods are full **of** it.
   A Such **as**?
   B Well, processed cheese, **for** example. Which is sad, because I eat a lot **of** cheese.

3. *A* What foods do manufacturers add sugar **to**? And what do they add it **for**?
   B Oh, they add it **to** almost everything – **from** soups **to** cereals. I mean, you need to look **at** the label to find out. That's what I always look **at**. Look out **for** corn syrup, too. That's a kind **of** sugar. People have gotten used to the taste, I guess.

④ Unit 9, Lesson C   Stress in expressions

Notice which words have the main stress in the bold expression in each sentence.	Expressions like this often have this stress.
▪ ■ *As far as I'm **concerned**, money is everything.* ▪ ■ *As far as success is **concerned**, it's important.* ▪ ■ *When it comes to **money**, I'm successful.* ▪ ■ *In terms of **money**, I'm pretty successful.*	▪ ■ *As far as I **know**, my friends are happy.* **Stressing *I* means "it's only my view."** ▪ ■ *As far as **I** know, they're happy.*

A 🔊 CD 3.35 **Read and listen to the information above. Repeat the example sentences.**

B 🔊 CD 3.36 **Listen. Circle the stressed words in the bold expressions. Then listen and repeat.**

1. As (far) as I can (tell), most of my friends are happy in terms of their social lives.
2. **As far as I'm concerned,** anyone can be happy. You just have to *choose* to be happy.
3. **When it comes to happiness,** it's probably much more important than being successful.
4. **As far as I know,** most successful people have worked very hard. They deserve their success.
5. **As far as I'm concerned,** there's no point being successful if you're not happy.
6. **As far as my friends are concerned,** they're all very ambitious in terms of their careers.

About you **C** Pair work **Discuss the sentences in Exercise B. Which views do you agree with?**

"Yeah. As far as I know, most of my friends are happy and enjoy what they're doing."

④ Unit 10, Lesson B   Silent vowels

Notice how one vowel in each of these words is "silent" or very reduced.

trav~~e~~ling	fam~~i~~ly	bus~~i~~ness	int~~e~~resting

A 🔊 CD 4.06 **Read and listen to the information above. Repeat the example words.**

B 🔊 CD 4.07 **Listen. Draw a line (/) through the silent vowel in the words in bold. Then listen again and repeat the questions.**

1. What's the most **interesting** place you've ever visited?
2. What's your **favorite** place to visit in your town or city?
3. What would your **preference** be: to stay at a friend's house or in a hotel?
4. When you go away, what's the most **valuable** thing you take with you?
5. Do you **generally** go away with your **family** or with your friends?
6. On **average**, how many trips a year do you take?
7. Do you know anyone who goes away on **business** a lot?
8. What's the best thing about **traveling**? And the worst?
9. What do you do in the **evenings** when you're not at work or in class?
10. Do you always go to the same place in your free time, or do you go to **different** places?

About you **C** Pair work **Take turns asking and answering the questions in Exercise B. Then find a new partner. Tell him or her your first partner's answers to the questions.**

④ Unit 11, Lesson C Consonant groups

> Notice that when two or more consonant sounds are together, one consonant sound (often *t, th, d,* or *k*) is sometimes not pronounced.*
>
> **In the middle of words**   **Across two words**
>
> I **asked my** parents.   I **don't know**.   I **just got** it.
> It **costs too** much.   It's a **gift for** you.   It's **next Saturday**.
> It was a few **months ago**.   It was a **gold bracelet**.   I always **send them** a card.
>
> *Grammatical endings like the *-s* or *-ed* of verbs are usually pronounced.

A ◀)) CD 4.23 **Read and listen to the information above. Repeat the example sentences.**

B ◀)) CD 4.24 **Read these conversations. Look at the words in bold. Draw a line (/) through the consonants that are not pronounced. Then listen, check, and repeat.**

1. *A* What's the **best gift** you've ever received?
   B My parents gave me a **gold necklace**. They gave it to me **last May** for my graduation. It was the **most beautiful** gift I've ever gotten.

2. *A* Do you always buy your **best friends** a birthday card?
   B No way! It **costs too** much. Sometimes I **send them** an email.

3. *A* When was the **last time** you got a gift?
   B I **don't know**. Let's see . . . well, a few **months ago**. I **just got** some chocolates.

4. *A* Your birthday's **next Saturday**, isn't it? Do you know what you'll be getting?
   B Actually, it's **next Sunday**, but I've **asked my** parents not to buy me anything this year.

About you   **C**   **Pair work**   **Practice the conversations in Exercise B. Practice again, giving your own answers.**

④ Unit 12, Lesson A Stress and intonation

> Notice how new information gets the main stress in a conversation. The voice goes up on the main stress and then falls or continues to rise.
>
> **Words already in the conversation are often**   **Contrasting ideas are often stressed.**
> **not stressed in the responses.**
>
> *A* My **sister** wants to study **math**.   *A* I'm really **bad** at **French**.
>
> *B* So is your sister **good** at math?   *B* Aren't you **good** at languages?
>
> *A* **Yeah**, she's **incredibly** good at math.   *A* **No**! I'm **terrible** at languages.

A ◀)) CD 4.30 **Read and listen to the information above. Repeat the example conversations.**

B ◀)) CD 4.31 **Listen. The stressed words in the first lines are in bold. Circle the words with the main stress in the responses. Then practice with a partner.**

1. *A* I'm not very **good** at learning **languages**.
   B Really? Well, learning languages is difficult.
   A Yeah. It's extremely difficult.

2. *A* One of my **classmates** has a real **talent** for **music**.
   B I wish I had a talent for music!
   A Yeah. I can't even sing in tune.
   B Well, I can't sing in tune or play an instrument or anything.

Questions

	Information questions	Yes-No questions
present of *be*	*How's your English class this year?*	*Is it fun?*
past of *be*	*Where **was** your mother born?*	***Were** both your parents born here?*
simple present	*How often **do** your parents **call** you?*	***Does** everyone in your family **have** a cell phone?*
simple past	*What time **did** you **get up** today?*	***Did** you **get up** early?*
present continuous	*Why **are** you **studying** English?*	***Are** you **studying** English for your job?*
past continuous	*Where **were** you **living** in 2010?*	***Were** you **living** here?*
present perfect	*Which cities **have** you **been** to?*	***Has** your family ever **lived** abroad?*
present perfect continuous	*How long **have** you **been studying** English?*	***Have** you **been studying** English for a long time?*
modal verbs	*What **should** you **say** no to more often?*	***Can** you **say** no to chocolate?*

- *Who* and *What* can be the subject of an information question. They take a singular verb.
  ***Who** sits next to you in class?*
  ***What** made you decide to study English?*

- The subject can also be a question word + noun. The verb agrees with the noun.
  ***What word** describes you best?*
  ***Which cities** are the most beautiful?*

A Complete the questions. Use the forms on the left with the verbs in parentheses.

present of *be*
1. Where _____ your family from originally? (be)
2. _____ your parents from another city? (be)

past of *be*
3. What _____ your favorite game when you were little? (be)
4. _____ you good at sports as a child? (be)

simple present
5. How many people _____ you _____ in your neighborhood? (know)
6. _____ your best friend _____ near you? (live)
7. Which friend _____ the most time at your house? (spend)
8. What _____ you and your friends _____ on the weekend? (do)

simple past
9. When _____ you _____ home last night? (get)
10. _____ you _____ with your friends last night? (go out)

present continuous
11. What _____ you _____ for exercise now? (do)
12. _____ you _____ enough exercise these days? (get)

past continuous
13. What _____ you _____ at this time yesterday? (do)
14. _____ you _____ with your friends yesterday? (hang out)

present perfect
15. How long _____ you _____ your best friend? (know)
16. _____ your best friend ever _____ you angry? (make)

present perfect continuous
17. How _____ your English class _____ _____ this year? (go)
18. _____ you _____ _____ a lot? (learn)

modal verbs
19. _____ you _____ English better than your friends? (can / speak)
20. In your opinion, how much time _____ you _____ practicing English every day? (should / spend)

About you

B Write your own answers to the questions. Give as much information as you can.

My father is originally from Ecuador and my mother was born in Bolivia, but we live in Colombia now. My sisters and I were all born here.

❶ Frequency expressions

- In the simple present, frequency adverbs usually go after the subject in affirmative statements and after *don't* and *doesn't* in negative statements. In the present continuous, they go after *am, is, are (not)*.
  *My sister **rarely** uses email.*　　　*She doesn't **often** use a computer.*
  *My kids are **constantly** texting.*　　*They're not **always** talking on the phone.*

- Frequency adverbs usually go after modal verbs, although other patterns are possible.
  *I'll **usually** log on to my social network site after dinner.*

- These adverbs can go before the subject: *sometimes, usually, often, normally, generally, occasionally*.
  ***Occasionally** my son will email a family member.*

- Longer expressions often go at the end of a sentence: *once / twice a day, all the time, every once in a while.*
  *We talk on the phone **twice a week**.*

> **Common errors**
>
> Don't put an adverb between a verb and its object.
> *I **often** check my email late at night.* (NOT *I check often my email.*)

About you

Add the words and expressions to the sentences. Then rewrite the sentences so they are true for you.

1. I make phone calls. (never / after 10:00 p.m.) <u>I never make phone calls after 10:00 p.m.</u>
   <u>Occasionally I make phone calls after 10:00 p.m.</u>

2. My dad will text me. (occasionally / during his lunch break) _____

3. My sister checks her email. (normally / before breakfast) _____

4. I send personal letters. (rarely / these days) _____

5. I instant message my friends. (generally / late at night) _____

6. My best friend is sending me text messages. (constantly / during the day) _____

❷ State verbs

> **In conversation . . .**
>
> People often use *love* and *like* in the continuous to talk about news.
> *"I'm loving my new job."*

- In general, use these verbs in the simple form – not the continuous form – when they describe states: *agree, believe, know, mean, like, love, hate, look, seem, feel, sound, understand.*
  *I **know** I **don't need** a new phone, but I really **want** a red one.*
  *"He **doesn't seem** happy." "I **agree**. He **looks** a little upset today."*
  *What kind of music **do** you **like**?* (NOT *What kind of music are you liking?*)

- Some verbs have a different meaning in the simple and continuous forms: *have, see, think.*
  ***Do** you **have** any children?*　　　　BUT ***Are** you **having** a nice time?* (at a party)
  *I **see** the problem.*　　　　　　　　BUT *I'**m seeing** someone right now.*
  *What **do** you **think** of this class?*　BUT *You look happy. What **are** you **thinking** about?*

A Complete the questions with the verbs given. Use the simple present or present continuous.

1. What _____ the word *eccentric* _____ ? (mean)
2. _____ you _____ that you can make new friends through a social network? (believe)
3. What _____ you _____ about right now? (think)
4. _____ everyone in your family _____ how to send text messages? (know)
5. _____ your parents _____ profiles on a social network? (have)

About you

B Write your own answers to the questions. Give as much information as you can.

Verbs in subject and object relative clauses

- In relative clauses, *who*, *that*, and *which* can be the subject or object of the verb.
  Use a singular verb with a singular subject and a plural verb with a plural subject.

Subject relative clauses

		subject	verb	object
Defining	There's a TV show	*that*	*arranges*	plastic surgery.
	TV shows	*that*	*arrange*	plastic surgery **are** often criticized by doctors.

Non-defining Celebrity magazines, **which need** to attract readers, **publish** some incredible stories.
                  My brother, **who loves** celebrity gossip, **reads** celebrity magazines all the time.

Object relative clauses

		object	subject	verb
Defining	People read about the clothes	(*that*)	celebrities	*wear*.
	I'm interested in the people	(*who/that*) ^{whom}	my favorite actor	*dates*.

Non-defining Reality shows, **which** I never watch, by the way, **have** millions of viewers.

- *Which* clauses that comment on a previous clause can be subject or object relative clauses.
  As a subject, *which* takes a singular verb.
  Celebrity magazines sometimes invent stories, **which is** pretty shocking.
  Some people believe everything they read, **which** I find very scary.

> **Common errors**
>
> Don't repeat the subject or object in a relative clause.
> The actor who was on TV last week has . . . (NOT ~~The actor who he was on TV last week has~~ . . .)
> The actor (that) I saw on TV last week has . . . (NOT ~~The actor (that) I saw him on TV last week has~~ . . .)

Complete the sentences with a singular or plural form of the verbs in parentheses.

1. In some cities, you can go on a "celebrity bus tour," which _____ (take) you through the neighborhoods of famous people and _____ (show) you their houses.

2. A celebrity who _____ (want) to avoid photographers _____ (have to) keep his or her plans secret.

3. Someone who _____ (be) obsessed with a celebrity often _____ (try) to look like that person.

4. Famous people who _____ (prefer) to protect their privacy _____ (try) to keep photographers away from their homes.

5. A photographer who _____ (chase) a celebrity in a car _____ (be) just reckless.

6. Celebrities often appear on talk shows, which _____ (not pay) them very much but _____ (give) them valuable publicity.

7. Fashion designers, who _____ (need) publicity, often _____ (lend) actors clothes to wear on TV.

8. One popular fashion designer, who _____ (work) a lot with celebrities, often _____ (lend) people her clothes to wear on TV.

9. Actors who _____ (get) arrested often _____ (use) the publicity, which just _____ (show) that "There's no such thing as bad publicity."

1 Using *that* clauses

- You can use different nouns with *that* clauses to present a point, such as a problem, or a fact, etc. You can omit *that* in speaking, but in general include *that* in your formal writing.

The problem is
The fact / reality is *that children watch too much television.*
The point / thing is

The **biggest / main problem is** *that children who watch too much TV can become overweight.*
The **odd / amazing thing is** *that kids who watch too much TV are often aggressive at school.*

- You can add more information to *problem* or *thing* by using preposition + noun or + *-ing* form.
The problem **with watching too much television** *is that it keeps you from getting exercise.*
The worst thing **about TV** *these days is that kids watch it while they're eating.*

> **Writing vs. Conversation**
>
> Avoid using *The thing is . . .* in formal writing.

Rewrite these sentences by introducing them with the information in parentheses.

1. Kids can learn about current events by watching TV. (That's one good thing.)

   One good thing is that kids can learn about current events by watching TV.

2. Very young children learn a lot from watching educational programs. (That's the reality.)
3. Some children learn more about history from television than at school. (That's the interesting thing.)
4. They don't care about the shows their children watch. (That's the problem with parents today.)

2 *what* clauses

- You can use *what* clauses to emphasize a point as an opinion.
Children are spending more and more time in front of the TV. This is surprising / clear. →
What's surprising / clear *is that children are spending more and more time in front of the TV.*
Children see a lot of violence on TV. That bothers me. →
What bothers me *is that children see a lot of violence on TV.*

> **In conversation . . .**
>
> These *what* clauses are common ways of making a point.
> *What I'm saying is that . . .*
> *What I'm trying to say is that . . .*

A Rewrite these sentences by starting them with a *what* clause that gives the information in parentheses.

1. Television keeps children from getting enough exercise.
   (That bothers me.)

   What bothers me is that . . .

2. Children need to play and be creative, too. (That's what I'm saying.)
3. Kids watch a lot of violent TV shows, and that can make them aggressive. (That's really scary.)
4. Even educational TV shows prevent kids from exercising. (That's clear.)

About you

B Write down five of your own ideas about the influence of television on children. Use the expressions in the box to introduce your ideas.

> The biggest problem with watching television is . . .   The good thing about television is . . .
> The point is . . .   What bothers me is . . .   What I'm trying to say is . . .

Time expressions with the simple past and present perfect

- You can use time expressions like these with the simple past to indicate a completed time in the past.
- You can use time expressions like these with the present perfect to indicate a "time up to now" which is not yet complete.

I worked on a farm . . .		*I've had a lot of problems . . .*	
yesterday.	*the year before last.*	*lately.*	*over the past few years.*
last week.	*a couple of years ago.*	*so far.*	*in the last few days.*
in the fall.	*at the end of July.*	*to date.*	*since last year.*
earlier this year.	*when I was 20.*	*in my life.*	*since we last spoke.*
right after college.		*up until now.*	

- You can use some time expressions with both the simple past and the present perfect:
  today, this week / month / year, for (quite) a while, for a long time, recently.
  We had some bad luck this year. (The speaker is referring to a point in the past.)
  We've had some bad luck this year. (The speaker sees this year as a period of time up to now.)
  We've been busy recently. (The speaker may not be busy now but considers this relevant now.)

- Time expressions usually go at the beginning or end of a statement.
  Yesterday *I ran into an old friend.* OR *I ran into an old friend* **yesterday**.

- Use *for* with a period of time. Use *since* with a phrase or a clause which gives a point in time.
  I've lived here **for** *many years /* **since** *1995 /* **since** *I was a child.*

Common errors

- Don't put a time expression between the verb and the object.
  We bought a new television **last week**. (NOT ~~We bought last week a new television~~.)
- Avoid putting the time expressions above (except *recently*) between the subject and the verb.
  She got married **right after college**. (NOT ~~She right after college got married~~.)

A Complete the sentences with the simple past or present perfect of the verbs in parentheses.

1. My sister <u>moved</u> (move) to Chicago earlier this year, and so far things <u>have gone</u> (go) pretty well for her. What's great is that she _____ (find) a job right after she got there.
2. My parents _____ (travel) a lot over the past few years. To date they _____ (visit) five different countries. The year before last, they _____ (take) a trip to South Africa.
3. I _____ (be) extremely busy in the last few days. I _____ (not have) a minute to take a break up until now.
4. My best friend _____ (have) some bad luck since he finished school. Last year, for example, he _____ (lose) his job, and he _____ (be) out of work for a long time. He has another job now, but the thing is that he _____ (not be) happy with it recently.
5. I _____ (be) pretty lucky since I got this job. The really amazing thing is that I _____ (get) two raises so far.
6. A lot of things _____ (happen) in my life since we last spoke. First of all, I _____ (meet) someone wonderful in the spring, and in fact we _____ (get) married just last month

About you

B Write four sentences about yourself or people you know. Use the ideas from above.

A new couple has just moved into the apartment next to us.

Time expressions with the past perfect

- You can use the following time expressions with the past perfect.

already / still / yet
*By the time I got to the restaurant, most people had **already** eaten.*
*When I left for class, I **still** hadn't completed my assignment, so I finished it on the bus.*
*My best friend hadn't arrived **yet**, but I couldn't wait any longer, so I went home.*

(not) until after
*I did**n't** find my watch **until after** I'd bought a new one.*

by the time
*I was exhausted **by the time** I'd finished cleaning the house.*

never . . . before
*She was a great teacher. I learned things that I'd **never** understood **before**.*

earlier / previously / years ago
*I got a stomachache from something I'd eaten **earlier**.*
*It was a problem I'd had **previously**, so I knew what caused it.*
*I knew exactly what to do because I'd seen a doctor about it **years ago**.*

A **Complete the sentences with appropriate time expressions in the box.**

by the time	earlier	never . . . before	until after

1. Last summer I took a vacation in Australia. I didn't know much about the country because I'd _____ been there _____ , but I was really excited about the trip.
2. A month before I left, things started to go wrong. I lost my camera, and I didn't find it _____ I'd bought a new one.
3. I finally found my old camera in my suitcase! I'd put it there _____ so I wouldn't forget it.
4. The week before the trip, my boss gave me an urgent project to complete. I was exhausted _____ I'd finished it.

already	previously	still	yet

5. The day I left, I felt stressed because I _____ hadn't packed my suitcase. It took a long time to fit everything in.
6. A friend of mine drove me to the airport. He'd driven there a few times _____ , so he thought he knew the way. But he got lost!
7. By the time I got to the gate, most of the passengers had _____ boarded the plane.
8. Luckily, they hadn't closed the gate _____ , and I was able to get on the flight. In the end, everything worked out fine. I guess I learned that it almost always does!

About you

B **Write 5–10 sentences about an interesting experience you've had. Use the past perfect and time expressions.**

Last week I went to a new club. All my friends had already been there, but I hadn't . . .

1 Making uncountable nouns countable

- Uncountable nouns are often names of materials or of groups of things. You can use *a piece of* to refer to an example or a part of these uncountable nouns: *a piece of paper / plastic / clothing / jewelry / furniture / music / equipment / information / software / advice / evidence.*
  Can I give you **a piece of advice**? When you buy **a new piece of equipment**, check the warranty.

- With some uncountable nouns, you need to use a different countable noun to refer to an example or a part: *travel – trip; cash – coin* or *bill; feedback – comment; luggage – bag; work – job* or *position.*
  My job includes a lot of international **travel**. I go on nine or ten business **trips** a year.
  My boss's **feedback** is very valuable. Her **comments** are always useful.

> **Common errors**
>
> Use (*How*) *much* with uncountable nouns and (*How*) *many* with plural countable nouns.
> Don't take **too much luggage / too many bags**. (NOT . . . ~~too many luggages~~)
> **How much travel / How many trips** are you planning? (NOT ~~How many travels . . .~~)

Complete the sentences with a countable noun like the uncountable noun in bold. Add *a, a piece of,* or *piece of* if necessary. Some have more than one answer.

1. Be sure to ask for **advice** before a job interview. Here's one important piece of advice: Only ask the interviewer questions that show your interest in the job.
2. If you're looking for rewarding **work**, think about applying for _____ in health care.
3. It's nice to have exercise **equipment** at home. One useful _____ is an exercise bike.
4. **Travel** can be expensive. When you plan _____ , compare prices on the Internet.
5. Don't carry too much **luggage** when you travel. Just take one _____ with you.
6. Some **jewelry** is expensive, so before you buy _____ , make sure it's something you like.

2 More about uncountable nouns

- Academic subjects and sports that end in *-s* are usually singular: *economics, genetics, mathematics, physics, politics; aerobics, gymnastics. News* also takes a singular verb.
  Physics was my favorite subject in high school.
  The **news isn't** good, I'm afraid.

- Some nouns are both countable and uncountable but they have different meanings, e.g. *business, competition, experience, paper, time, work.*
  My mother has always worked in **business**. She has owned several **businesses**.
  I have a lot of **experience** using dangerous equipment. I've had some scary **experiences**.

About you

Circle the correct words. Then write your own answers to the questions.

1. Are job candidates facing stiff **competition / competitions** these days?
2. Has it ever taken you **a long time / long time** to find a job?
3. Do you have **an experience / experience** preparing a résumé?
4. **Is / Are** mathematics a field that you're interested in?
5. **Do / Does** economics give people useful knowledge for a career in business?
6. Have you ever thought of starting **a business / business**?
7. Do you think that politics **interest / interests** young people as a career?
8. **Do / Does** the news ever depress you?

More about the definite article

- Use *the* with these common locations, especially after the prepositions *at* and *to*: *the office, the factory, the store, the mall, the gym, the library, the park, the pool, the post office, the bank.*
  *I'd like to have exercise equipment **at the office**. I never have time to go **to the gym**.*
  *Some companies install ATMs so that employees don't have to go **to the bank**.*

- Don't use *the* with these common locations, especially after the prepositions *at, to, in, before*, and *after*: *home, bed, work, school, college, class, prison, jail.*
  *I arrive **at work** early so that I can leave early to pick up my children **after school**.*
  *Some companies offer special training programs for people who have been **in prison**.*
  *Many employees work during the day and go **to college** at night.*

- Don't use *the* before meals. You can use an article when you describe a particular meal.
  *I had **breakfast** late, so I didn't eat much for **lunch**.*
  ***The lunch** we had at that new café wasn't very good. It was **an expensive lunch**, too.*

> **Common errors**
>
> *It was late, so I went **to bed**.* (NOT . . . *so I ~~went to the bed~~.*)
> *She couldn't go **to work** because she was sick.* (NOT *She couldn't ~~go to the work~~ . . .*)

A Complete these conversations with *the, a, an,* or (-) if no word is necessary.

1. *A* Around what time do you go to ____-____ bed at night?
   B Oh, I'm always in _____ bed by 10:00, because I have to be at _____ factory at 8.

2. *A* Did you have _____ breakfast this morning?
   B Yes, but I'm having _____ light lunch, because I'm going out for _____ expensive dinner.

3. *A* Have you ever wanted to take a nap after _____ big lunch?
   B Occasionally I'll do that at _____ home, but there's no place to sleep at _____ work.

4. *A* Do you do anything regularly for exercise, like go to _____ gym?
   B Well, sometimes I go for a run in _____ park, and every so often I go to _____ pool for a swim.

5. *A* Have you ever taken a pet with you to _____ work or to _____ school?
   B Actually, when I was in _____ college, a guy used to bring a pet rat to _____ class. The teacher never knew.

6. *A* Do you go straight home after _____ work?
   B Well, it seems like I always have something to do, like stop at _____ store to pick up something for _____ dinner or go to _____ bank for some cash.

7. *A* Do you ever do anything fun after _____ class, like go to a restaurant?
   B Um, sometimes I go out for _____ dinner with some classmates.

8. *A* Would you like to have flexible hours at _____ office?
   B Yeah, I'd like to be able to pick up my kids after _____ school.

About you | **B** Write your own answers to the questions above.

I usually go to bed around 10:30.

1 Continuous forms for conditions

- You can use past continuous forms to introduce hypothetical situations in the present.
  If you **were hoping** to get a job with a charity, you might want to volunteer first.
  If you **were planning** to change the world, where would you start?

- You can use past perfect continuous forms to introduce hypothetical situations in the past.
  If the Salwens **had been living** in a small house, they wouldn't have been able to raise so much.
  Hannah might not have seen the homeless man if she **hadn't been looking** out the window.

About you

Complete the questions with a continuous form of the verbs. Then answer the questions.

1. If you and your classmates _____ to raise money for a good cause, how would you do it? (try)
2. If you _____ so hard, what would you have done differently last year? (not work)
3. If you _____ about giving to a charity, what organization would you choose? Why? (think)
4. What would you do if you _____ down the street and you saw a homeless person? (walk)
5. If you _____ to help your community, what would you do? (plan)

2 *even if* and *unless* to talk about conditions

- You can use *even* to add special emphasis to a condition introduced by *if*.
  I think I would give to charity **even if** I didn't have much money.
  Even if I had saved some money last year, I wouldn't have given it to a charity.

- You can use *unless* to introduce what needs to happen or be true for something else to happen.
  It means "except if."
  I wouldn't give money to charity **unless** I were a millionaire (**except if** I were a millionaire).
  = I would **only** give money to charity **if** I were a millionaire.

- You can use the same verb forms with *even if* and *unless* as with *if* clauses.
  I **wouldn't sell** my house unless it **were / was** really necessary.
  The Salwens **would have raised** money for charity even if Hannah **hadn't seen** the man that day.

Common errors

Don't use **unless** when the event in the *if* clause actually happened.
If they hadn't sold their house, they wouldn't be as close now. (NOT ~~Unless they had sold . . .~~)

About you

Complete the answers with the clauses in the box. More than one answer may be possible.

| I didn't want them. | I had a very good job. | I had to put the donation on my credit card. |
| I only had a few things. | I wanted time off work. | I couldn't find a job when I got back. |

1. **A** Would you give money to charity if you were out of work?
   B Absolutely. I would do it even if _____
   C I don't think so. I would never do it unless _____

2. **A** Would you ever give up a good position if you had a chance to spend a year traveling?
   B Sure. I wouldn't miss a chance like that unless _____
   C Never. I wouldn't give up a good position even if _____

3. **A** Would you give away your belongings if you had the chance to help someone?
   B I don't think so. I wouldn't give my things away unless _____
   C Yes, I would. I'd give my things away even if _____

1 Use of *wish* with *would*

- You can use *wish* followed by a clause with *would* in order to comment on a situation you would like to change.
  You're always leaving the lights on! → *I **wish** you **wouldn't leave** the lights on.*
  Why can't the kids spend less money on soda? → *I wish the kids **would spend** less money on soda.*

- You can comment on general situations using *people* or *they* in the clause with *would*.
  *I wish **they'd stop** tearing down the historic buildings in our neighborhood.*
  *I wish **people would learn** to recycle their bottles and cans.*

Common errors

Don't confuse *wish* and *hope*.
*I **hope** this information will be helpful to you.* (NOT ~~I wish this information would be helpful to you.~~)

A Comment on the situations below. Write sentences with *I wish* + a clause with *would*.

1. You use so much water! <u>I wish you wouldn't use so much water!</u>
2. You never recycle your newspapers. _____
3. Why don't people use public transportation more? _____
4. Why can't people be more polite on the bus? _____
5. They need to do something about water pollution. _____
6. People are always throwing their litter on the streets. _____

About you **B Write five sentences about situations you would like to change. Begin each sentence with *I wish* and include *would* or *wouldn't*.**

2 Strong wishes with *If only*

- You can use *If only* to introduce a strong wish, which is either difficult or impossible to achieve. The verb forms that follow *If only* are the same as those that follow *I wish*.
  I wish people were more generous. → ***If only** people **were** more generous.*
  I wish people would care about the homeless. → ***If only** people **would care** about the homeless.*
  I wish we could predict the future. → ***If only** we **could predict** the future.*

- In writing, add a main clause to a sentence with *if only*.
  *If only people cared more about the homeless, **we might eradicate the problem**.*
  *If only we could predict the future, **we would all be a lot richer**.*

Common errors

Don't confuse *if only* and *only if*.
*I would miss work **only if** I were sick.* OR *I would **only** miss work **if** I were sick* (NOT ~~I would miss work if only I were sick.~~)

A Use *If only* to rewrite these thoughts as strong wishes. Some have more than one answer.

1. Why can't we find a way to end all wars? <u>If only we could find a way to end all wars!</u>
2. I don't know why people don't recycle more! _____
3. People are so narrow-minded about some things. _____
4. I wish we could predict natural disasters better. _____
5. I wish they would create more jobs for the unemployed. _____
6. I wish I hadn't quit my job. _____

About you **B Write five strong wishes of your own. Use *If only*.**

1 Plans and intentions with *be going to* and *will*

- You can use the future with *be going to* to talk about your plans or intentions when you have already made decisions. Use *will* for decisions you make at the moment of speaking.
  I'm going to be working from home, so *I'm going to get* a laptop. I think **I'll look for** one today.

- You can use *will* to state decisions in stores and restaurants, to offer help, or to make promises.
  I'll take this dress.   **I'll have** the fish.   **I'll open** the door.   **I won't tell** anyone.

- You can use the future continuous to tell people about plans that affect them or to go over plans you've agreed on. You can also use it to politely ask people about their own plans.
  I'll be calling you later. (= We already agreed on this.)   **I'll call** you later. (= I just decided.)
  Will you **be paying** with a credit card or a debit card?

> **Common errors**
>
> Use *I'll* + verb to make an offer.
> **I'll call** you tonight. (NOT ~~I call~~ you tonight.)

Circle the most appropriate expressions. Say why you chose each expression.

It's a plan they've agreed on.

A   Sorry to disturb you. I just wanted to remind you that **I'll be leaving** / **I'll leave** early tonight, like we agreed. **I'm going to take** / **I'll take** a friend out to dinner for her birthday.

B   OK . . . Actually, it's Tuesday today, right? So **I'll leave** / **I'm going to be leaving** the office late tonight as usual. So . . . yeah, **I take care of** / **I'll take care of** anything that comes up.

A   Thanks. So **I'm going to see** / **I'll see** you tomorrow morning, then.

B   Well, tomorrow's busy. **Will you be coming in** / **Are you going to come in** at 8:00, as usual?

A   If there's a lot to do, **I'm going to get** / **I'll get** here by 7:00. **I won't be** / **I'm not going to be** late, I promise.

2 Present forms in clauses that refer to the future

- Use the present in clauses that begin with *when*, *before*, *after*, *until*, or *as soon as* to refer to the future.
  Before we **get to** the movie theater, I'm going to stop at an ATM. I'll need some cash **when** we **get** there.
  I won't be able to do anything **until** I **eat**. I'll buy something **as soon as** we **get** to the theater.

- Use the present in clauses with *unless*, *as long as*, *so long as*, *providing (that)*, and *provided (that)* that refer to the future. These expressions introduce something that needs to happen or be true so that something else can happen.
  I can pay **as long as** / **so long as** we **go** to a café that takes debit cards. OR I **can't** pay **unless** we **go** . . .
  They won't charge interest **provided (that)** / **providing (that)** you **pay** the bill in full.

- Use the present in clauses with *in case*, which introduces a possibility that you want to be ready for.
  I'm going to take all my credit cards **in case** they **don't accept** one of them.

About you

Combine the sentences using the words given. Then make three sentences true for you.

1. I'll lend you some money. You'll have to pay me back next week, though. (as long as)
    I'll lend you some money as long as you pay me back next week.

2. I'm not going to be taking a vacation next summer. I probably won't get a raise. (unless)

3. I won't be able to apply for a credit card right away. First, I'll need to get a full-time job. (until)

4. I'm going to take a lot of cash. They might not accept credit cards. (in case)

5. Our grocery store will give us a discount. We'll have to pay in cash, however. (provided that)

① More on necessity modals

- You can use *should* (*not*), *ought* (*not*) *to*, and *had better* (*not*) to say what is advisable. Use *had better* in specific situations.
  You **should / ought to** check the equipment before a presentation. You **shouldn't** begin until you check it.
  You **'d better** get going – it's almost 10:30. You **'d better not** be late for class again.

- Use *must* (*not*) to say what is necessary. *Must* is mainly used in formal notices and announcements.
  You **must** turn off your cell phone before the lecture. You **must not** use a cell phone during the lecture.

- You can use *have to* and *need to* to say what is necessary in the affirmative. In the negative, however, these expressions are used to say what is NOT necessary.
  You **have to / need to** carry a driver's license when you drive. = It's necessary.
  But you **don't have to / don't need to** carry your passport. = It's not necessary.

About you

Complete the sentences with a modal form from the box. Often more than one answer is possible. Then write four sentences to describe rules or advice for your city.

need to	have to	must	'd better	should	ought to
don't need to	don't have to	must not	'd better not	shouldn't	

1. Here, the law says you ___must / have to / need to___ wear a helmet when you ride a motorcycle.
2. Many countries have a law that says you _____ wear a seat belt when you're riding in a car. Here, it's only necessary if you're sitting in the front seat – you _____ wear one in the back.
3. In many places, you _____ use your cell phone when you drive. It's against the law.
4. In most countries, you _____ stop your car for a flashing red light, but you _____ stop for a flashing yellow light. You _____ slow down, however.
5. You _____ look both ways before crossing a street. It's not a law, though.
6. We _____ go out tonight. There's going to be a big storm. We _____ stay home.

② Possibility modals in the affirmative and negative

- Use *may* (*not*), *might* (*not*), and *must* (*not*) to make guesses. *Not* is generally not contracted.
  We **may / might** have to end this meeting early. = It's possible we'll have to . . .
  We **may not / might not** have time for a lot of questions. = It's possible we won't have time . . .
  The principal isn't here. She **must** be busy today. = It's likely she's . . .
  The meeting is almost over. The principal **must not** be coming. = It's likely she's not coming.

- You can also use *could* to talk about possibilities, but it often becomes *can't* in the negative and means "it's not possible."
  The projector is brand new. It **can't be** broken. = It's not possible that it's broken.
  But it **could be** unplugged. = It's possible that it's unplugged.

Circle the appropriate modal verbs in the sentences.

1. The elevator's not working. I'm afraid we (**might**)/ **must** have to use the stairs.
2. My camera won't turn on. I suppose the battery **could / can** need recharging. Wait a minute. It simply **might not / can't** be the battery. I just recharged it last night!
3. My oven's not working. I **may not / can't** be able to get it fixed. I **might / must** need a new one.
4. My sister's not answering her cell phone. I think she **might not / could** have her cell phone with her. Or maybe the battery **could / must not** be dead. Or her phone **may not / must** be on.

❶ Objects with separable phrasal verbs

- With separable phrasal verbs, you can put noun objects before or after the particle, but long noun objects generally go after the particle.
  *Don't forget to turn off **the TV.** / Don't forget to turn **the TV** off.*
  *Don't forget to turn off **the TV, the computer, and all the lights in the living room and kitchen.***

- Object pronouns (*me, you, him, it,* etc.) always go before the particle. However, indefinite pronouns (*something, anybody,* etc.) and possessive pronouns (*mine, yours,* etc.) can go after the particle.
  *My roommate borrowed my belt, and she never gave **it** back.*
  *She's always borrowing my stuff, and she never gives back **anything** / gives **anything** back.*
  *My room is dirty, but I won't clean **it** up unless you clean up **yours** / you clean **yours** up.*

About you

Complete the sentences with the objects and verbs given. More than one answer may be possible. Then rewrite the sentences to make them true for you.

1. Before I go to bed, I always _____ . (everything / put away)
2. If I'm late, I try hard not to _____ . (my parents and my sister / wake up)
3. When I get up, I always _____ first. (the television / turn on)
4. If I borrow something, I try to _____ as soon as possible. (it / give back)
5. I never leave things on the floor. I always _____ . (everything / pick up)
6. I don't _____ . (bottles, cans, or any food packaging / throw away)

❷ Phrasal verbs followed by the *-ing* form of the verb

- You can use an *-ing* form after many phrasal verbs. The *-ing* form follows the particle.
  *I've almost given up **trying** to get along with my roommates. I may end up **moving** out.*

- Some verbs consist of a verb, a particle, and a preposition. The *-ing* form follows the preposition.
  *My brother never gets around to **doing** the dishes. He gets away with **leaving** them.*

> **Common errors**
>
> Don't use an infinitive or base form of the verb after a particle or preposition.
> *We're looking forward **to seeing** you.* (NOT ~~We're looking forward to see you.~~)

A **Rewrite the sentences. Replace the words in bold with a correct form of a phrasal verb in the box. Write the verb in parentheses in the correct form.**

end up   get around to   get out of   give up   keep on   look forward to   put off   take care of

1. My roommate never **finds the time** (do) any chores at the apartment.
2. He always **delays** (do) the dishes and says he'll do them later.
3. So I **finally** (do) the dishes all by myself.
4. He manages to **avoid** (shop) for food by going out of town on the weekends.
5. I have to **take responsibility for** (buy) all the groceries.
6. People tell me I should **continue** (try) to work things out with him.
7. Anyhow I've **stopped** (try) to talk to him about it.
8. I'm **excited about** (move) out of the apartment at the end of the semester.

B **Write about someone you know. Is he or she helpful around the house?**

More patterns with infinitives and *it* clauses

- You can use *too* before an adjective + infinitive, especially *late, young, early, busy, small, old, long, good, tired, easy, hard,* and *difficult.*
  It's never **too late** to learn new things.   I was **too young** to remember my grandmother.

- You can add *for* + person after the adjective, especially after *hard, difficult,* and *easy.*
  It's difficult / hard **for me** to make decisions.   It's not easy **for a lot of people** to raise children.

- You can use *to* or *for* + person with *interesting, fascinating,* and *important.*
  It's interesting **to me / for me** to watch parents with their children.
  It's important **to many people / for many people** to live near their families.

- People frequently use *not* with these adjectives beginning with *un-, in-,* or *im-,* especially in academic writing: *uncommon, impossible,* and *unusual.* The adjective can be followed directly by an infinitive or by *for* + person.
  It's **not uncommon** to feel sad when your children leave home to go to college.
  It's **not unusual** for families to argue about money.

A   **Rewrite these statements adding the ideas in parentheses.**

1. Parents often put a lot of pressure on their kids. (It's not unusual.)
   <u>It's not unusual for parents to put a lot of pressure on their kids.</u>

2. Some parents let their kids have free time for themselves. (It's very important.)
   _____

3. Children often think that their parents are narrow-minded. (It's not uncommon.)
   _____

4. I couldn't understand my parents' views when I was younger. (It was difficult.)
   _____

5. Parents often can't understand why their children are fighting with each other. (It's not easy.)
   _____

6. I enjoy seeing how different families handle discipline. (It's always interesting.)
   _____

7. Brothers and sisters sometimes go on fighting even after they leave home. (It's not unusual.)
   _____

8. You should always apologize to a family member if you've had a fight. (It's never too late.)
   _____

9. Kids shouldn't move back in with their parents after they finish college. (It's probably not good.)
   _____

10. College graduates frequently can't find jobs, though. (It's sometimes too hard.)
    _____

About you   **B**   **Use these expressions to introduce five of your ideas about family life.**

> It wasn't easy for me . . .   It's not uncommon for children . . .   It's not unusual for families . . .
> It's too difficult for me . . .   It's very important for parents . . .

Question forms in the passive

- In most passive questions, the auxiliary verb (*is, were, have,* etc.) or modal verb (*will, can,* etc.) comes before the subject.

Statement	Yes-No question	Information question
The population **is expected** to rise.	**Is** the population **expected** to rise?	When **is** it **expected** to rise?
The issue **is being discussed**.	**Is** the issue **being discussed**?	Where **is** it **being discussed**?
The idea **was developed** at Columbia.	**Was** the idea **developed** at Columbia?	Where **was** it **developed**?
Crops **have been grown** in water.	**Have** crops **been grown** in water?	How long **have** they **been grown** in water?
Water **will be recycled**.	**Will** water **be recycled**?	How **will** it **be recycled**?

- When the question word is the subject, the auxiliary or modal verb does not change position.
Vertical farming **is going to be discussed** next week. → What**'s going to be discussed** next week?
An expert in vertical farming **will be invited** to speak. → Who **will be invited** to speak?

- Information questions about the "doer" can end in *by.*
Vertical farming **was developed by** Despommier. → Who **was** vertical farming **developed by**?

A Complete these *yes-no* questions in the passive for the responses given.

1. A ___Is the population expected___ to increase in the future?
   B Yes, the population is expected to increase by 3 to 4 billion people in the next 50 years.

2. A _____ to feed this population?
   B Yes, more food can definitely be produced, but it won't be easy.

3. A _____ to increase the food supply?
   B Actually, several methods have been developed. One is called vertical farming.

4. A _____ anywhere at the moment?
   B Yes, vertical farming is being used in a number of places. But the method is still experimental.

B Complete the information questions in the passive.

1. A How long ___have crops been grown in water___ ?
   B Crops have been grown in water since ancient times.

2. A What _____ ?
   B This method of farming is called hydroponics.

3. A Who _____ ?
   B Hydroponics was first used by the Egyptians, the Aztecs, and the Chinese in ancient times.

4. A Where _____ ?
   B Most hydroponic crops are grown in greenhouses.

5. A How _____ ?
   B Land can be conserved by building high-rise hydroponic greenhouses in urban areas.

6. A What kind of costs _____ ?
   B Transportation costs would be reduced by urban vertical farming.

❶ Verb + object + infinitive

- Many verbs follow the pattern of verb + object + infinitive: *advise, ask, encourage, expect, force, get* (= *persuade*), *invite, persuade, remind, tell, want, warn, would like.*
  My doctor **wants me to eat** less meat and fat.
  The government is **encouraging people to eat** more fruits and vegetables.
  BUT The government is **discouraging people from eating** too much fat.

- Notice the position of *not.*
  The doctor warned me **not** to eat too much fat.   He advised me **not** to go on any extreme diets.

> **Common errors**
>
> Do not use a *that* clause after the verb *want.*
> I **want all my friends to have** a healthy diet. (NOT I ~~want that all my friends have~~ . . .)

About you

Unscramble these sentences. Then choose four sentences and rewrite them with your own ideas or information.

1. is encouraging / their eating habits / the government / to improve / people
   The government is encouraging people to improve their eating habits.
2. to pay / us / a special tax / the government / may force / on sugar-filled drinks
3. students / my college / is discouraging / from / energy drinks / drinking
4. during the school day / schools / unhealthy snacks / don't want / to eat / children
5. not / me / to eat / my doctor / too much junk food / advised
6. to eat / are always reminding / a good breakfast / my parents / me
7. me / to stop / has persuaded / my best friend / eating meat
8. is trying to get / my brother / some weight / to lose / me

❷ More verb patterns

- Some verbs can follow the pattern of verb + object + adjective. Examples are *make* and *keep.*
  Trying to stay healthy **keeps me busy.**
  Complicated instructions **make some diets hard** to follow.

- Verbs that express likes and dislikes can also follow this pattern. Examples are *like, would like, hate, prefer,* and *find.*
  I **find some cheese too salty.**   I **don't like my tea cold.**   I **prefer it really hot.**
  He **likes his fish baked** or **fried.**   He doesn't **like it raw.**

About you

Complete these sentences with the appropriate form of a verb from the box. Then rewrite the sentences to make them true for you.

| find   keep   like   make   ✓ prefer |

1. My father hates eating raw vegetables. He __prefers__ his vegetables cooked.
2. I never drink coffee after noon. It _____ me awake at night.
3. I avoid eating pasta for lunch. It _____ me sleepy all afternoon.
4. My brother eats a lot of junk food. He _____ a healthy diet very boring.
5. A friend of mine puts chili peppers in all her cooking. She _____ her food hot and spicy.

❶ Singular or plural verbs with determiners

- Use a singular verb with *each*, *every*, and *neither* + countable noun or the pronoun *one*.
  Each child / Every child **is** *unique and special, and each one / every one* **needs** *individual attention.*
  I have two children, and neither child **has** *any interest in sports. Neither one* **plays** *sports.*

- Use a singular verb with *no* + singular countable or uncountable noun. Use a plural verb with *no* + plural noun.
  No success **comes** *easily.   No job* **is** *perfect.   Unfortunately, no good jobs* **are** *available right now.*

- People mostly use a plural verb after *neither of* and *none of*. In formal writing, people use a singular verb.
  Informal: *Neither of my parents* **have studied** *English. None of their friends* **have learned** *English, either.*
  Formal: *Neither of my parents* **has studied** *English. None of their friends* **has learned** *English, either.*

About you

Circle the correct verb in each sentence. Sometimes both forms can be correct. Then choose three sentences and rewrite them with your own ideas or information.

1. Both of my brothers **has** / ⟨**have**⟩ finished college, but neither one **has** / **have** found a job yet. No companies **is** / **are** hiring people right now.
2. All successful people **knows** / **know** that every failure **presents** / **present** an opportunity.
3. I've had two jobs. Neither of them **was** / **were** perfect, but each one **was** / **were** interesting.
4. All of my friends **is** / **are** focused on their work. None of them **wants** / **want** to get married.
5. Neither of my parents **wants** / **want** me to be an entrepreneur. Both of them **has** / **have** advised me to study for a profession.
6. No job **is** / **are** ever completely secure. Every employee **needs** / **need** to save money "for a rainy day."

❷ Determiners with and without *of*

- You can use *all*, *each*, *every*, *both*, *neither*, *some*, *a few*, *several*, *many*, and *most* before a noun.
  Every job *is different.* **A few jobs** *seem easy, but* **most jobs** *are challenging in some way.*

- When most of these determiners are followed by another determiner + noun or by an object pronoun, add *of*. With *all* and *both*, *of* is optional before a noun. *A lot of* always includes *of*. After *every*, use *one of*.
  Each of my children *is different.* **Each of them** *has a different job, but* **every one of** *them is happy.*
  All (of) the people *at work want to do well.* **All of us** *work hard.* **A lot of people / us** *work weekends.*
  Both (of) my parents *have interesting careers.* **Neither of them** *wants / want to retire.*

- Use *no* before a noun. Use *none of* + determiner + noun or *none of* + object pronoun.
  No employees *are unhappy.* **None of the employees / them** *is / are unhappy.*

About you

Complete the sentences with the words in the box. Add *of* if necessary. In some, more than one word is possible. Then rewrite the sentences with your own ideas or information.

all	both	each	every	every one	most	neither	no	none

1. I have five close friends, and ___all of___ them have jobs. _____ them is unemployed.
2. _____ jobs require training, but for my current job, _____ formal training was necessary.
3. _____ student in my English course is serious, and _____ them ever miss a class.
4. _____ my parents enjoy being retired. _____ them wish they could keep on working.
5. _____ the people in my family love sports, but _____ us plays a different sport.
6. I'm not married, but _____ my sisters are. _____ sister has any children yet, though.

❶ Verbs followed by an *-ing* form or an infinitive

- Use *forget*, *remember*, and *regret* + an *-ing* form to mean "remember / forget / regret that someone did something." You can also use these verbs with an infinitive to mean "remember / forget / regret something that someone needs or needed to do."
  *I'll never **forget going up** to get my college diploma.* BUT *I **forgot to shake** the president's hand.*
  *I **remember thanking** my professor as I left.* BUT *I always **remember to say** thank you.*

- You can use *stop* and *try* + an *-ing* form or an infinitive, but they have different meanings.
  *I've **stopped drinking** soda.* (= I don't drink it now.)
  BUT *I **stopped to pick up** some fruit juice at the store.* (**to** = in order to)
  *I **tried giving up** coffee for a whole year, but then I started drinking it again.* (**try** = experiment with)
  BUT *I **tried to give up** sweets, but I just couldn't do it.* (**try** = try without success)

About you

Complete this anecdote with the correct form of the verbs given. Then write a short anecdote about something that happened to you.

I'll never forget <u>hiking</u> (hike) through the Amazon rain forest. It had been my dream to go there. I was on a tour and at one point, I stopped _____ (get) some pictures of tropical birds. After a while, I couldn't hear the voices of the other hikers, so I stopped _____ (take) pictures and tried _____ (catch up with) the group. Unfortunately, I couldn't find the path. I tried _____ (yell) for help several times, but no one heard me. I looked for my GPS device but realized I had forgotten _____ (put) it in my pack that day. I hadn't remembered _____ (bring) my map, either. I remember _____ (think) that I'd never find my group again. Luckily, our guide stopped _____ (count) the hikers and noticed I was missing. He led the whole group back to find me. He was very annoyed, and I have to say I regretted _____ (take) those pictures. My happiest moment turned into my scariest.

❷ Verbs of perception + object + base form or *-ing* form

- After the verbs *feel*, *see*, *watch*, *notice*, and *hear*, you can use an object + the base form of a verb to describe a complete event.
  *I **watched** my friends **leave** the restaurant. I **heard** someone **say**, "See you soon."*
  *I **saw** my sister **call** a taxi and **felt** her **take** my arm and **guide** me to it.*

- You can also use an object + an *-ing* form after these verbs to describe an event in progress or an event that takes place over a longer period of time.
  *I **heard** people **singing**. I went in the room and **saw** all my friends **standing** around the piano.*

A Rewrite these sentences using the verbs of perception given.

1. Some strange things were happening as I walked up to my house. (noticed)
   I noticed some strange things happening as I walked up to my house.
2. Someone turned off the lights in the living room. (saw)
3. Someone was closing the curtains. (noticed)
4. People were talking to each other softly. (could hear)
5. Somebody yelled "Surprise!" when I walked into the living room. (heard)
6. Several people were holding up a big birthday cake. (saw)

About you

B Write an anecdote about a happy moment. Use verbs of perception.

1 Reported speech: verbs and pronouns

- When you report things people say, you may need to change the pronouns in the reported sentence.
  "**I** left **my** camera on the plane." → Karen said that **she** had left **her** camera on the plane.
  "**We**'re happy to carry **your** bags." → The guides said that **they** were happy to carry **my/our** bags.

- The verb in the reported sentence often "shifts back." You do not always need to change the simple past or past continuous. The past perfect does not change.
  "**I'm** really **enjoying** the trip." → Rob said that he **was** really **enjoying** the trip.
  "**I don't like** the hotel, though." → He told me that he **didn't like** the hotel, though.
  "**I wasn't feeling** well." → He explained that he **hadn't been feeling** well. (OR **wasn't feeling**)
  "**I met up with** an old friend." → He said that he **had met up with** / **met** an old friend.
  "**I've seen** some amazing things." → He told me that he **'d seen** some amazing things.
  "**I hadn't been** there before." → He said that he **hadn't been** there before.

A Report the things that people said after a trip. There may be more than one correct answer.

1. Karen: "I'm planning to go back to Florida. I've never enjoyed a vacation so much!"
   Karen said _____ and _____ .

2. Joe and Sue: "The airline made us check our luggage and lost it. We've never had that happen before."
   Joe and Sue said _____ . They said _____ .

3. Sandra: "I met my boyfriend on vacation. He was sitting next to me on the plane."
   Sandra told me _____ . She said _____ .

4. Ana: "I had a great time in India. I hadn't been there before."
   Ana said _____ . She said _____ .

5. Guy: "My mom didn't like the food. That surprised me."
   He said _____ . He said _____ .

About you

B Write five sentences about trips you've taken in the past, and give them to a partner. Report your partner's comments.

2 Reported speech: time and place expressions

- Time and place expressions often change in the reported sentence.

  next week → the following week or the week after   this morning → that morning   here → there
  tomorrow → the following day or the day after   today → that day
  yesterday → the previous day or the day before   now → then
  last year → the year before   then → then or after that

  "We're going to the beach **this** morning." → He said they were going to the beach **that** morning.
  "**Yesterday** we went to a farm." → He said that they had gone to a farm **the day before**.

Report this extract from Rona's blog. Rewrite the sentences.

Another day in Tuscany . . . We're eating breakfast outside this morning. We couldn't do that yesterday because there was a huge thunderstorm. It's beautiful here. This afternoon we're going to a farm and we're going to pick olives. Then we're going to learn how they make olive oil. Tomorrow we're visiting our friends. We saw them last year back home. It'll be the first time we've been to their home in Italy. Then next week we're going to drive to the coast. We're having a fabulous time!

Rona said that they were eating breakfast outside that morning.

❶ Reported speech: other reporting verbs

- You can use different verbs to report the things people say, especially in writing. To report statements, you can use verbs such as *add, answer, claim, complain, comment, confirm, explain, inform, mention, predict, promise, remark, remind, reply, say, state,* and *tell.*

  With *add, answer, claim, comment, confirm, predict, remark, reply,* and *state,* use a *that* clause.
  "The flight's at 8:00 a.m. You should check in by 7:00 a.m."
  She **confirmed** (that) the flight was at 8:00 a.m. and **added** (that) we should check in by 7:00 a.m.

  With *inform, remind,* and *tell,* use an indirect object and a *that* clause.
  "The flight's full." The agent **informed** me (that) the flight was full.

  With *comment, complain, explain, mention, say,* and *reply,* you can use a *that* clause or *to* + person + a *that* clause.
  "My room is noisy." I **complained** (to the receptionist) (that) my room was noisy.

- To report questions, you can use *ask, inquire* (more formal), *want to know,* and *wonder.*
  "Are you leaving?" He **wanted to know** if I was leaving. / He **inquired** whether I was leaving.

- To report instructions, you can use *advise, instruct, order, persuade, remind,* and *warn.*
  "Don't forget your hat." She **advised** me not to forget my hat. / She **reminded** me to take my hat.

Complete the sentences so they have a similar meaning. Use the words given.

1. The tour agent said to us, "Don't go off the trail." He also said, "Take some food."
   The tour agent _____ (warned) the trail. He also _____ (reminded) some food.
2. The check-in agent asked me, "Are you traveling alone?" and "Did you pack your bags yourself?"
   The check-in agent _____ (wanted to know). She also _____ (inquired).
3. The tour guide said, "Drink plenty of water." He said, "It will be a tough walk."
   The tour guide _____ (advised). He _____ (added).
4. One passenger said, "The flight's been delayed for four hours. We should get a voucher for a free meal."
   One passenger _____ (complained). He also _____ (mentioned).

❷ Reported speech: reporting verb forms

- When the reporting verb is in the present tense, the verb often does not need to "shift back" because the information may still be true or relevant to the present time.
  "I'm having a great time." ➔ She says she's having a great time.

- People often use the past continuous to report news. You can use the present tense or the present perfect in the reported speech if the information is still true.
  "The airlines have raised their prices." ➔ He **was saying** the airlines have raised their prices.

A Imagine you have just heard these comments. Report each one. Start with the words given.

1. "I'm traveling on business right now. I'm sitting in the airport in Beijing." *He says . . .*
2. "The flights are delayed because of the snow. We'll be arriving late." *She says . . .*
3. "I had a great trip. I saw dolphins and some amazing birds." *He was saying . . .*
4. "The government is promoting tourism. They don't want to lose tourist dollars." *She was saying . . .*

About you

B Write five pieces of news. Then give them to a partner. Report your partner's news.

1 More on relative clauses

- A defining relative clause defines or gives essential information about a noun. The sentence needs the relative clause to complete its meaning.

  *Spring is the time **when many people get married**.*
  *The hotel **where my parents had their reception** closed.*
  *I have an uncle **whose marriage was arranged**.*

- A non-defining relative clause gives extra information about a noun. The sentence has a complete meaning without the relative clause. Notice the commas.

  *People like to get married in the spring, **when it's warmer**.*
  *There was a garden, **where the photos were taken**.*
  *He had strict parents, **whose aim was to find him a bride**.*

Common errors

Do not use *which* for possession before a noun.
*We went to a hotel, **whose** name I've forgotten.* (NOT ~~which name~~ . . .)

Rewrite each pair of sentences as one sentence. Start with the words given. Use relative clauses with *when*, *where*, or *whose*. Add commas where necessary.

1. I have several friends. Their wedding ceremonies were outside.
   I have several friends <u>whose wedding ceremonies were outside.</u>
2. The hotel has just appeared in a bridal magazine. We got married there.
   The hotel _____
3. The best season to get married is winter. The trees are covered in snow.
   The best season to get married is winter _____
4. I have conservative parents. Their main concern is to find a husband for me.
   I have conservative parents _____
5. After the ceremony, we went to a Japanese restaurant. We ate sushi.
   After the ceremony, _____

2 Prepositions in relative clauses

- In spoken or informal English, relative clauses can end with a preposition.

  *I married a co-worker who I'd shared an office **with**.*
  *We met at a golf club, which we both belonged **to**.*

- In formal English, prepositions can start a relative clause. Notice the use of *whom* for people and *which* (not *that*) for things.

  *I married a co-worker **with whom** I'd shared an office.*
  *We met at a golf club, **to which** we both belonged.*

- You can often rephrase a relative clause that ends with a preposition of location by using *where*.

  *That's the place that we went **to** for our photos.*
  OR *That's the place **where** we went for our photos.*

- A preposition of location can also start the relative clause in more formal English.

  *The Royal is the hotel **in / at** which we stayed.*
  OR *The Royal is the hotel we stayed **in / at**. (less formal)*

Rewrite the sentences. Make the comments in 1–3 less formal. Sometimes there is more than one answer. Sentences 4–6 are extracts from a letter of complaint. Make them more formal.

1. The Ritz is the restaurant to which we are going for the rehearsal dinner.
2. I want to marry a person with whom I share a lot of interests.
3. My wife and I met at a homeless shelter at which we both volunteered.
4. The dinner at the reception, which we had paid a lot of money for, was cold.
5. We complained to the hotel manager, who we had an argument with.
6. The question which we want an answer to is, "Why was the meal cold?"

❶ More on verb + direct object + prepositional phrase

• With these verbs, use *for* in the prepositional phrase: *bake, buy, cook, draw, find, make,* and *paint*.	*Will you bake a cake **for** me?* *I'm painting a picture **for** my father.*
• With most other verbs, use *to*: *give, hand, lend, offer, owe, pay, read, send, show,* and *write*.	*I didn't send a gift **to** him this year.* *We handed all our money **to** the clerk.*
• With *bring* and *take*, you can use *for* or *to*, but the meaning is different.	*I've brought some flowers **for** you.* (= They're a gift.) *Can I borrow your laptop? I'll bring it back **to** you later.*

About you

Rewrite the sentences using a direct object + prepositional phrase. Then use the ideas to write true sentences of your own.

1. I always bake my sister a cake on her birthday.
2. I never give my friends money. I prefer to hand them a nicely wrapped gift.
3. When friends invite you for dinner, it's nice to offer your host a small gift.
4. On special occasions, I'll often cook my family a nice meal.
5. If you want to give a friend who has everything a gift, a magazine subscription is a good idea.
6. When I get greeting cards, I always show my family the messages.
7. When I have to send someone a gift in the mail, I always choose something small.
8. I once made a friend an unusual gift. I drew him a picture of his cat.
9. My parents once bought me an underwater camera for my birthday.

❷ Passive sentences

- In the passive, either the indirect object or the direct object can become the subject of the sentence.
- Compare this active sentence with the two passive sentences below.

subject	active verb	indirect object	direct object
My aunt	*gave*	*me*	*this ring.*

Indirect object as subject	Direct object as subject
I was given this ring (by my aunt). This pattern is more common.	*This ring was given to me (by my aunt).* This pattern is less common and often more formal.

Rewrite these sentences in the passive form. Start with the words given.

1. The school gave us certificates when we completed the course. *We . . .*
   We were given certificates (by the school) when we completed the course.
2. My father's company gave him a clock when he retired. *A clock . . .*
3. Someone sent my sister a gift card for her birthday. *My sister . . .*
4. One of my friends owes me a lot of money. *I . . .*
5. Someone handed me a microphone so I could make a speech at my party. *A microphone . . .*
6. My mother always gave us a piece of jewelry for our birthdays. *We . . .*

1 *well* + adjective

- You can use *well* before the adjectives below. It means "very" or "very much." Add a hyphen when *well* + adjective comes before a noun.
  I'm **well aware** of my abilities. I'm **well educated** and **well trained**.
  I'm also a **well-organized** and **well-informed** person.
  He wasn't **well prepared** for the exam. He was **well short of** the 90 percent he needed.

- You can use *well* in a number of fixed expressions, e.g., *well off, well known, well thought-out, well behaved, well written,* and *well dressed*.
  My teacher said my poem was **well written**. He said it was a **well-written** piece.
  She must be very **well off** now that she's a **well-known** architect.

About you   **Complete the sentences with the expressions in the box. Do you agree? Write sentences expressing your own views.**

well educated	well informed	well-known	well off	well-organized	well prepared
well thought-out	well-written				

1. It's important to have a _____ work space. You can save a lot of time looking for things.
2. Many people aren't very _____ these days. They don't read the news or know what's going on.
3. You should be _____ before any interview. Find out what you can about the job first.
4. People often say that students can't produce a _____ essay or one that's _____ .
5. To be _____ , you need to learn art, music, and languages – not just math and science.
6. People who are _____ , have to work very hard. Isn't that a _____ fact?

2 Adverb and adjective collocations

- Certain adverbs are commonly used with certain adjectives. Here are some common combinations.
  = 100 percent   **completely:** *different, new, unknown, separate, safe, unrealistic*
           entirely: *different, new, sure, possible, clear, appropriate, accurate*
           totally: *different, wrong, false, honest, convinced, unacceptable, irrelevant*
  = nearly 100 percent   **virtually:** *impossible, unknown, identical, unchanged, nonexistent*
  = very   **highly:** *qualified, unlikely, effective, skilled, respected, educated, intelligent*
  = in many places   **widely:** *available, known, accepted, respected*

A   **Complete the sentences with an adverb from above. There may be more than one answer.**

1. Being good with people is a _____ different kind of intelligence from being good at math.
2. Smart people aren't all _____ educated. It's _____ possible to be smart and uneducated.
3. I'm not _____ convinced that intelligence is knowing lots of facts. It's _____ wrong.
4. Latin is _____ nonexistent in schools now. It's _____ irrelevant in today's world.
5. It's _____ impossible to have every type of intelligence. In fact, it's _____ unknown.
6. You have to be _____ intelligent or _____ qualified to be a _____ respected person.
7. It's a _____ known fact that listening to music can help children with their math ability.

About you   **B**   **Do you agree with the statements above? Write sentences expressing your own views.**

1. I agree. They require totally different kinds of skills. I think . . .

❶ Patterns with comparatives

- You can use nouns, pronouns, or clauses after *than* and *as*. Notice the verb forms in the clauses.

*Bryan cycles faster than **his teammates**.*	*They don't cycle as fast as **Bryan**.*
*He's faster than **them**.*	*They're not as fast as **him**.*
*He's faster than **they are**.*	*They're not as fast as **he is**.*
*He cycles faster than **they do**.*	*They don't cycle as fast as **he does**.*
*He trains harder than **he did**.*	*He didn't use to train as hard as **he does** now.*
*He's faster than **he used to be**. / **he was**.*	*He's cycling further than **he used to**. / **he did**.*
*Nurdan practices less often than **she should**.*	*She plays as often as **she can**.*
*She's improved more slowly than **she hoped**.*	*She hasn't improved as much as **she'd like**.*

Common errors

Use *than*, not *that*, in comparisons.
*He's faster **than** his teammates.* (NOT . . . *faster ~~that his teammates~~*.)

About you

Complete the second sentences. Sometimes more than one option is possible. Then use the topic of each sentence above to write your own true sentences.

1. I'm better than my classmates at mental math. They're not as good _____ .
2. My sister reads faster than anyone in the family. We can't read as fast _____ .
3. My English hasn't improved as much as I'd like. I'm not as fluent _____ .
4. I'm training much harder this year for the marathon. I now run much faster _____ .
5. Both my parents are learning Italian. But my father doesn't practice as often _____ .
6. My friend Ana understands people really well. My other friends aren't as understanding _____ .
7. One guy in our class can play the guitar really well. No one can play it as well _____ .
8. My brother's swimming has improved. He's more confident _____ .

❷ More patterns with comparatives

- Comparatives are often repeated with *and* to talk about changing situations.
  *Work just gets **busier and busier**. I'm finding it **more and more difficult** to catch up.*

- Comparatives are often used in the pattern *the* + comparative, *the* + comparative to show the effect of one event on another. In this pattern, *more* is often an adverb.
  The harder *you practice an instrument,* **the better** *you get.* (= If you practice harder, you get better.)
  The more *I thought about it,* **the more nervous / the less confident** *I'd feel.*

A **Rewrite the sentences starting with the words given.**

1. If you read more, you learn more. *The more* . . .   The more you read, the more you learn.
2. If you do something, you like it better. *The more* . . .
3. If you work hard, you feel happy. *The harder* . . .
4. As you get older, life becomes more rewarding. *The older* . . .
5. If you practice a skill more, it becomes easier. *The more* . . .
6. Getting into college is increasingly difficult. *It's getting more and* . . .
7. Beating records in most sports is getting harder. *It's becoming harder and* . . .
8. When I find out more about politics, I like it less. *The more* . . .

About you

B **Do you agree with the sentences above? Write your own view and give examples.**

Illustration credits

11: (cartoon) Liza Donnelly; **20:** (podcast icon) hleib/Shutterstock; **27:** (cartoon) Liza Donnelly; **29:** (flip pad) Jupiter Images/Getty Images; **36:** (cartoon) Liza Donnelly; **39:** (datebook) AXL/Shutterstock; **48:** (cartoon) Liza Donnelly; **60:** (background) CGTextures; **69:** (cartoon) Liza Donnelly; **80:** (cartoon) Liza Donnelly; **91:** (cartoon) Liza Donnelly; **93:** (tablet) Tatiana Popova/Shutterstock, (valentine heart) Kraska/Shutterstock, (heart) ancroft/Shutterstock; **95:** (cartoon) Liza Donnelly; **106:** (paper texture) Roman Sigaev/Shutterstock; **109:** (cartoon) Liza Donnelly; **116:** (papers) Robyn Mackenzie/iStockphoto; **122:** (top border) Heidi Kalyani/iStockphoto, (dragon background) ponsulak kunsub/Shutterstock; **135:** (bottom right) glo/Shutterstock

Photography credits

10: (top right from left to right) Sergej Razvodovskij/Shutterstock, SuriyaPhoto/Shutterstock, (middle left) Photosani/Shutterstock, (middle right) Booka/Shutterstock; **11:** Jeff Thrower/Shutterstock; **12:** (background) Alphaspirit/Shutterstock, (clockwise from top left) rubberball/Getty Images, Somos Photography/Veer, Payless Images/Shutterstock, Joshua Hodge Photography/iStockphoto; **14:** Fabrice Malzieu; **15:** Fabrice Malzieu; **16:** (top right) Martin Carlsson/iStockphoto, (top right photo shoot) charity myers/iStockphoto, (bottom right) 4x6/iStockphoto; **17:** (left) Ablestock.com/Thinkstock, (right) iStockphoto/Thinkstock; **19:** Jupiter Images/Thinkstock; **20:** (Lady Gaga) Helga Esteb/Shutterstock.com, (magazine cover) Maria Deseo/PhotoEdit, (monitor) Fotonium/Shutterstock, (paparazzi) Losevsky Pavel/Shutterstock, (middle) Jeff Schultes/Shutterstock, (middle background) echo3005/Shutterstock; **22:** (middle left) Karina Kononenko/Shutterstock, (top right) Howard Kingsnorth/Getty Images; **24:** (man and woman) Fabrice Malzieu, (café background) Shvaygert Ekaterina/Shutterstock; **25:** Fabrice Malzieu; **26:** (left wire) MalDix/Shutterstock, (right wire) donatas1205/Shutterstock, (background) ilolab/Shutterstock, (top right) Stockbyte/Thinkstock; **27:** (bottom left) jcjgphotography/Shutterstock; **29:** Jupiter Images/Thinkstock; **30:** (top right, people talking) Gina Sanders/Shutterstock, (top right) Viktor Gmyria/Shutterstock, (blog image) Shutterstock, (bookshelf) Ferenc Szelepcsenyi/Shutterstock, (middle left) Creatas Images/Thinkstock, (middle center) Gabe Palmer/Getty Images, (middle right) Huchen Lu/iStockphoto; **32:** (browser window) Shutterstock, (girl studying) Jack Hollingsworth/Thinkstock; **34:** Fabrice Malzieu; **35:** Fabrice Malzieu; **36:** (newspaper) Hemera/Thinkstock, (coffee beans) Gtranquillity/Shutterstock; **37:** (bottom) Tupungato/Shutterstock.com; **42:** (classifieds) Alex Slobodkin/iStockphoto, (businessman, top right) Dmitriy Shironosov/Shutterstock, (mother and daughter) Kzenon/Shutterstock, (middle left) Shutterstock; **44:** (top left to right) StockLite/Shutterstock, Collage Photography/Veer, c./Shutterstock, Jupiter Images/Getty Images, wavebreakmedia ltd./Shutterstock, (background) kakin/Shutterstock, (haircut) Jupiter Images/Thinkstock; **45:** Deklofenak/Shutterstock; **46:** Fabrice Malzieu; **47:** Fabrice Malzieu; **48:** (background) re_bekka/Shutterstock; **49:** (middle right) takayuki/Shutterstock, (bottom right) Sideways Design/Shutterstock; **51:** (bottom) mtkang/Shutterstock, (poster) Benoit Chartron/iStockphoto; **52:** (top, clockwise left to right) Aneal Vohra/Photolibrary, kak2s/Shutterstock, mangostock/Shutterstock, (fence) Johannes Kornelius/Shutterstock, (middle right) © Allison Shirreffs; **54:** (top background) James Thew/Shutterstock, (middle from left to right) Ocean Photography/Veer, (clockwise from bottom left) Phase4Photography/Shutterstock, michellegibson/iStockphoto, Tyler Olson/Shutterstock; **56:** (middle) Fabrice Malzieu, (top left) Pakhnyushcha/Shutterstock, (top middle) Jupiterimages/Thinkstock, (top right) Distinctive Images/Shutterstock; **57:** (middle) Fabrice Malzieu, (top right) © Steve Debenport/iStockphoto, (ribbon) Robyn Mackenzie/Shutte; **58:** (background) Tanor/Shutterstock, (top right) © Mercy Ships/Debra Bell, (bottom left) © Mercy Ships/John Rolland; **59:** © Mercy Ships/John Rolland; **60:** (top center) Blend Images/Shutterstock, (bottom left) Goodshoot/Thinkstock, (bottom middle) Karel Gallas/Shutterstock, (bottom right) Brand X Pictures/Thinkstock; **61:** (bottom right) Jupiter Images/Thinkstock; **62:** (girl in 3D glasses) Nejron Photo/Shutterstock, (money in phone) Slavoljub Pantelic/Shutterstock, (robot) Julien Tromeur/Shutterstock, (African American professor) Hemera Technologies/Thinkstock, (Amanda) Andresr/Shutterstock, (Oliver) iodrakon/Shutterstock, (Sam) Phil Date/Shutterstock, (Judith) holbox/Shutterstock; **63:** Valentyn Volkov/Shutterstock; **64:** IT Stock/Thinkstock; **65:** razihusin/Shutterstock; **66:** Fabrice Malzieu; **67:** Fabrice Malzieu; **68:** James Thew/Shutterstock; **71:** Kuzma/shutterstock; **74:** (top from left to right) Stockbyte/Thinkstock Images, PM Images/Getty Images, (cork board) tdixon 8875/Shutterstock, (push pins) Tshooter/Shutterstock; **76:** (grass) Junker/Shutterstock, (top left) Linda Kloosterhof/iStockphoto, (top middle) Ryan McVay/Thinkstock, (top right) Andy Dean Photography/Shutterstock, (middle clockwise from left to right) Thinkstock Images, digitalskillet/iStockphoto, Bill Noll/iStockphoto, Comstock Images/Thinkstock; **77:** Brandy Taylor/iStockphoto; **78:** (top right) Fabrice Malzieu; **79:** Fabrice Malzieu, (bottom right) Ariel Skelley/Getty Images; **81:** Darren Hubley/Shutterstock; **83:** (top right) konstantynov/Shutterstock, (top left) Cheryl Graham/iStockphoto, (left headshot) Zurijeta/Shutterstock, (tablet) ra2 studio/Shutterstock, (family, bottom left) wong yu liang/Shutterstock; **84:** (chemist) Blaj Gabriel/Shutterstock, (food) Valentyn Volkov/Shutterstock, (middle left to right) Rick Bowmer/AP Images, David Oldfield/Thinkstock, Brenda Carson/Shutterstock, Blake Kurasek; **85:** Blake Kurasek; **86:** (peppers) Stephen Mcsweeny/Shutterstock, (pineapple) Marek Mnich/iStockphoto, (apple and raisins) bogdan ionescu/Shutterstock, (kiwis and mangoes) Robyn Mackenzie/iStockphoto, (mushrooms) B.G. Smith/Shutterstock, (man doing yoga) Comstock Images/Thinkstock, (blueberries and cherries) alejandro dans neergaard/Shutterstock, (ginger) Stockbyte/Thinkstock, (tea) matka_Wariatka/Shutterstock, (avocado) Nattika/Shutterstock, (tofu) Cameramannz/Shutterstock; **88:** Fabrice Malzieu; **89:** (top) Fabrice Malzieu, (middle left to right) Michel Porro/Getty Images, "ShootingCompany/Alamy," Pixsooz/Shutterstock, Holly Farrell/ABC via Getty Images, ABC via Getty Images; **90:** (honey) Geanina Bechea/Shutterstock, (honey stick) kontur-vid/Shutterstock, (top left to right) Rich Pedroncelli/AP Images, Hemera/Thinkstock, gmalandra/iStockphoto, Karen Moskowitz/Getty Images; **93:** (top left) Alila Sao Mai/Shutterstock, (top middle) hkannn/Shutterstock, (top right) hkannn/Shutterstock, (middle left) Ionia/Shutterstock, (middle right) nld/Shutterstock, (poster) Picsfive/Shutterstock, (blueberries) odze/Shutterstock, (broccoli) Cogipix/Shutterstock, (tomatoes) monticello/Shutterstock; **94:** (graduate) Stephen Coburn/Shutterstock, (sign) Pincasso/Shutterstock, (Rachael Ray) ABC via Getty Images, (Mark Zuckerberg) Bloomberg via Getty Images; **96:** (middle right) Moodboard Premium/Glow Images, (sand) CGTextures, (clams) Jacinta/Shutterstock; **98-99:** Sarah Cole; **100:** (background) oksana.perkins/Shutterstock, (top left) AridOcean/Shutterstock; **101:** (middle right) MELBA PHOTO AGENCY/Alamy, (map) Silvano audisio/Shutterstock; **103:** (magazine) Dan Gerber/Shutterstock, (bottom right) wrangler/Shutterstock; **106:** (top plane) Lars Christensen/Shutterstock, (atlas) slobo/iStockphoto, (passport) Arvind Balaraman/Shutterstock, (top right) Roman Sigaev/Shutterstock, (Bolivia mountain) Robert Harding Images/Glow Images, (tourists) Ozimages/Alamy, (middle plane) Paul Kingsley/Alamy, (map) Olinchuk/Shutterstock; **107:** (middle right) Ivan Sgualdini/Shutterstock, (bottom left to right) amie Marshall - Tribaleye Images/Getty Images, MARTIN ALIPAZ/epa/Corbis, Harald Toepfer/Shutterstock, Baloncici/Shutterstock, Kapu/Shutterstock; **108:** (eye mask) Guangyu Cai/iStockphoto, (ear plugs) Anthony DiChello/Shutterstock, (flashlight) karbunar/Shutterstock, (clockwise right) © battles/iStockphoto, (candles) Brooke Fuller/Shutterstock, (clockwise right to left) ClickPop/Shutterstock, (iPad frame) Opachevsky Irina/Shutterstock, (tea) Akinshin/Dreamstime.com, (background) AKaiser/Shutterstock, (bottom top left) Ken Hurst/Shutterstock, (bottom left middle) CREATISTA/Shutterstock, (bottom left) Supri Suharjoto/Shutterstock, (bottom top right) iStockphoto/Thinkstock, (bottom right middle) Thinkstock Images, (bottom right) Creatas Images/Thinkstock; **110:** (middle left) Fabrice Malzieu, (background) argus/Shutterstock, (spacecraft) DM7/Shutterstock; **111:** Fabrice Malzieu; **112:** (leaf) hddigital/Shutterstock, (background) Terrance Emerson/Shutterstock, (orangutan) Uryadnikov Sergey/Shutterstock; **113:** aida ricciardiello/Shutterstock; **115:** (laptop) Chris Baynham/Shutterstock, (screenshot) Steve Broer/Shutterstock; **116:** (top right) Sara Winter/iStockphoto, (gifts) Hintau Aliaksei/Shutterstock, (bride) Chris Gramly/iStockphoto, (top right) Andresr/Shutterstock, (cupcake) Ruth Black/Shutterstock, (bottom left) Danny Zhan/AP Images; **118:** (top left to right) Ariel Skelley/Getty Images, (top left to right) Monkey Business Images/Getty Images, (top right to left) Corbis RF/Glow Images, (top right) bikeriderlondon/Shutterstock, (top background) kaarsten/Shutterstock, (bottom background) kakin/Shutterstock, (bottom right) frender/iStockphoto; **119:** Irina Nartova/Shutterstock; **120:** Fabrice Malzieu; **121:** Fabrice Malzieu; (cake) GraÃ§a Victoria/Shutterstock; **122:** (middle left) Tito Wong/Shutterstock, (middle right) David Hunter/Photolibrary; **123:** (top right) Lonely Planet Images/Alamy, (bottom right) Mike Thomas; **125:** (laptop) andersphoto/Shutterstock, (married couple) Brand X Pictures/Thinkstock; **126:** (Einstein) Library of Congress, (violin) Vanja Jimmy Ivosevic/Shutterstock, (art) fotoecho/Shutterstock, (frame) Hannamariah/Shutterstock, (hand) DenisNata/Shutterstock, (bottom right) Kurhan/Shutterstock; **127:** Kris Connor/Getty Images; **128:** (top left) Superstock/Glow Images, (bottom left) Galina Barskaya/iStockphoto, (bottom right) Jeremy Woodhouse/Getty Images; **130:** (middle) Fabrice Malzieu, (top right) james cheadle/Alamy; **131:** (top) Fabrice Malzieu, (middle left) Jupiterimages/Thinkstock, (middle center) Photos.com/Thinkstock, (middle right) NBAE/Getty Images; **132:** (background) Graeme Shannon/Shutterstock, (top left) Thos Robinson/Getty Images, (bottom right) photo courtesy of Chris Waddell; **133:** (bottom right) photo courtesy of Charlotte Cox, (gold medal) Kuzmin Andrey/Shutterstock; **134:** (top right) photo courtesy of Gladys Sandiford; **135:** glo/Shutterstock; **136:** (left to right) Zigy Kalveny-Charles Thatcher/Getty Images, Jeff Greenberg/PhotoEdit, Creatas/Thinkstock

Text credits

Every effort has been made to trace the owners of copyrighted material in this book. We would be grateful to hear from anyone who recognizes his or her copyrighted material and who is unacknowledged. We will be pleased to make the necessary corrections in future editions of the book.

Corpus

Development of this publication has made use of the Cambridge English Corpus (CEC). The CEC is a computer database of contemporary spoken and written English, which currently stands at over one billion words. It includes British English, American English and other varieties of English. It also includes the Cambridge Learner Corpus, developed in collaboration with the University of Cambridge ESOL Examinations. Cambridge University Press has built up the CEC to provide evidence about language use that helps to produce better language teaching materials.